LONDONIST

DRINKS

Published by AA Publishing, a trading name of AA Media Limited,
Grove House, Lutyens Close, Basingstoke, Hampshire RG24 8AG, UK

First published in 2019
10 9 8 7 6 5 4 3 2 1

© AA Media Ltd 2019
Text © Londonist Ltd
For a full list of illustrators, contributors and copyright holders see page 192

ISBN: 978-0-7495-8196-1

Publisher: Phil Carroll
Editor: Rebecca Needes
Designer: Elizabeth Baldin
Concept design: Ben Brannan
Repro: Ian Little
Production: Martyn Harris
Art Director: James Tims

Printed and bound in Dubai by Oriental Press

This book was typeset in Garden Essential and Plantain Light

A05648

CONTENTS

Foreword   7

Pubs named after fictional characters
by Harry Rosehill   8

12 great bars in railway arches
by Maire Connor   12

Made in London
by Will Noble   15

Did London invent the cocktail?
by Steve Manktelow, cocktail expert
from GOAT Chelsea   17

Tea in London: a potted history
by Laura Reynolds   18

Recreate Karl Marx's rowdy Tottenham Court
Road pub crawl by Matt Brown   23

Drink like a spy in the roaring 20s
by Timothy Phillips   25

A martini fit for James Bond
by Steve Manktelow   27

Sports bars that are actually good
by Will Noble   28

Peculiar pub interiors
by Matt Brown   30

How many Red Lions are there in London?
by Matt Brown   32

The marvellous universe of the micropub
by Darryl Chamberlain   34

The London pub that's in a nursery rhyme
by Matt Brown   38

London toilets you can drink in
by Harry Rosehill   41

Sink the best martinis in London
by Lydia Manch   43

A drink that Paddington would totally go for
by Ben O'Norum   45

Did you know... Six of London's tube stations
are named after pubs by Matt Brown   46

A riverside crawl of the Thames
by Matt Brown   49

Seek out a city speakeasy
by Will Noble   52

An oenophile's odyssey
by Maire Connor   56

Get quizzical
by Harry Rosehill   60

Drink your way around the world
by Will Noble   62

10 of the best Wetherspoons
by Will Noble   65

A tale of two gin crazes (and a hazy bit in between)
by Steve Manktelow   67

CONTENTS *continued*

Pimm's: created in London as a legal loophole
by Steve Manktelow   69

The Docklands light ale-way
by Matt Brown   70

London's strangest pub names
by Matt Brown and Will Noble   72

Drink in the view – bars with stunning vistas
by Laura Reynolds   74

*Quaff your way through the kings and queens
of England* by Matt Brown   77

The fatal London beer flood
by Matt Brown   83

A swift one in London's hotel bars
by Lydia Manch   84

The cocktail with its own poem
by Ben O'Norum   87

A history of drinking chocolate in London
by Laura Reynolds   88

The pub: all things to all people
by Matt Brown   91

Drink your way through the rainbow
by Matt Brown   93

The curious world of London's gentlemen's clubs
by Maire Connor   97

Deserter do the Oliver Reed pub crawl
by Deserter   100

Highballs on high buildings: London's best rooftop bars
by Laura Reynolds   103

Where's my tap water from?
by Matt Brown   106

*Drink your way around London like
Charles Dickens* by Matt Brown   107

The celebratory drink with a mournful birth
by Ben O'Norum   109

A Circle line pub crawl
by Sam Cullen   110

Catch a theatre show… in the pub
by Harry Rosehill   116

Strange brews: London's weirdest drinks
by Laura Reynolds   119

Most haunted pubs
by Ben O'Norum   121

Bars beneath your feet
by Lettie McKie and Maire Connor   124

How London became utterly addicted to coffee
by Laura Reynolds   126

A cocktail to 'wake you up and f**k you up'
by Ben O'Norum   129

Which is London's oldest pub?
by Peter Watts   130

An ode to the milk round
by Will Noble   133

Bars that float
by Laura Reynolds   135

A punch that pines for London
by Steve Manktelow   137

Where to drink when you're not drinking
by Laura Reynolds   138

Working men's clubs: still a thing in London
by Harry Rosehill   142

Bizarre and beautiful drinking traditions
by Harry Rosehill   146

A Blue Posts pub crawl
by Matt Brown   148

Fictional pubs: an imaginary crawl
by Will Noble   151

The bartender and the star
by Will Noble   153

London's most extravagant drinking experiences
by Maire Connor   154

The best pubs near London's train stations
by Matt Brown   156

Inside the Beefeaters' private pub in the
Tower of London by Will Noble   162

15 of the best craft beer pubs in London
by Dave Haste   163

It happened down the pub…
by Matt Brown   170

The legendary Londonist 12 days of Christmas
pub crawl by Matt Brown   171

What have Tom and Jerry got to do with eggnog?
by Steve Manktelow   175

Where to get a drink when the city's sleeping
by Harry Rosehill   176

Record-breaking pubs: highest, smallest, priciest…
by Matt Brown   178

**Liquid history: a chronology of key events
in London drinking   180**

About the artists   184

Index   189

Credits   192

FOREWORD

Have you ever noticed that the centre of the London Underground map forms a bottle?
From its neck, which opens up between Liverpool Street and Tower Hill, the Thames
seems to flow – some marvellous pale blue elixir.

Like many cities, London pivots around liquid. Long before a single brick was placed – or a single order was placed at the bar for that matter – the Thames and its tributaries were waiting, ready to quench the thirst of countless Londoners. Except, it turns out, that Londoners hankered after something stronger.

In 1954, an ancient Roman temple, rededicated to the wine deity Bacchus, was discovered in the City. Londinium's residents staved off the stresses of urban life with a bracer, and it's been a ritual ever since. Beer, of course, went on to become Londoners' poison of choice. Its best-known brand is London Pride, brewed at the side of the Thames and made with Thames water.

It stands to reason *Londonist* loves a tipple too – so much, that we made our own IPA on the Bermondsey Beer Mile. And then we thought: if we can write a beer label, how difficult can it be to write an entire book on booze?

In *Londonist Drinks*, we meet the inventors of iconic cocktails, and the ghouls who hang around the corners of creaky boozers. Embark on whimsical pub crawls, and call in at bars from the pages of fiction. Sip sparkling thirst-quenchers on the rooftops of skyscrapers, and delve into the dank depths of railway arches to sup on strange delights.

It's not all intoxicating potions. London itself dallied with temperance – seek out the Victorian fountains scattered about the city. Everyone should take a breather now and again, and so we've sprinkled this book with mint tea, milkrounds, kombucha and that classic – tap water.

We hope you'll take this book down the pub with you and pore over it with a pint of London porter. Maybe you'll read other bits in bed with a sore head. We don't recommend that you down it in one go though. Please enjoy responsibly.

Will Noble, *Londonist* Editor

P.S. The irony of writing a book on drinking for the AA has not escaped us.

What is *Londonist*? Established as *The Big Smoker* in 2004, *Londonist* has become one of the go-to places for Londoners and people visiting London. Events, food and drink, history, transport, trivia – we cover everything you need to know about the capital, celebrating its quirks, eccentricities, hidden and surprising bits along the way.
Check us out:
londonist.com   f facebook.com/londonistcom   @Londonist   londonist_com

PUBS NAMED AFTER FICTIONAL CHARACTERS

Children's poetry, a nimble-fingered folk legend and a dog from a Laurel and Hardy film give some of London's pubs their names.

Well, it's more imaginative than calling your boozer The Red Lion, isn't it? (Discover the rampant pride of Red Lions that resides in London on page 32).

The Artful Dodger, Tower Hill

Despite its namesake, we've never had trouble with pickpockets at The Artful Dodger. In fact, it's a rather comely, homely Victorian boozer. For those who know Oliver Twist and his companions from the musical, rather than the novel, you might have difficulty recognising the original incarnation of Dodger. He isn't as charming as in later versions, and it's alluded to that he winds up in a penal colony in Australia.

The location of a pub with this name is somewhat questionable. The nearby Tower of London gets mentioned in a whopping nine Dickens books, but *Oliver Twist* isn't one of them. Still, you can get a glimpse of it on your right, as you zoom out of Tower Gateway on the DLR.
47 Royal Mint Street, E1 8LG

Betsey Trotwood, Clerkenwell

The second Dickens character to grace this list, this one is a little more obscure than the Dodger. Betsey Trotwood is David Copperfield's great-aunt in… you guessed it, *David Copperfield*. Betsey initially doesn't take any interest in David because he's male and she's sworn off the entire sex. Eventually, she comes round to the little charmer.

Betsey Trotwood the pub has an illustration of Betsey hanging up outside, but that's where the connection ends – men are allowed to drink here. We recommend visiting the Betsey if you're looking for a Clerkenwell pub with live music, comedy, or even poetry recitals.
56 Farringdon Road, EC1R 3BL

Illustration by MEL SMITH DESIGNS

Brave Sir Robin, Crouch Hill

Brave, brave, brave, brave Sir Robin – that's four braves for those of you who are counting. Remember the ironically named Brave Sir Robin and his band of narrating minstrels from *Monty Python and the Holy Grail*? The man who was supposedly unafraid at the prospect of having his eyes gouged out or his elbows broken… until, at the first sign of danger, he turns tail and makes a run for it: "Brave Sir Robin ran away".

The pub lies around the corner from Crouch Hill station and, unlike the man it's named after, you won't want to flee. Spend the afternoon curled up on the sofa bravely working your way through the outrageously large beer selection. There are 20 casks and kegs on rotation.

29 Crouch Hill, N4 4AP

The Laughing Gravy, Waterloo

The Laughing Gravy on Blackfriars Road is now more of a bar-restaurant than pub, but its past life – and the fact that you can still get a decent drink – earns it a spot on this list. The somewhat odd name references a Laurel and Hardy short from 1930, in which the hapless pair frantically try to hide their dog – named Laughing Gravy – from their hilariously splenetic landlord.

The Laughing Gravy is a great shout if you're looking to avoid the mega-crowds

in Waterloo as a show files out from The Old Vic. If you eat, be ready for a seasonal menu that's unafraid of getting experimental. If you stick to the bar, order a pint of Fourpure's oatmeal stout. Oh, and if you watch the film: beware its shockingly grizzly ending.

154 Blackfriars Road, SE1 8EN

The Mad Bishop & Bear, Paddington

So here we have a half and half-er. One half – The Mad Bishop – isn't drawn from fiction. The story goes that Great Western Railway found a plot of land, which it thought perfect for its marquee station, but dreaded the thought of negotiating with the landowner – which just so happened to be Westminster Abbey. Except the church gave away the land for a pittance, something that the railway people clearly thought "mad".

The second half of this pub's moniker is completely fictional, although you might forget that upon walking round the station. Michael Bond's *Paddington Bear* has a statue, a bench and this pub, all dedicated to him. As for the pub's menu? Not a marmalade sandwich in sight.

Paddington Station, W2 1HB (see page 160 also)

The Moby Dick, Rotherhithe

Everyone's favourite fictional whale has a pub named after it in London's Docklands. There have been a few whales spotted swimming up the Thames, which we suspect is what this name

pays homage to. In 2018 a beluga, who the media playfully dubbed 'Benny' was spotted in the Thames. Benny's shimmering paleness recalls Moby Dick as described in the novel: "It was the whiteness of the whale that appalled me".

The pub itself bears little relation to a great white whale. Apart from its cavernous size that is; the modern Fuller's joint has two floors for you to nurse your pint on.

6 Russell Place, SE16 1PL

The Owl & Hitchhiker, Holloway Road

This Holloway Road pub objectively wins the fictional characters in names competition – because it has not one, but two entirely separate works of fiction (and their characters) in its name. First comes the Owl, of 'The Owl and the Pussycat' fame.

The latter part of the pub's name is an homage to Douglas Adams' wacky sci-fi series, *The Hitchhiker's Guide to the Galaxy*. Apart from a penchant for silliness, what connects these two rather disparate works is the authors: both lived in the Holloway Road area at one stage in their life.

It would be all too easy to have a brilliant pub name, combined with a rather boring boozer, but fortunately The Owl & Hitchhiker does not fall afoul of that potential pitfall. Cartoons are scribbled over the bar, plus there's a Don't Panic sign, and a wooden owl.

471 Holloway Road, N7 6LE

The Owl & The Pussycat, Ealing/ Shoreditch

Two Owl and the Pussycat pubs can be found in London, both inspired by Edward Lear's masterpiece about a waterborne inter-species elopement. The Owl & The Pussycat micropub in Ealing takes up residence in a former children's bookshop. Amusingly, the pub's website has an employee of the month competition. By December 2018 the Pussycat had won the title 15 times, compared to the Owl's paltry 10.

The other Owl and Pussycat lives in buzzy Shoreditch. Indeed, as the swell of people spills out onto the street each Friday, this pub is the source of some of that buzz. This is much more than a post-work drinking hole though – pies, roasts and fish and chips are on the menu. If it's solely booze you require, head upstairs to The Jago cocktail bar. It's named after the semi-fictitious slum from Arthur Morrison's *A Child of the Jago*.

The Owl & The Pussycat (Ealing micropub), 106 Northfield Avenue, W13 9RT

The Owl & Pussycat (Shoreditch), 34 Redchurch Street, E2 7DP

The Resting Hare

This one's a little questionable. The team behind The Resting Hare claim not to have named the pub after Aesop's fable. Instead it's said to come from local Victorian architect Thomas Cubbitt, who noticed the tameness of hares in the area while on his morning constitutional. The poet W B Yeats, who lived in the area in the 1920s, similarly wrote of "a handsome grey hare taking rest". But… it's called The Resting Hare. Do you honestly expect that not to spark images of a hare taking a nap mid-race as a tortoise edges past?

Think about this conundrum as you peruse The Resting Hare's drink selection – a bountiful 15 taps to select from. If you're an Aesop purist, just a 10 minute walk away is pan-Asian restaurant Hare & Tortoise in the Brunswick Centre. Surely that's named after the fable?

The Resting Hare, 8 Woburn Walk, WC1H 0JL

Hare & Tortoise, 11–13 Brunswick Square, WC1N 1AF

Robin Hood, Enfield/ Sutton/Bexleyheath

London is very much not Nottingham, yet the heroic outlaw still has a few pubs in London named after him. Well, Robin Hood is one of England's most enduring folk heroes – his tale spread far and wide, by ballads, books, cartoons, plus a few dodgy blockbusters.

All three of the Robin Hood pubs we've found live in London's outer boroughs. Maybe those dwelling in the likes of Mayfair and Chelsea aren't too comfortable with the idea of someone stealing from the rich and giving to the poor?

Robin Hood & Little John, 78 Lion Road, DA6 8PF

The Robin Hood, The Ridgeway, EN2 8AP

Robin Hood, 52 West Street, SM1 1SH

The Walrus & The Carpenter, Monument

Edward Lear isn't the only surrealist poet whose work adorns a London pub sign. Lewis Carroll's 'The Walrus and the Carpenter', from *Through the Looking Glass, and What Alice Found There*, shares that honour. The poem is recited by Tweedle Dee and Tweedle Dum, and the two characters in the poem trick a group of oysters away from safety so the Walrus and the Carpenter can slurp them up. Lovely stuff.

This is the ideal pub to kick back in with a pint after clambering up 311 steps to the summit of The Monument, which is just a hop, skip and jump away. Grub will be necessary – an all-round refuel is in order after that climbing – so it's lucky that these guys are, in their own words, 'proper connoisseurs of sausages and chops'. There are other options for the sausage-averse, although no oysters. Apologies to all walruses and carpenters who might be reading.

45 Monument Street, EC3R 8BU

12 GREAT BARS IN RAILWAY ARCHES

With all that exposed brickwork and domed metallic ceilings, railway arches boast a bonafide industrial chic aesthetic. It's no wonder that plenty of the city's trendiest watering holes are located here.

Beneath the purr of engines and the screech of wheels on steel tracks, many a vibrant London business thrives. Within the arches, longstanding traders ranging from motorbike repair shops to furniture restorers rub shoulders with creative start-ups: craft breweries, art galleries, and even a Korean barbershop/cafe.

For decades, the comparatively affordable rents and malleable spaces offered by Network Rail have attracted many small businesses unafraid of a bit of elbow grease (tenants are responsible for much of the interior maintenance) – bars amongst them. Read on for some of our favourites.

40 Maltby Street, Bermondsey

After a busy Saturday spent at Maltby Street Market, perusing posh condiments and stuffing your face with gourmet brownies, plonk yourself, and your shopping bags, down at number 40 for a well-deserved glass of vino. The bar is tacked on to the Gergovie Wine warehouse, so if your evening aperitivo doesn't quite quench your thirst, you can pick up a bottle or two to take home with you.
40 Maltby Street, SE1 3PA

Bar Story, Peckham

Who's up for a £4 negroni, then? Since it opened back in 2003, this wallet-friendly Peckham cocktail bar has become a local institution, beloved for its expertly mixed drinks, wood-fired oven pizzas, and a no-frills, laid-back vibe. Rock up between 6pm and 7pm any day of the week and get two cocktails for as little as £7. If it's too crowded, pop over to the archway opposite – a bar called Peckham Springs. Its eponymous cocktail references a certain episode of *Only Fools and Horses*.
213 Blenheim Grove, SE15 4QL

Bermondsey Beer Mile

It's a pilgrimage for craft beer connoisseurs everywhere and a way to incorporate some exercise into what inevitably amounts to a full-on sesh. The Bermondsey Beer Mile is your chance to knock back the best artisanal brews the capital has to offer, via the legion of brewery taprooms and bottle shops that occupy this winding stretch of railway arches.

As you squeeze your way through the crowds on a Saturday (most of the breweries aren't open to the public during the week), it's hard to believe that the area's first brewery, Kernel, moved in a mere decade ago. Since then, Bermondsey has become the epicentre of London's craft beer revolution. Thanks to recent expansion you're currently looking at a two-mile bar crawl – wear comfy shoes.

Where to start? you may well ask. We'd say Fourpure – it's at the quieter end of the 'mile'. They also brewed our 2018 *Londonist* Session IPA, so we might be a bit biased.

Buster Mantis, Deptford

Seconds from Deptford Station, this laid-back Jamaican-inspired bar – named for the island nation's first prime minister – is the perfect place to kill some time waiting for your train. Watch out though: too much of their infamously potent rum punch and you could find your journey plans totally derailed. The venue has become a staple of the underground jazz scene, hosting legendary midweek jams which incorporate everything from west African rhythms to future soul, grime and Afrofuturist spoken word.
**3–4 Resolution Way,
SE8 4NT**

Camden Town Brewery

Curious about the life-cycle of your Camden Hells? Let Camden Town Brewery give you the low-down on how their libations make their way to your charmingly squat pint glass. End up in the taproom onsite to sample the fruits of their labour. Oh, and if you can make it to one of the 'tank parties' – where you can quaff pints of unfiltered Hells lager from 60-hectolitre tanks – do.
55–59 Wilkin Street Mews, NW5 3NN

Draughts, Hackney and Waterloo

The rhythmic rumble of the Overground intermingles with cries of outrage arising from a particularly acrimonious round of Articulate at London's first ever board game cafe. Draughts, which opened after a phenomenally successful Kickstarter campaign back in 2014, stocks more than 800 games as well as a decent selection of booze. Go forth and chug craft beer over a game of Cluedo, master Monopoly while nursing a glass of Merlot, or opt for a quiet cuppa and a round of Connect 4.

Its second venue, which opened in Waterloo in 2018, also resides in a railway arch; part of the famous Waterloo Vaults and Leake Street area.
**Arch 337, Acton Mews, E8 4EA
Arch 16, Leake Street, SE1 7NN**

Doodle Bar, Bermondsey

Embrace your inner Picasso at this bar, which invites you to scribble all over the walls. After Doodle Bar was pushed out of Battersea to make way for luxury flats, it found a new home on Bermondsey's Druid Street. There's also a ping pong table for the more athletically inclined, plus more than 20 types of gin to really bring out that competitive spirit.
60 Druid Street, SE1 2EZ

Little Nan's, Deptford

If you're a sucker for all things kitsch, you'll love Little Nan's. Named in tribute to owner Tristan's late grandmother, this cocktail bar takes Pat Butcher as its muse: think animal print fabric, Union Jacks, and a menagerie of delightfully wacky knick-knacks. They even play the *EastEnders* theme at closing time. In the wrong hands, this could all come off unbearably twee, but it retains the authentic, homespun feel that made it a truly unique southeast London gem. The drinks menu is a lot of fun; pop in for a teapot cocktail named after Lady Di, or a spiked slushy.
Arches 13–15, Deptford Market Yard, SE8 4BX

Mother Kelly's, Bethnal Green

You're spoilt for choice at this NYC-style taproom, which boasts more than 20 ever-changing brews on tap, plus half-a-dozen fridges chock-full of bottles and cans (none of your bog-standard off-licence tinnies here). At the bar, you can find all sorts of colourful concoctions, from amber IPAs to a ruby red Krier lambic. Mother Kelly's gets bonus points for its numerical menu. So if you're not quite sure how to ask for a half of, say, Brouwerij 't IJ, you can just quote the tap number instead and avoid outing yourself as a beer novice. Win.
251 Paradise Row, E2 9LE (also Vauxhall, see page 168)

Night Tales, Hackney

An exotic world of sensory delights lies inside the charcoal-black arches of Hackney's aptly named Bohemia Place. Here, you'll find one heck of a sound system, an agave bar, and a brilliantly illuminated Japanese-inspired terrace complete with luxury day beds (in case you need a lie-down). Night Tales is more than just a pretty face, though, and has welcomed the likes of Four Tet, Django Django and Groove Armada to its decks.
14 Bohemia Place, E8 1DU

Renegade, Bethnal Green

Sick of the same old sauvignon blanc? Make a beeline for urban winery Renegade (see page 59). True to its name, you can expect to find all sorts of characterful libations here, concocted in small batches with minimal human intervention. In the taproom, candles flicker atop benches and barrels and the air is heady with the aroma of fermenting fruit. All the ingredients for a night of good old-fashioned Bacchanalian revelry.
Arch 12, Gales Gardens, E2 0EJ

The Wanstead Tap, Forest Gate

Who would've thought you'd find one of London's widest range of craft brews in the midst of a load of garages in Forest Gate? For those after something a little stronger, you'll be pleased to hear that the Wanstead Tap also pours out local, small-batch spirits. And if you're after a dose of culture, the bar hosts regular discussions, short film screenings, and intimate gigs.
Arch 352, Winchelsea Road, E7 0AQ

If any of these tickle your fancy, go full steam ahead and start exploring, because change could be afoot for London's railway arches. In 2018, Network Rail sold its portfolio to a pair of property investors – Blackstone and Telereal Trillium – for a cool £1.5 billion. The sale provoked considerable controversy, with some taking the view that Network Rail should retain the rental income and use it to fund crucial infrastructure maintenance. Others took issue with the choice of buyer.

The MD of Telereal Trillium has taken pains to allay fears of increasing rents and profit chasing, telling the press that the company will be taking a tenant-centric approach to business, including support for struggling trader tenants. He also announced the company's intention to reopen hundreds of the capital's vacant arches. Whether these are made affordable for small businesses – and whether the incoming owner's pledge to protect existing traders is honoured – remains to be seen.

MADE IN LONDON

*Every man and his drunk dog know that London's craft beer scene is positively fermenting –
the city now accommodates more than 100 breweries. But in the nooks and crannies of those industrial
sheds and railway arches, it's more than just beer that's being concocted for your supping pleasure…*

Cider – made in London Bridge

London's recent relationship with cider has been sour: pubs dedicated to the apple nectar, like the Cider Tap and Chimes of Pimlico, closed down. Could it be that the drink is just too wholesomely rural for us urbane lot? Enter Hawkes – self-professed 'Saviours of Cider' – and creators of Urban Orchard, an ineffably quaffable brew, crafted in their cidery beneath the railway arches on Druid Street. Come for a tour, stay to pour the contents of an apple tree down your neck. If you happen to be cider-wary, order a Hawkes Lovechild – it's a beer-cider hybrid.

Hawkes, 96 Druid Street, SE1 2HQ

Coca-Cola – made in Edmonton and Sidcup

We always thought that Coca-Cola was made by Santa, then personally delivered in a fairy light-strewn articulated truck, too. But it turns out that the highly moreish syrup juice is made in plenty of places, two of them in London. Edmonton's Coca-Cola factory has been in business since 1974, churning out 50 million cases of soft drink each year (other fizzy elixirs they make include Diet Coke, Dr Pepper, Sprite, Lilt and Fanta). Sidcup's setup is even older – it started cranking out Coke in 1961. Also making Cherry Coke, Schweppes and the controversial Vanilla Coke, the Sidcup plant fills up more than 80 cans/bottles every second. Neither factory is open to the public – your teeth will be relieved to hear that.

Mead – made in Peckham

Mead: isn't it some sort of medieval Lucozade, quaffed chiefly by knights, post dragon-slaying workout? Anyway, that's what we thought until Gosnells came along. Now you can find the fermented-honey-elixir poured cold from the tap at this Peckham industrial estate, which neighbours a place that sells neon rainbow doe spines (well, you can never have enough). Gosnells' is lighter than traditional meads – and their varieties include dry-hopped and barrel-aged. Ask nicely, and they'll tell you how to make a Peckham Lemonade cocktail.

Gosnells, Unit 2, Print Village, Chadwick Road, SE15 4PU

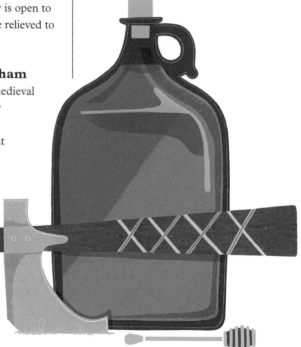

Sake – made in Peckham

It began with a wedding. Actually, it began with a hazy night out in a Farringdon tiki bar. It was here that Tom and Lucy hooked up, which led them to get married. At their wedding, they served up their home brew sake. "It was surprisingly not terrible," remembers Tom – a ringing endorsement that inspired the pair to establish London's first sake brewery, Kanpai (it means 'dry your cup'). The somewhat laborious task of turning rice, water, yeast and koji (a 'magic mould') into liquid deliciousness takes place on a Peckham industrial estate. All that's required of you is to rock up at the weekend, pull up a stool and relish it. Kanpai!

Kanpai, Unit 2a–2, 133 Copeland Road, SE15 3SN

Vodka – made in Hackney Downs

The London ether is again redolent with the whiff of juniper: gin is king once more. As for vodka – you'll have to head waaay east to find that. Not quite as far as Moscow – we're talking Hackney Downs. Nestled under the station here is Our/London's micro-distillery, where they craft vodka using British wheat, and a yeast originally found in wine production. Take a tour, then sink an icy vodka martini, while cheersing Anglo-Russian relations.

Our/London, Arch 435 & 436, Spurstowe Road, E8 1LS

Wine – made in Enfield, Brompton, Bethnal Green and Battersea

Medieval Londoners planted vineyards in London, the richer folk quaffing the stuff from gold-lined coconut shells. Sometimes diluted with vinegar, it was probably more mouth-puckering than that abomination you once bought from Tesco for £2.70. Since then, our vino-making credentials have slipped even further into the abyss, i.e. we stopped making it altogether. That is, until the past few years when a few London wineries stepped forwards.

Forty Hall dialled back the years by opening what it claims to be London's first commercial vineyard since medieval times (see page 58). At 10 acres, the operation is a community affair – run and managed by locals. If you want to get hands-on with the grapes, the vineyard is always on the lookout for volunteers.

At last count, there are four more wineries in London. Brompton's London Cru hand-selects grapes from European vineyards, magicking them into small batches of wine down an alleyway in SW6. To add to the Londony vibe, they're named things like Barbican Barbera and Baker St Bacchus. Renegade London Wine in Bethnal Green (see page 59) is named as such because 'they don't play by the rules'. By which we mean they don't play by Europe's appellation rules. The results of this flouter mentality are delicious vegan and vegetarian wines.

There are TWO wineries in Battersea, as well – Blackbook (not, unfortunately, a nod to Dylan Moran's vino-guzzling character in London-set sitcom *Black Books*) and Vagabond Wines. We suspect that by the time this book is published, there'll be even more wineries.

Forty Hall Vineyard, Enfield, EN2 9HA
London Cru, 21–27 Seagrave Road, Fulham, SW6 1RP
Renegade London Wine, Arch 12, Gales Gardens, E2 0EJ
Blackbook Winery, Arch 41, London Stone Business Estate, Broughton Street, SW8 3QR
Vagabond Wines, Unit 12, Circus Village West, Circus Road West, Phase 1 Battersea Power Station, SW11 8EZ

DID LONDON INVENT THE COCKTAIL?

For more than 200 years, everyone believed the cocktail was an American invention from 1806. Then someone found a reference to a 'cocktail' from three years earlier. It was a jab at then-prime minister, Pitt the Younger. A London newspaper referred to his drinks tab at the Axe & Gate Tavern; on it was a "cocktail – (vulgarly called ginger)". Savoy bartender Harry Craddock, meanwhile, ~~recounted~~ invented a story involving Aztec kings, American generals, Mexican walking fish and a beautiful dancer called Coctel. Maybe we'll never know who – or where – invented the first cocktail. Anyway, Charles Francatelli, chief cook to Queen Victoria, released a cook's guide in 1861 with a chapter on cocktails. Here's his recipe for a 'Cock-tail'.

Make a No. 1016. COCK-TAIL

Put three lumps of sugar in a tumbler with a dessert spoonful of Savory and Moore's essence of Jamaica ginger, and a wineglassful of brandy.
Fill up with hot water.

Or, for a modern-day duplicate:

4 parts (50ml) Cognac
One 2cm lump of fresh ginger, crushed
1 part sugar syrup
Stir with boiling hot water and strain into a glass

TEA IN LONDON: A POTTED HISTORY

Londoners have had a long, steamy love affair with tea, despite coffee getting a head-start. Pour yourself a cuppa and pore over this history of our beloved brew.

Who brought tea to London and when?

The first tea in England was shipped in from China, by the infamous East India Company. The shipping and trade company was founded in 1600 by Queen Elizabeth I with the purpose of exploring the East. In 1848, the company sent botanist Robert Fortune into India to establish tea plantations there (you may have heard of his Darjeeling plantation, still going strong today). Varieties from other countries including Ceylon (now Sri Lanka) soon followed. The East India Company name has been revived by a modern company selling fine foods from all over the world – and is 100% less involved with slavery.

Believe it or not, tea was first sold in England from a coffee house owned by one Thomas Garway in Exchange Alley in the City of London. That was around 1657–8. Samuel Pepys had his first taste in 1660 – a diary entry reads:

"I did send for a cup of tee (a China drink) of which I never had drank before".

Queen Catherine of Braganza, Portuguese wife of King Charles II, had been accustomed to taking tea in her native country. Once tea made it to England, she helped to popularise it among the wealthy upper classes, most of whom had never heard of it up until this point.

Tea houses never caught on in the way that chocolate houses and coffee houses did, largely because it was easier for people to prepare tea in their own homes (tea only required boiling water, whereas special equipment was needed for the preparation of coffee and cocoa).

During the Industrial Revolution, tea became more readily available. With sugar and milk added it was seen as an efficient way to keep workforces energised for hours of intense physical labour. The chocolate biscuit, alas, didn't rock up till 1925.

Here are some of the London locations linked with tea's rise in popularity:

Twinings, 216 Strand

Mention 'tea' and 'London' and the name 'Twinings' will soon follow. The company has a tea shop and museum on Strand. The narrow corridor of a shop opened in 1706, and is to tea drinkers what libraries are to book lovers; floor-to-ceiling shelves laden with bags, boxes and tins of teas from around the world. Jane Austen came here – it welcomed women back in the days when the city's coffee houses were men-only – and Earl Grey tea was first marketed under that name here.

The royal warrant sits above the door, as does the company's logo – the world's oldest commercial logo in continuous use since it was designed in 1787.

Earl Grey's portrait, National Portrait Gallery

If Earl Grey is your tea tipple of choice, pay tribute to its namesake: a portrait of Charles Grey, the 2nd Earl Grey, can be found in Room 20 of the National Portrait Gallery. Alas, he has in his hand a letter rather than a cuppa.

The origins of Earl Grey tea, flavoured with bergamot oil, are debated.

Illustration by TRIBAMBUKA

The most widely agreed story is that it came about as a drink to be consumed at Howick Hall, the Grey family's Northumberland residence. Bergamot was added to tea to offset lime in the local water, and Lady Grey found it so popular with guests that the recipe was passed to Twinings, who marketed it under the name 'Earl Grey'.

The *Cutty Sark* tea clipper, Greenwich

Greenwich's *Cutty Sark* is the world's only surviving extreme tea clipper ship (extreme clippers had sharper bows than regular clippers, making them zippier). Despite suffering from a fire in 2007, 90% of the ship's hull is original. Its maiden voyage was in 1870, taking wine, spirits and beer to Shanghai and returning with 1.3 million pounds of tea. The voyage lasted a stomach-churning eight months.

Once steam travel became more prevalent, *Cutty Sark* was switched to other duties, including shuttling wool between England and Australia. Under the name *Ferreira*, *Cutty Sark* was damaged in a gale on the way into Falmouth Harbour, bringing an end to her seafaring days but beginning a campaign to restore her.

Also, how many ships can say they have a train station named after them?

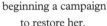

London's tea warehouses and docks

By the 19th century, tea was so popular that great shipments of it were flooding into Britain. Tea clipper ships raced back to the Port of London in an attempt to be the first to unload their cargo, most famously in the Great Tea Race of 1866 in which two ships finished the 14,000 mile journey just 28 minutes apart.

Several London docks were used by tea ships and clippers to unload and store the goods, including St Katharine Docks. In its peak, 32,000 tons of tea came through here every year – now commemorated by a plaque.

Hay's Wharf (now Hay's Galleria) and Shad Thames, both on the south bank of the Thames, were also tea warehouses. In the 19th century, around 80% of the dry goods imported to London arrived in Hay's Wharf – also known as as the 'larder of London'. The offices above the shops and restaurants today were formerly warehouse space where tea would have been stored.

Shad Thames, built in the 1870s, was one of the biggest warehouse complexes in London, and received much of the tea, coffee, spices and other goods arriving in the capital. Today, the apartment buildings are named after these products – one of them Tea Trade Wharf.

Horniman Museum and the Horniman Tea Company

Forest Hill's Horniman Museum doesn't appear at first to have much to do with tea, but its founder Frederick John Horniman made his fortune as a tea trader in Victorian times.

The business – which the family sold in 1918 but still trades as Horniman's Tea today (mainly sold in Spain) – was founded by Frederick's father, John Horniman, in 1826. Until this point, tea was sold loose, but Frederick began selling it packaged, to keep it fresh. (He, alas, didn't invent the tea bag – that was down to an American.)

While travelling the globe sourcing the best leaves, Frederick collected all kinds of zany objects from the countries he visited, thus creating the foundations of today's museum.

You may have noticed a pub in Hay's Galleria called Horniman at Hays. That's a nod to the fact that Horniman's Tea used to be traded at Hay's Wharf. Raise a pint (or cuppa) to him next time you're in the area.

Bramah Tea and Coffee Museum

For a few years, London had a museum dedicated to tea and coffee, covering the trade history of the commodities. If you look closely at certain pedestrian signposts around Shad Thames today, you'll still see directions to the now-defunct Bramah Tea and Coffee Museum. It was opened by tea expert Edward Bramah in 1992, first at Butler's Wharf before later moving to Southwark Street. It closed following Bramah's death in 2008 and never reopened.

Tea brand ghost signs around London

London has several ghost signs (adverts painted onto buildings and walls that have faded over the years) relating to tea.

'James Ashby & Sons Ltd Embassy Tea & Coffee' can be made out on the side of 195–205 Union Street in Southwark. Although the building was under threat in 2008, it was still standing – and the sign still mostly visible – in 2018. The harder-to-read logo above the writing is that of Rose Brand Fine Teas.

The Mazawattee Tea Company was run by the Densham family, who grew their business in 18th-century London. They were based in south London, including Purley and Croydon, and a sign advertising the brand can still be seen from the platform at Sydenham station.

Well-known tea brand Lipton lingers over the entrance to Deptford Market Yard. More synonymous with iced tea today, the company started out when Glaswegian Sir Thomas Lipton purchased tea fields in Ceylon in 1890. Lipton doesn't have any particular connection to the Deptford area, so this was likely just a billboard advertising the product to locals.

David Garrick's tea service at the V&A

Thespian David Garrick – namesake of the Garrick Theatre – travelled extensively for his work, and collected many fine objects, including a tea service now on display at the V&A. The museum acquired it in 2011, and believes that Garrick bought it in Paris in 1764. An intricate oak carry case, lined with paper board and silk, contains a blue-, green-, red- and white-patterned ceramic tea set. Despite damage to the case (since restored), the ceramic is in good nick, with the painters' marks of François Fontelliau and Louis Jean Thévenet.

Afternoon tea in London

Tea is more than a drink these days – afternoon tea is an event in itself, beloved by tourists with a taste for cakes and Instagramming. The Duchess of Bedford dreamed up the idea for afternoon tea in 1840 as a way to fill the long gap between lunch and dinner, and although it wasn't invented here in London – the Duchess was in residence at Woburn Abbey at the time – it soon caught on among London's upper classes. Perhaps the most famous today is afternoon tea at The Ritz, a selection of finger sandwiches, scones, clotted cream, pastries and cakes, served up in the hotel's lavish Palm Court restaurant. An impressive selection of 18 different types of loose-leaf tea are available to accompany your tiered treats.

From the traditional to the bizarre, 21st-century Londoners have a wealth of afternoon teas to choose from. Themed offerings are popular, including the Sanderson Hotel's Mad Hatter Afternoon Tea, and a *Charlie and the Chocolate Factory* affair at One Aldwych.

Where to buy and drink tea in London today

21st-century tea-drinking in London is a multi-faceted beast. For the finest tea experiences, we recommend the following:

Tea House Theatre, Vauxhall: The clue's in the name for this one – tea shop by day, theatre by night, all in a former pub. More than 30 teas are on the cafe menu, from good old Yorkshire tea to black, green and oolong varieties.

Postcard Teas, Bond Street: More than 100 varieties of tea are available at this shop, which includes the date and location where the tea was picked on each label.

Twinings, Strand: We've mentioned Twinings before, but for the best experience visit the Loose Tea Bar when you arrive, and sip on your chosen tea while you browse the rest of the shop.

Fortnum & Mason, Piccadilly: If it's good enough for the Queen, it's good enough for us. The grocer to the Royal Family has been selling tea for more than 300 years, with blends named after various monarchs throughout this period. Green tea, white tea, oolong tea, black tea, infusions tea… it's all there, along with teapots, and other tea drinking gadgets and accessories. Buy it downstairs to drink at home, or head upstairs to The Gallery restaurant to indulge in-store.

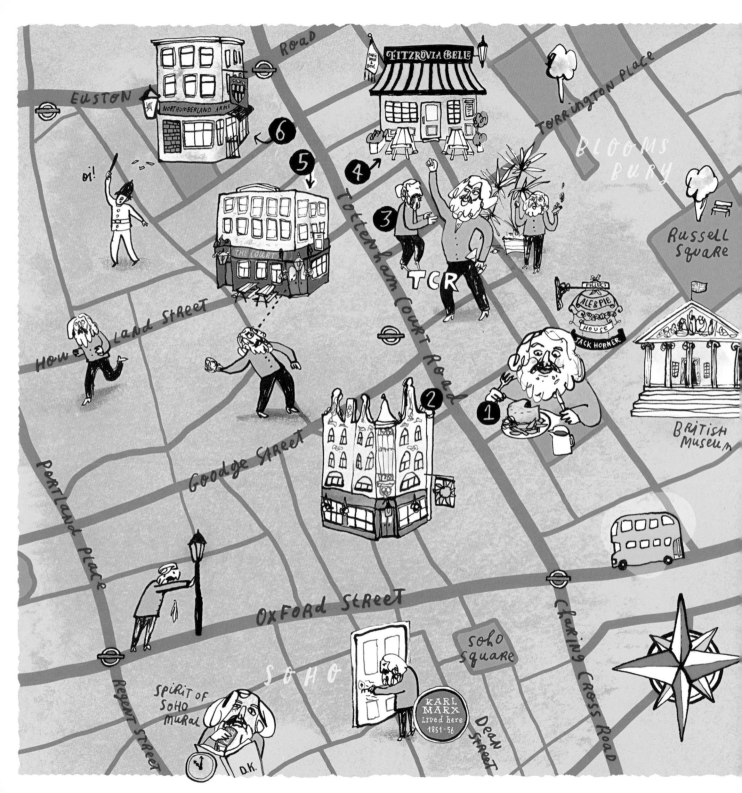

RECREATE KARL MARX'S ROWDY TOTTENHAM COURT ROAD PUB CRAWL

Karl Marx: Thinker, philosopher, theorist, sociologist… and drunken yob.
That's right, the beardy communist was something of a drinker.

One night in the late 1850s, Marx embarked upon a famous pub crawl that would see him arguing with the locals before running down the street smashing gas lamps.

Gathering together some boozy friends, the young(ish) Marx endeavoured to 'take something' in every saloon between Oxford Street and Hampstead Road… that is, to have a drink in every pub along Tottenham Court Road.

The challenge would have been somewhat more intoxicating in Marx's day, when at least 18 pubs lined the street. Today there are just six, but we can still have a beery old time following in his footsteps.

The Jack Horner

The Jack Horner sits, appropriately, on a corner. And like its nursery-rhyme namesake, it has a fondness for pies. Stick your thumb (or fork) into any from a range that includes chicken madras, stargazy, and good old steak 'n' ale. Beer is by Fullers, with six on cask including a guest. Otherwise, it's a fairly unassuming bar with the brewery's usual trick of dark wood, brass trimmings and random prints of ye olde London. Known as the Bedford in Marx's time, this is not a bad place to start.
234–236 Tottenham Court Road, W1T 7QJ

The Rising Sun

An L-shaped stalwart of TCR, the Rising Sun is gloriously Victorian. Marx surely popped in here on his fateful bender. He'd certainly feel at home today. The bar is a relic of bygone days, with an oxblood (or communist red?) ceiling and tactile wallpaper that must have been painted over a hundred times and looks like it's melting. An incongruous fruit machine stands in the corner – the proletarians have nothing to lose but their change. The beer selection is decent and variable. This place has its flaws, but enjoy the decor, for the Rising Sun is perhaps the most characterful stop on our crawl.
46 Tottenham Court Road, W1T 2ED

Illustration by NANNA KOEKOEK

TCR Lounge Bar

Remarkably, TCR Lounge Bar is the only stop on our crawl that wasn't a pub in Marx's day. The website says this is a 'style bar'. Maybe once upon a time, but now the TCR looks a little dated and careworn. It's not without its merits – a lively scene on a Friday night, and a little-known beer garden (rare in these parts) hidden round the back. It does have a spacious, relaxed feel on a weekday afternoon, and more of a buzz in the evening, with thumping music. It's caught somewhere between a pub and a bar. The drink selection tends more toward the latter, with lagers and cocktails being the house 'thing'. This would be the point on the crawl where Marx would be getting a bit jolly – perhaps making puns about 'glass struggles' – but we still have a way to go.

183 Tottenham Court Road, W1T 7PE

The Fitzrovia Belle

Marx would have known this place as the Mortimer Arms, but it now associates itself with Fitzrovia, despite being – to most people's perceptions – on the wrong side of TCR (though technically in the Fitzrovia conservation area). Tiny front room, lengthy back room, and all is abuzz. This sports pub has guest bedrooms upstairs, which might be just the thing after a riotous night out.

174 Tottenham Court Road, W1T 7NT

The Court

The Court tends to attract a young crowd, drawn from UCL and the nearby teaching hospital – though the copious passing trade brings in all-comers. With burgers, curries, pies and other favourites at superbly low prices, it's no wonder that this is a student haunt. Unless you're a massive grumpian, you can't help but smile along with the positive mood in this place. If Marx were here, this is the point he'd start tugging at his beard with nascent thoughts about smashing things.

108a Tottenham Court Road, W1T 5AA

The Northumberland Arms

It's hard to classify the Northumberland. It's a fairly small pub with lofty ideas. The menu flourishes words like 'organic', 'fresh' and 'handmade', while the background music is cool-as-a-communist-cucumber. The beers are mainstream, but good mainstream. This diminutive drinking space is tight and cosy, and it would be easy to eavesdrop on comrades at the next table. As the most northerly pub on Tottenham Court Road (both now and in the 1850s), it's possible that Marx ended his crawl in this very space. The beer must have been talking by this point: 'outlaw private property', 'abolish religion', 'rise up and smash the capitalist gas lights!'.

Having completed the Karl Marx pub crawl, it is but a two-minute walk to Warren Street station. Please do not smash the lamps.

119 Tottenham Court Road, W1T 5AW

DRINK LIKE A SPY
IN THE ROARING 20S

Looking for a location for a clandestine meeting? Londonist *has your back.*

Spies and secret agents have always liked meeting in public places. It's more anonymous – safer, even. Sensitive conversations can get lost in the general hubbub of other diners and drinkers. (So, of course, can the addition of radioactive polonium-210 to a man's cup of tea, as London discovered when Aleksandr Litvinenko was poisoned in the Pine Bar of the Millennium Hotel in 2006.)

The British government has gradually been declassifying the MI5 archives, held at the National Archives in Kew. They're brimming with unexpected details about the lives of British Intelligence officers and the people they spied on – including information about where spies liked to dine, drink and let their hair down.

Most of these establishments are in central London, which has always been Britain's principal magnet for spies. But the suburbs feature one or two important locations too: secret agents must be willing to go wherever their orders take them. Several of the businesses still exist today. If you happen to find yourself in one, cast your eye round to check whether any of your fellow customers might be hiding a secret or two.

Then again, if they were doing their job properly, how would you know?

Bodega Wine House, Bedford Street (closed 1970s)

A forerunner of later chains like All Bar One, the Bodega specialised in wine rather than beer. It had an ornate interior spread over many floors and was colloquially known as the Marble Halls. It was popular with writers, journalists and actors – which is probably why, in early 1925, W N Ewer, a leading journalist, decided to use it to meet a potential British Intelligence informant. In addition to his work at the *Daily Herald* newspaper, Ewer was a Soviet spy. In the best traditions of intelligence tradecraft, he instructed his secret service contact to 'carry with you or be reading a copy of the *Daily Herald*'.

Claridge's, Mayfair

In the 1920s, Claridge's developed a reputation as the favourite haunt for well-to-do flappers and bright young things. Simultaneously its airy lobbies and exclusive dining rooms were available to Soviet revolutionaries. In the summer of 1920, the leading Russian Communist

Lev Kamenev took to lunching here during his whirlwind romance with Clare Sheridan, a sculptor who happened to be Winston Churchill's cousin. Kamenev was present in London for peace talks with the British government, but British Intelligence suspected that he was trying to recruit Sheridan as a means of getting the goss on Churchill, who was then a cabinet minister. MI5 arranged for a friend of Sheridan's, Sidney Russell Cooke, who was also a former officer of the service, to join her and Kamenev at the hotel restaurant and report back on what went on.

Café Royal, Regent Street

A Victorian institution that thrived in the Roaring Twenties, the Café Royal was another place where Kamenev and Sheridan liked to dine out. At a slightly later date, in the mid-1920s, it was also a favourite drinking spot of Wilfred Macartney, a one-time millionaire who became a convicted jewel thief when his inheritance ran out. After getting caught, Macartney converted to Communism, (much to the surprise of his close friends), and went on to sell British military secrets to the Russians for money. His MI5 file described him as an inveterate imbiber of the Café Royal's hot grogs. He thought he was good at covering his tracks, but he was actually watched every step of the way by the intelligence agencies and eventually his espionage landed him in jail for a 10-year stretch.

The Dolphin, Uxbridge

Less celebrated and less central than other spots, the Dolphin pub on the Grand Union Canal in Uxbridge nonetheless played a starring role in a key episode in British history, the ARCOS raid. In May 1927, British police raided the Soviet Union's main diplomatic office in the City of London, which was known as the ARCOS building. The government expelled 400 Soviet citizens after the raid accusing them of involvement in spying and other seditious activities. The tip-off that sparked the raid came from a former British employee of the Soviets, Edward Langston, who said that he had seen classified British documents inside the building. Langston's new job was as the landlord of the Dolphin pub and it was from here that he monitored the news of the raid and its aftermath, worrying greatly about the possibility of reprisals. Soviet secret agents did indeed work out his identity and run him to ground. He sent a telegram to MI5 asking for a revolver to protect himself.

Frolics, Regent Street (closed mid-1920s)

This 1920s nightclub on Regent's Place was popular with people searching for somewhere to drink and dance after the pubs closed. Restrictive licensing laws meant that nightclubs were subject to regular police attention because **they sold** hard liquor out-of-hours. But Frolics went one better and attracted surveillance from British Intelligence when an MI5 informant pointed out that it had become the favourite 'night haunt' of female Soviet spies in London. Allegedly, these women were trying to 'get into touch with British officers and young men of good standing' at the club in the hope of starting affairs with them and recruiting them to the Communist cause.

Lyon's Corner Houses, various locations (last one closed 1977)

This celebrated chain of teashops, with their 'Nippy' waitresses, was owned by the ancestors of Nigella Lawson. The Soviet secret agent Walter Dale liked to meet his moles inside Special Branch at the Corner House near Bank tube station. Over tea, and perhaps the occasional slice of cake, he received tip-offs about future secret operations as well as documents from Special Branch's confidential archives. All of these he passed on to Moscow.

Pinoli's, Wardour Street (closed 1949)

Pinoli's was a Soho institution, a large restaurant in the Grand-Café style that catered to a wide range of tastes and pockets. In late 1920 it was the scene of an event that British Intelligence watched with microscopic interest: the end-of-year dinner of the influential Hampstead branch of the Communist Party of Great Britain. Details of the evening were gathered meticulously by the authorities, who were extremely worried to discover that the guest of honour was a Soviet spy called Nikolai Klyshko. Somewhat excessively, Special Branch sent full particulars of the soirée to the British cabinet, down to the contents of the set menu, which included tomato soup and lamb cutlets. Festivities apparently ended with a rousing rendition of 'The Red Flag'.

The Savoy, Strand

With its renowned Savoy Orpheans Band and American Bar, The Savoy summed up the height of jazz-age glamour. It was also the perfect setting to demonstrate one's membership of the international elite. That was what Jacob Kirchenstein and his wife Vallie wanted to achieve when they stayed here after arriving in London from New York in late 1922. Jacob was posing as a shipping agent and wanted to look wealthy and sophisticated. In reality, he was preparing to work as a Soviet secret agent. Moscow had sent him to Britain in order to coordinate a network of spies across the British Empire and to steal military secrets. Thanks to the cover he created with the help of The Savoy, he was able to operate undetected by MI5 and other intelligence agencies for several years.

A MARTINI FIT FOR JAMES BOND

Numerous scientific studies have concluded that James Bond has an alcohol problem. Not really the level-headed gentleman you want gambling for world security in a casino in the south of France, is it? Of all the drinks Bond has casual relationships with, the best-known is the Vesper martini. He orders it in *Casino Royale** – and never again. It appears that Bond's taste in cocktails lasts as long as his taste in women.

Make a Vesper martini
6 parts gin. *We would choose a masculine gin like Duck and Crutch with its nutmeg and walnut notes*
2 parts vodka. *It really should be Russian*
1 part Lillet Blanc

Martini purists shy away from shaking martinis, which dilutes the drink a little more, and chills it better. But be a devil, shake vigorously over a little ice, and serve with a twist of lemon peel, while saying something witty. Or order one at DUKES (see pages 43 and 85), the Mayfair bar where Fleming is thought to have come up with Bond's tipple.

*He also orders a Heineken in the 2006 film. Seriously, James?

SPORTS BARS THAT ARE ACTUALLY GOOD

Your team is playing. Your person is boxing. Your horse is running. Your country is… swimming?
We all love a bit of The Sports. But are there actually any decent sports bars in London?

You know, ones that don't charge you a fortune to watch the Europa League quarter-final, or try to dissolve your taste buds with exorbitant Danish lager? As you may have guessed from the title of this article, the answer is yes. Let the reading commence!

Bar Kick, Shoreditch

Footy gets a dose of Continental class at Bar Kick – a hangout scattered with Formica tables, and draped in international football scarves. The drinks are not your usual fare; we have literally ordered a sidecar here during a Man U match, and the barman didn't bat an eyelid. When there isn't a match on, give your wrist a workout on the fussball tables (spinning's cheating). Sister bar Cafe Kick, on Exmouth Market, is an equally worthy hipster-footy haven.
127 Shoreditch High Street, E1 6JE

The Faltering Fullback, Finsbury

It may have bicycles dangling from the ceiling, but The Faltering Fullback's sport of choice is rugby. You'll have to turn up early for a chance of bagging a seat in this cosy, gimcrack-festooned boozer. But for those who value character over comfort, crowding around the horseshoe bar and craning your neck up at the TVs is all part of the experience. Sink a pint of the Black Stuff and soak it up with a Thai curry (no Irish stew on the menu here). The pub garden feels more like a mini rainforest, and tends to be inhabited with half of north London, whether the sun's out or not.
19 Perth Road, Finsbury Park, N4 3HB

Golazio, Walworth

Remember that Channel 4 football show from the 90s, *Football Italia*? The founders of Golazio certainly did – they created this modish Walworth bar around their obsession, plastering it with retro Italy kits, and playing Serie A games (current and vintage) on a projector. They screen Premier League footie, too. Far from being a novelty bar, Golazio serves up piping hot pizza by the slice (beats a packet of salt and vinegar), and you can get your gob around a 12-strong Italian craft beer selection. Some of it is punchier than a bout of *Calcio fiorentino*. For some reason though, when we were last there, they switched the football over to the rugby. Referee!
59 Camberwell Road, SE5 0EZ

Greenwood, Victoria

Football. NFL. Boxing. Rugby. You name it, Greenwood probably screens it. After all, it does have about twelve billion screens (not to mention a couple of stuffed zebra heads). This being Victoria, there is an urbane, gentlemen's club theme going on; the space-age lighting and mid-century sideboards make it feel like the kind of establishment in which Don Draper would sip an old fashioned, while watching the Mets. Book a table, and get in some sharing platters (pizza, croquettes, buffalo wings). They're named Get the Ball Rolling, The Gloves are Off and The Whole Nine Yards. Sports references, innit.

170 Victoria Street, Westminster, SW1E 5LB

Hamlet Bar, East Dulwich

An afternoon at Dulwich Hamlet is a must for anyone, football fan or no. The locals' self-aware middle-class chants (including the only ones, to our knowledge, to contain the word 'Plantagenet') should frankly be released as an album. Now happily relocated to their former East Dulwich ground, Hamlet have opened the club bar seven days a week. Here you can shoot pool while ogling sports on the TV. Order an Edgar Kail Pale Ale, named after their legendary forward, and brewed exclusively for the club.

Another bar-in-a-stadium that has our seal of approval: Leyton Orient Supporters Club. It's good for pre-match raffles, real ale and homemade butties. Actually, it's one of the friendliest bars we've been in, period. Finally, there's the bar at Spurs' new stadium – the Goal Line Bar. At 65 metres, it claims to be the longest bar in Europe, and magically serves pints from the bottom up. And not just your average lager; it's well stocked with in-house microbrewery Beavertown's delicious offerings.

Champion Hill Stadium, Edgar Kail Way, SE22 8BD

Look Mum, No Hands!, Old Street

Right. Here's another establishment with cycles hanging from the ceiling – and this one IS bike related. A coffee shop/repair workshop/merch boutique, Look Mum, No Hands! is one of many cycle cafes peddling – or should that be pedalling – their wares in London. And though this isn't a sports bar per se, you can watch major cycling events – not least the Tour de France – unfold on a big screen here. They also show cycling documentaries, followed by Q&As. Our first question would be: "Sorry, how do you fix a puncture again?"

49 Old Street, EC1V 9HX

The Porterhouse, Covent Garden

12 levels of beer, live music and a van-load of TVs make The Porterhouse a veritable Fun House of booze. When World Cups, Six Nations, Wimbledon et al are on, the beer flows (it's their own beer, too – try the oyster stout, with real oyster juice in it), and the good times roll. After the sport's done and dusted, the real party happens: live bands, perched on the mezzanine, belt out feel-good hits, and everything is right with the world. If England (or Ireland – it's an Irish pub) are victorious, start concocting those excuses for not making it into work tomorrow.

21–22 Maiden Lane, WC2E 7NA

Radicals & Victuallers, Angel

One of our biggest beefs with the common-or-garden sports bar is that the beer offering is often one of *those* godawful lagers or *that* ubiquitous stout, and not much in between. Radicals & Victuallers doesn't suffer from such a problem – partly because it's a bar that screens sport, rather than a full-time sports bar. A range of tasty brews from the likes of Tiny Rebel, Thornbridge and Brewdog plays out well with anyone who appreciates a decent pint. We find that it's marginally more palatable to watch your team get walloped 4-0 if you're supping a Welsh tropical pale ale.

59 Upper Street, N1 0NY

The Sydney Arms, Chelsea

Grizzled racing commentator John McCririck is no stranger to the Sydney Arms, an upmarket boozer which brands itself 'London's Racing Pub'. Five screens blare out all the important gee gee races, plus a healthy mix of rugby and football. They do a roaring trade in fizz here (these are horse people. In CHELSEA), and the wine list is more accomplished than pretty much any sports bar in London. On big race days, prepare to be fascinated by the array of fascinators. There'll be no shortage of tips flying around too. If you win big, celebrate with the £95 bottle of Laurent Perrier rosé.

70 Sydney Street, Chelsea, SW3 6NJ

PECULIAR PUB INTERIORS

Dead cats, drunken Teletubbies and a fossilised turd.
It's amazing what you can find inside a London pub.

The Blackfriar, Blackfriars

An unofficial waiting room for Thameslink 'services' (see page 156), The Blackfriar is a jewel both inside and out. The interior is decorated with dozens of murals, sculptures and reliefs showing friars going about their monkish business. Be sure to stick your head into the barrel-roofed dining area, perhaps the most opulent pub room in central London.
174 Queen Victoria Street, EC4V 4EG

The Champion, Fitzrovia

This sturdy Sam Smith's pub is enlivened by a series of tinted glass windows depicting sporting champions of yore. The eye is immediately drawn to hirsute cricketer WG Grace. Other champs include Channel swimmer Matthew Webb, boxer Bob Fitzsimmons and jockey Fred Archer. Further Victorian celebs such as Florence Nightingale and David Livingstone are also commemorated.
12–13 Wells Street, W1T 3PA

The Churchill Arms, Notting Hill

The Churchill (see page 115 also) is eccentric both inside and out. The exterior is a riot of hanging baskets. Colourful inflorescence almost entirely obscures the pub. Inside, too, there's little hint of the fabric of the building, with several giga-Steptoes (the SI unit of clutter) suspended from the ceiling. Pots, pans, porcelain commodes, sporting gear, lamps, royal memorabilia, bunting and assorted Churchillian gimcracks all dangle overhead. The back room resembles the exterior, with more

plants than a post-apocalyptic Homebase. To awkwardly paraphrase Churchill, 'Never in the field of pub decoration has so much been displayed to so many, in such a tight space'.
119 Kensington Church Street, W8 7LN

Dirty Dicks, Bishopsgate

With a Carry On-style sense of humour, Dirty Dicks eschews its expected apostrophe, leading to plentiful sniggers. Named after an 18th-century hoarder, the pub long kept its cellar bar in a state of artful tattiness, with mummified animals and giant cobwebs all part of the charm. The cellar was cleaned up a decade or so ago, but you can still admire the shrivelled up cats, rats and squirrels in a display cabinet downstairs. Taxidermy can be found in many a London pub, but you ain't seen nothing quite like the emaciated felines of Dirty Dicks. Just don't do an image search if anybody else is looking.
202 Bishopsgate, EC2M 4NR

The George and Dragon, Acton

No feature, individually taken, is particularly unusual about this 18th-century inn. It's the combination of old and new that make it such a revelation. The front room is a pure slice of history, with rich, dark wood panelling, a golden bust and a three-quarter length portrait of a cavalier. You then pass through another ye olde room with a period fireplace and emerge into the back bar. This could not be more different. Dubbed the 'Dragonfly Brewery', the former dining room is dominated by huge copper fermentation tanks and two oversized, half-nude nymph statues. We've never seen a contrast quite like it.
183 High Street, W3 9DJ

The Grenadier, Belgravia

This charming mews pub is a former officers' mess and wears its military credentials on its sleeve, with old uniforms and regimental keepsakes dotted about. Most memorable, though, is the ceiling decoration. An old tradition (see page 147) invites patrons to pin signed dollar bills to the plasterwork. These are said to be for 'Cedric', whose spirit (see page 121) haunts the pub every September, if the legends are to be believed.
18 Wilton Row, SW1X 7NR

Lord Nelson, Southwark

This funtime pub looks like it was decorated by a group of pissed-up students. The back room is painted like a nursery, with giant pansies and buttercups climbing the walls, overshadowing grinning snails and Teletubbies. The main bar, meanwhile, is a temple to popular culture. A Simpson's spiderpig crawls along the ceiling, doing whatever a spiderpig does. Gizmo from *Gremlins* superintends the lager taps. Snoopy, Mario and Cartman are all present and incorrect. Don't be surprised if you leave with a traffic cone on your head.
243 Union Street, SE1 0LR

The Seven Stars, Carey Street

It's not so much the interior of this tiny old pub that's a bit weird, but the window displays. At first, you'll spy a dusty menagerie of stuffed birds, lone feathers and ostrich eggs… odd things to find in a pub window, but nothing too outrageous. Then you notice that one of the skulls wears a barrister's wig. This braincase of jurisprudence peers down on a smaller rodent skull, this time wearing a spectacle… yes, in the singular, for the eyepiece has one lens and two arms. A fossilised turd resides nearby. This surreal bricolage is labelled 'The Cabinet of Largesse'. We've never yet enquired what it all means. We're not sure we want to know.
53–54 Carey Street, WC2A 2JB

The Sherlock Holmes, Charing Cross

Downstairs, you'll find a handsome but elementary bar with the usual beers of the Greene King chain. But follow the clues to the upstairs room, and you're in for a singular treat. Here stands a life-sized recreation of Holmes's study, rescued from the 1951 Festival of Britain. Fans of the detective will delight in spotting the numerous props from the canon. Even if you don't care for Victorian sleuthing, it's worth a look for the dummy of Holmes alone, which resembles an emaciated Vladimir Putin.
10 Northumberland Street, WC2N 5DB

HOW MANY RED LIONS ARE THERE IN LONDON?

The Red Lion is widely regarded as Britain's most common pub name. The Pubs Galore website, a crowdsourced site that keeps track of pub closures and openings, counts 567 at the time of writing.

So, how many Red Lions can be found in London? We count 26, if you include variations like Ye Olde Red Lion (Cheam), Red Lion and Sun (Highgate) and the Red Lion and Pineapple in Acton – part of the Wetherspoon chain, whose peculiar name recalls two earlier pubs in the area. If we pare things back to venues called simply 'The Red Lion', then we reckon on 21.

The crimson feline can be found right across the capital, from Bromley to Enfield to Uxbridge, but central London has more than its fair share. The closest are both in St James's, a mere five-minute walk from one another (and both thoroughly charming).

The Red Lion in Whitehall is technically the prime minister's local – it's the closest pub to 10 Downing Street. It also contains a 'division bell', which rings every time Members of the House of Commons need to put down the pint and go cast a vote. Do not mistake it for the fire alarm.

No one is sure quite why the country has so many Red Lions. Some writers note that the beast is among the most common devices on coats of arms – hence, the widespread name probably has many origins that can be traced back to different nobles and landowners.

Still, 26 Red Lions is fewer than we'd have guessed. Indeed, pubs called the Prince of Wales are more numerous, with at least 31 active pubs across the capital. Who'd have thought he'd be so popular?

Illustration by ANDY COUNCIL.

THE MARVELLOUS UNIVERSE OF THE MICROPUB

Pull up a chair, grab a pint, put your phone away, and rediscover the art of enjoying a drink and some conversation. Beautiful.

Micropubs began life in Kent in the mid-2000s as an alternative to mainstream boozers where the music was too loud, the smell of roasts got up your nostrils and the telly proved too much of a distraction. The first one, the Butcher's Arms, opened near Canterbury in 2005 and has inspired more than 300 others across the country.

These early pint-sized pubs followed a simple philosophy. They concentrated on a rotating line-up of cask ales, they usually had only one room, and you wouldn't find a TV or music in them – and Lord forbid you should chat on your phone. London's first micropub, The Door Hinge, opened in Welling in 2013, and follows this formula closely, with a smashed-up Nokia on the wall serving as a strict reminder to keep your phone switched off.

The micropub has already evolved from those Kentish roots. Ciders, wines and spirits are on the menu now – all chosen with the same care as the ales. Others have borrowed features from the micropub's close cousin, the bottle shop. Some have quizzes and live music. One (no names, no pack drill) even broke all the rules and

put a TV in for the 2018 World Cup. What would the purists say?

Now there are more than 20 micropubs in and around London. The beers are normally beautifully kept – and you can try before you buy. Board games and resident dogs feature heavily too. These places are nearly all run by just one or two people – many are shut on Mondays to give them a day off – and there's a story behind most, be it a redundancy money investment, or simply a desire to give their own neighbourhood a decent place to go for a drink. Many are off the beaten track; all are well worth your time tracking down. Here are 11 to get you started.

The Beer Shop, Nunhead

There aren't many bars with their own running clubs, but pop into The Beer Shop on a Tuesday evening and you'll find the Runhead runners getting ready for their exertions – or toasting their efforts with a well-deserved ale. Based in an old corner shop unit, The Beer Shop treats cask and keg with equal reverence, and hosts street food pop-ups and beer tastings. A family friendly hangout during the daytime, you're as likely to find a child with a colouring book as you are a hoary old beer fan ticking off an entry in his copy of *London Drinker*.
40 Nunhead Green, SE15 3QF

The Dodo, Hanwell

Don't believe dreams can come true? Head to Hanwell and visit Lucy Do, who got the micropub bug after chucking in a career in marketing. Two years later, she opened The Dodo, and it's gone from strength to strength, even collaborating with the nearby Weird Beard brewery. Even for a micropub, this is minuscule – you order from your seat to save space – but thoughtfully designed and oh-so friendly. The Dodo has become a community hub, and after a couple of hours spent in the company of Lucy and her partner Alex, you can feel like a part of the Hanwell Massive. If Crossrail's got you contemplating a move to Hanwell, The Dodo might just seal the deal.

57 Boston Road, W7 3TR

The Hangar Micropub, Sidcup

Sidcup is London's micropub capital, and it's hard to choose between the options here. The Hangar is the newest, and developed a devoted following within weeks. You'd think this quiet shopping parade would resist the arrival of a micropub, but The Hangar has pulled it off by offering a mouthwatering range of ales and wines. Unusually for a micropub, there are even a couple of lagers on the menu. A Monday evening quiz features a game of hoopla. A wonderful place to visit on its own, or as part of a tour around the local micropub scene: there are two others (The Halfway House and The Broken Drum) within walking distance, while The Hackney Carriage and Hopper's Hut are a short 51 bus ride away.

37 The Oval, DA15 9ER

The Hop and Vine, Ruislip

At other end of the high street from the tube station – stroll past the Wimpy and the British Legion – sits perhaps the classiest of London's micropubs. You can order a cheese board to go with your beer, for goodness' sake. In another age, this would have been a wine bar, maybe even a coffee shop, but today, we'll happily settle for its wide range of gravity beers with a couple of keg beers too, as well as bottles and cans. On our visit, the owners had just returned from a holiday: "Welcome back – we missed you!" read a sign on the wall. It's not just the beer that leaves you with a nice glow.

18 High Street, HA4 7AN

Gidea Park Micropub

If you're really fussy about what you tip down your neck, you can check what beers are available on Gidea Park Micropub's online beer board. Dominoes and darts keep you amused, while pork pies ward off an empty stomach. If you want to take a memento home, buy an old pump clip, with the proceeds going to charity. Havering Council originally refused permission for this to be converted from an accountants' office. Bet some of them now sneak in here for a crafty pint.

236 Main Road, RM2 5HA

The Kentish Belle, Bexleyheath

Somebody here likes trains. The pub is named after a train. It helps raise money to restore old trains. And it's right next to Bexleyheath station. But the Kentish Belle is an altogether pleasanter experience than riding with Southeastern. It's a space for everybody; alongside real ales and a range of gins, you'll find events from quizzes to bottle swaps, a cheese club and board games nights. You wonder quite what this corner of Bexleyheath did before this place opened in early 2018. The landlord, Nicholas Hair, has stuck his neck out in demanding change in the fusty old Campaign for Real Ale. If the way he runs the Kentish Belle is anything to go by, they should be listening.

8 Pickford Lane, DA7 4QW

Little Green Dragon, Winchmore Hill

Named after a long-gone pub down the road, it's the regulars who make the Little Green Dragon what it is. And there are loads of them – the place was already heaving before the Campaign for Real Ale named it its London Pub of the Year 2018. The pub's most eye-catching feature is a corner of old bus memorabilia – the owner dusted off a pair of old bus seats to install, and then customers donated artefacts such as flyers for long-gone coach trips to Spurs and Arsenal matches. A cosy little bolt-hole worth a long bus ride to get to.

928 Green Lanes, N21 2AD

One Inn the Wood, Petts Wood

Petts Wood, between Bromley and Orpington, is where Daylight Saving Time was born. Inventor William Willett came up with the idea while riding his horse early one morning and seeing how many blinds were down. Thanks to him, you can enjoy languid summer evenings at One Inn The Wood, which specialises in Kent beers, ciders and wines. There are also Kent pork pies… even the crisps are from Kent. It's a little way off the Sidcup micropub cluster, so often gets overlooked, but this gem won CAMRA's London Pub of the Year in 2015 and is a beer aficionados' favourite. The service is friendly, and so are the fellow customers.

205 Petts Wood Road, BR5 1LA

The Radius Arms, Whyteleafe

We've broken a rule here. This is actually a couple of hundred metres outside London. But the wonderful Radius Arms is so easy to get to – a few minutes' walk from Whyteleafe and Upper Warlingham stations, both in zone 6, and just a few minutes from East Croydon – that we'll turn a blind eye. On a Saturday night, it feels like half of Croydon's here, with a real jumble of ages and genders, and usually a little puppy cradled in someone's arms. When we visited, there was a strong beer (7% Estonian porter, anyone?), a light beer (a tasty 2.8% table beer) and a whole range in between. The Radius also does ciders, wines and spirits, while its fridge is stuffed with bottles and cans. The ceiling is cluttered with old pump clips, and the walls display a love of motor racing and aviation. If you've ever doubted the appeal of a micropub, this is the one to come to.

203 Godstone Road, CR3 0EL

The River Ale House, Greenwich

Forget selfies on the Meridian Line – this is the real reason to come to Greenwich. Owner Trevor Puddifoot used to run a lingerie shop in a beaten-up old parade before the internet took his passing trade away. In 2017, his shop was reborn as The River Ale House. It's quickly become a much-loved part of life in this overlooked end of Greenwich, closer to Ikea and the roar of the Blackwall Tunnel flyover than the museums and market.

The keen prices and friendly atmosphere mean The River often attracts a slightly younger crowd. It's also pooch-friendly – it's not unusual to see three or four in here at once – and a favourite stop-off for fans heading to and from Charlton matches at The Valley. The beer's always top-notch, and there are plenty of bottles, cans, wines, ciders and gins to choose from, as well as sausage rolls and Scotch eggs for soakage.

131 Woolwich Road, SE10 0RJ

Upminster Taproom

Another micropub that overcame opposition from Havering Council (what is going on at that town hall?), the Upminster Tap Room is an excellent reason to jump on a train from Fenchurch Street. Housed in a Scout hut-like building by a petrol station, it doesn't look much, but inside lies a beer nirvana. The guv'nor serves you from one of the tables and everybody stops for a chat. On one of our visits, he found himself defending the concept of income tax to one of the regulars. Thankfully the battle he endured to get this place opened hasn't curdled his good humour, nor his love of talking about music. There's plenty of cider, wine and prosecco on offer, plus flavoured vodkas. If you're ever out around the Essex end of the District line, the only way is the Taproom.
1b Sunnyside Gardens, RM14 3DT

Also worth a mention

The borough of Bexley is the spiritual home of the London micropub. **The Door Hinge** in Welling was the first, with a back-to-basics, blokey vibe. It was followed by **The Penny Farthing** in Crayford and **The Broken Drum** in Blackfen. All are worth a visit, as is the Bexley Brewery's micropub, the **Bird & Barrel** at Barnehurst. Elsewhere, opposite Hayes station – the one near Bromley – you'll find the **Real Ale Way**, where folk music shindigs are as much of a draw as the beer, wine and gin. In Eltham, **The Long Pond** is a friendly two-room micropub that is hugely popular. Over in Northfields, **The Owl & The Pussycat** – a former children's bookshop (see page 11) – sells its own beers from the Marko Paulo brewery, which is handily located behind the bar.

Slightly further afield

Just outside London – but still reachable on an Oyster card – is **The Cotton Mill** in Swanley, a micropub built in a converted toilet. If it's sunny, you can sit on the little green outside. There's also a mobile bar for hire, built from a horsebox. Pushing your Oyster card to the limit, Dorking – right at the end of the 465 bus route – is home to **Cobbetts Beer Shop and Micropub**, which only seats 12 people but sells a fantastic array of beers to drink in or take away (and, with that capacity, you might not have a choice). If you're keen enough to make it out that far, treat yourself to a day out in Margate, which has plenty of micropubs. The one to put at the top of the list is the **Harbour Arms**, in a former fisherman's hut. Accompany your brew with a cup of whelks.

Not quite micropubs, but definitely microbars

Generally speaking, if you see a row of taps on the wall behind the bar, you're in a craft beer bar, not a micropub. But a couple do blur the line, and again, it's south London leading the way. **The Rusty Bucket** in Eltham is converted from a long-closed 'proper' pub, sells both keg and cask, and has modelled itself on how micropubs work. **Beer Rebellion** in Peckham has a similar atmosphere – and they let you chose your own glass. In Anerley – down the hill from Crystal Palace Park – **The Douglas Fir** is the Gipsy Hill Brewery's 'microbar', selling its own (and guest) beers. And **The Sympathetic Ear**, at the Brixton end of Tulse Hill, is a small but perfectly formed bar from the Canopy brewery.

THE LONDON PUB THAT'S IN A NURSERY RHYME

Have you ever dined inside a nursery rhyme?
If you've eaten at The Eagle on City Road, then count yourself included.

The pub is mentioned in the well-known tune 'Pop Goes the Weasel'. Specifically: "Up and down the City Road, in and out The Eagle; that's the way the money goes, Pop! goes the weasel."

We've been in and out of The Eagle on many occasions. It has a convivial atmosphere, a handsome green-tiled exterior, advertising 'Barclay's Stout and Ales', and one of the few beer gardens near Old Street tube. Unlike in the rhyme, there's no tuppenny rice or treacle by the half-pound on the menu. There's plenty of pop, though.

Where did the tune come from?

Surprisingly, the earliest mention of 'Pop Goes the Weasel' ties it to Queen Victoria. A series of adverts from 1852 and 1853 promote lessons in the 'highly fashionable' dance, as 'introduced at her Majesty's private soiree'. The British Library holds a copy of the music sheet from 1853. It has a similar tune to today, though nobody knows who composed it.

It soon filtered down the social classes. Race horses were named after the song.

Street musicians sang it on every corner. In 1854, the line "pop goes the weasel!" was described by one commentator as an "idiotic exclamation so humiliating to the intelligence of our age and race". Manufactured outrage is, it seems, nothing new. By 1856, anger had turned to ennui, when a correspondent to the *Morning Post* wrote: "Sir, For many months, everybody has been bored to death with the eternal grinding of this ditty on street". It has since lodged deep in the psyche, and continued down to our own time as one of the classic English nursery rhymes.

What does it mean?

The nonsense lyrics were debated even when fresh, in the 1850s. They have found many interpretations. "Pop goes the weasel" might relate to a spinner's tool, rhyming slang for throat (weasel and stoat), the act of pawning silver plate, or the sudden movement of an actual weasel. Again, nobody knows.

Is it definitely our pub?

The part relevant to our drinking den seems clearer: "Up and down the City Road, in and out The Eagle". This is almost certainly a reference to the pub that still stands today. A version of 1855 clearly makes reference:

In the Bird of Conquest, made
first by Romans famous,
Though "Grecian" my saloon was called
By some ignoramus.
Up and down the City-road,
In and out The Eagle,
That's the way the money comes,
Pop goes the weasel.

The rhyme makes sense when we know that The Eagle was nicknamed the Grecian Saloon in the 1850s, and was run by a Mr Benjamin Conquest. 'Pop Goes the Weasel' might not have started on the City Road, but it was quickly associated with the venue.

So next time you're passing down City Road, or looking for a place to wet your whistle near Old Street, consider a trip to The Eagle. Just watch out for exploding mustelids.

Illustration by LIVI GOSLING ILLUSTRATION

london toilets
you can drink in

LONDON TOILETS YOU CAN DRINK IN

Our city is flush with water closets that've been transformed into watering holes. And so, ladies and gentlemen, (toilet) roll up, and prepare to spend somewhat more than a penny…

The Attendant, Fitzrovia

This public convenience served people from 1890 until the 1960s, when the site was left dormant for 50 years. Then The Attendant moved in, a delightful cafe serving your coffee and brunching needs (although, alas, no booze). Instead The Attendant is more wellness-focused: think matcha and chai lattes. Whatever you're drinking, be sure to have it at the old urinals – now tastefully converted into tables. (Also as the whole toilet is now a cafe, it actually has no toilet – there isn't room. So it's probably a good thing that The Attendant doesn't serve any booze.)
27a Foley Street, W1W 6DY

Bermondsey Arts Club, Bermondsey

Here at *Londonist*, we have a strong belief that what a toilet really needs is some jazz. Thankfully, the folks at lush art-deco styled Bermondsey Arts Club agree with us, as that's what awaits inside these former loos. The cocktail list here is extensive and changes regularly depending on the season. We recommend the Brazillian Tea Punch, a blend of cachaca and lemongrass to transport you across the globe – although who'd want to be anywhere other than a set of converted loos?
102a Tower Bridge Road, SE1 4TP

CellarDoor, Aldwych

This was once the most infamous gents in Theatreland – supposedly Oscar Wilde, John Gielgud and Joe Orton were all patrons – and is now a cocktail and burlesque bar (see page 54) with one of London's sauciest loos in it. What's so saucy about the loo? The cubicle door is entirely see-through until the latch is locked. If that all sounds a bit much for you then just head to the bar, where the staff can create whichever cocktail you so desire, whether it's on the menu or not. Expect the dancers to get up close and personal during the burlesque performances – like many others on this list, it's a tight squeeze inside.
Wellington Street, WC2E 7DN

Chiringuito

Chiringuito holds a special accolade in London, as the only tapas joint with a rooftop bar in a former lavvy. It might be a sign of the times to be eating patatas bravas in what was a loo in the heart of the old East End, but it's a tasty one. Despite the Spanish name and tapas format, Chiringuito's cuisine doesn't just hail from the Iberian Peninsula – there's a fair bit from Latin America too (note the ceviche). The rooftop delights in summer thanks to the immense location on Museum Gardens. It's even got a cocktail named after the park: basil infused vodka, elderflower liquor, fresh lime, sugar, egg white, mint and grapefruit bitters.
Bethnal Green Museum Gardens, Cambridge Heath Road, E2 9PA

Illustration by JANINA SCHRÖTER

The High Cross

For whatever reason, most former toilets opt for a bar set-up. Maybe they feel that punters need high-end cocktails to entice them into somewhere people used to spend a penny. The High Cross in Tottenham takes a different approach, and is a pub instead. This is welcome news for a huge area that's severely lacking in proper boozers, so if you're looking to sup a pint in a cosy confine with beautiful mock Tudor frontage, this is the spot. Also, they serve supreme Scotch eggs.

350 High Road, Tottenham, N17 9HT

Ladies and Gentlemen

Its name is a classy way to let people know that this bar is a former relief spot – Ladies and Gentleman does everything with a touch of humour and style. That includes the regularly changing puntastic sign at street level, which alerts passers-by to the bar's existence. And the cocktail names – like Two Grapes, One Shrub and a Cactus. Lest we forget, the tiles on the wall behind the drinks at the bar are bathroom classics. Speaking of drinks, that's the number one reason to visit. This place has booze that's varied and not too costly.

2 Highgate Road, Kentish Town, NW5 1QU

Restaurant Story

Not every former toilet wears its credentials on its sleeve. Case in point, Restaurant Story, which pays little homage to its Victoria toilet block past. The Michelin-starred dining experience comes from the mind of one of Britain's most exciting chefs, Tom Sellers. Drinks-wise, you don't get much of a say here. It's all decided by a sommelier who picks a selection of drinks – wines or cocktails – to accompany whatever tasting menu you're having. The focus on stories is a lovely touch; diners are asked to bring along a book to leave on their ever-filling bookshelves.

199 Tooley Street, SE1 2JX

WC

WC stands for wine and charcuterie. Wait, that's not right. WC stands for water closet. Or is it both? See what they did there? It sits directly beneath Clapham Common tube station. Just think – as the trains rumble overhead, you could be tucking into a stunning meat and cheeseboard with a glass of Merlot in one hand, in the very spot someone was relieving themselves 30 years ago. You can do more than just eat and drink in these former loos. There's also live music to enjoy on Monday and Sunday nights, mostly of the singer-songwriter variety. Just remember – here, all songs are toilet-break songs.

Clapham Common South Side, SW4 7AA

SINK THE BEST MARTINIS IN LONDON

The martini: an uncomplicated drink, and somehow one of the easiest to botch, too. We don't like to chance it, and prefer to get one of London's expert bartenders to mix us one.

Of course, it's not all about the gin/vodka and vermouth these days. Some of London's best martinis come with unexpected twists. And on that note, let's begin with one that's got marmalade in it.

The Breakfast Martini at The Anchor & Hope

The martinis at this constantly crowded gastropub are small, simple tumblers, all just as dry, wet, clean or dirty as you ask for, and all at about the £6 mark. Play it safe with a frosty dirty martini, or, if you're feeling adventurous, check out their version of the Breakfast Martini. It's a divisive marmalade-and-lemon-juice beast that's prone to being oversweet and treacley in the wrong hands. But these are very much the right hands. The ideal pick-me-up after three hours of Shakespeare at The Old Vic, across the road.

336 The Cut, Lambeth, SE1 8LP

The Coastal Martini at Anthracite

This is a bar specialising in martinis, and the bartenders know their (cocktail) onions. Place yourself in their hands and leave the choice (from a wide range) of gin/vodka/vermouth/garnish up to them. *Londonist*'s recommendation? The Coastal Martini. The gin's infused with samphire, the vermouth's infused with cured lemon. Black pepper tincture, seaweed flake and chilli are thrown in for good measure. It sounds complicated but adds up to a simple, briny chill. With a kick. Like a windswept English beach holiday in a glass.

Great Northern Hotel, St Pancras, N1C 4TB

The Turkish Coffee Martini at Dar in Tooting Broadway Market

For anybody who loves the idea of an Espresso Martini but can't stand the sickly syrupyness so many are laced with: this version from Mediterranean restaurant Dar is The One. Their titchy bar in Tooting Broadway Market stirs up a Turkish Coffee Martini, with all the grainy residue and fierce punch of a Turkish espresso, along with, well, a lot of booze. A velvety glass of sleeplessness.

29 Tooting High Street, Tooting, SW17 0RJ

The Vesper Martini at DUKES Bar

You might not have heard of barman Gilberto Preti, who's thought to have created the Vesper, but you'll almost certainly know of its most famous fictional drinker.

Preti was working in the bar of Dukes hotel just off St James's Street in the early 1950s when he created the drink for the first time, especially for author Ian Fleming. Fleming was so impressed with the cocktail's suave cred that he wrote it into *Casino Royale*. In the first Bond novel, 007 explains

to a barman how to make it: "Three measures of Gordon's (gin), one of vodka, half a measure of Kina Lillet (now called Lillet Blanc). Shake it very well until it's ice-cold, then add a large thin slice of lemon peel. Got it?".
35 St James's Place, St James's, SW1A 1NY (see page 27 also)

The Martiny at Every Cloud

This homey Hackney drinking den serves a small, perfectly formed martini to match. The Martiny is a double-shot glass served chilly and compelling. And it comes from a Jager machine that's been twisted to holier ends. We can surely all agree it's the most socially significant repurposing of tech since Arnold came back to save humanity in *Terminator 2*. It's £5. It's three for £12. It's strong, tiny, undeniable.
11a Morning Lane, Hackney, E9 6ND

The Redistilled Gibson Martini at The Gibson

This green-glaze tiled bar is named after a martini with the olive switched for a pickled onion, created for the artist Charles Dana Gibson in 1908. The same drink that Cary Grant knocks back pre-dinner in *North by Northwest*. Unsurprisingly, the Gibson is their headliner cocktail – and you can't argue with the gently vinegary sting of the standard version. But to take advantage of the bar's perfectionist and experimental ethos, go for the Redistilled Gibson Martini: gin and Noilly Prat, steeped for 72 hours with pickled onion, lemon zest and pickled spices. Though maybe avoid it on a first date.
44 Old Street, Clerkenwell, EC1V 9AQ

The classic martini at Hide Below

The martinis at this dimly lit, underground Mayfair bar don't look like anything out of the ordinary. But there's a cool smoothness to them: courtesy of the way they're stirred with frozen birch sap rather than ice, to silken the finish against your tongue. A touch of perfectionist hedonism to justify the steep price tags. Drink it at the bar, a sanded-down swoop of tree trunk.
85 Piccadilly, Mayfair, W1J 7NB

The Espresso Martini at The Martini Bar

Bitter espresso, small-batch vodka, brutalist architecture and high art. It's like the Barbican Martini Bar has taken all the most urbane tropes they could think of and fused them into this rich, black, night-owl martini. Drink up, and spend

the evening soaking in one of the on-site exhibitions or plays, wide-eyed.
Barbican Centre, Silk Street, Barbican, EC2Y 8DS

The Montgomery Martini at Mr Fogg's Gin Parlour

Said to be Hemingway's favourite version, the Montgomery's mostly a glass of gin with a vanishingly brief touch of vermouth. Sink back into a claw-footed chaise longue and enjoy Tanqueray gin, Noilly Prat vermouth and orange bitters in a ratio named after Field Marshall Montgomery – who would engage the enemy with a 15:1 advantage for his troops.
58 St Martin's Lane, Covent Garden, WC2N 4EA

The House Martini at The Ned's Library Bar

Stashed away in a bookish corner of swank-former-bank The Ned, The Library Bar proves that drink-driving isn't all bad, thanks to its martini trolley. Each beverage from this souped-up bar-on-wheels is studiously measured and mixed with the dedication of a Buckingham Palace butler attending to the Queen's nightcap. Poured out into chilled cut glass by a white-tuxedoed chap, you feel like royalty before you've taken the first sip.

The House Martini is a meaty gin classic, flecked with orange bitters. The Apricot Vesper is a subtly floral take on the Bond staple. We can't remember what our third martini was.
27 Poultry, City of London, EC2R 8AJ

A DRINK THAT PADDINGTON WOULD TOTALLY GO FOR

Salvatore Calabrese usually only had an espresso for breakfast before leaving for work at the Library Bar at the The Lanesborough Hotel. But one morning, his wife made him toast and marmalade, insisting he ate it before leaving. Calabrese ended up taking the jar to work with him, and this cocktail was the result. We always wondered why breakfast was the most important meal of the day.

Make a Breakfast Martini

Combine 50ml of gin, 12ml of triple sec and 12ml of fresh lemon juice, and shake over ice together with a spoonful of English marmalade. Strain and serve in a martini glass.

DID YOU KNOW... SIX OF LONDON'S TUBE STATIONS ARE NAMED AFTER PUBS

At least, we think so. Get your trivia hat on…

Most of the stops on the tube network have names whose origins stretch back hundreds of years. Some, like Wembley Park and Kennington, recall ancient landowners or chieftains. Others, such as Burnt Oak and Woodford, recall landscape features. And then there are the tube stations named after pubs. There are six, by our reckoning.

Angel

The Angel coaching inn long stood on an important crossroads to the north of London.

It primarily served travellers following the Great North Road (the modern A1, roughly speaking). From the mid-18th century, the Angel also found itself well placed on the New Road, now called Pentonville Road – an early bypass popular with animal drovers guiding their stock to Smithfield Market.

The inn dates back to ancient times, but seems to have changed its name to the Angel around 1614. It was here, in 1790, that Thomas Paine began writing *Rights of Man*, one of the most influential books of all time.

The Angel continued trading under different guises until well into the 20th century; the current building is from 1899. It is now a branch of the Co-Op bank. The inn lives on in the name of the tube station (opened in 1901), in a Wetherspoon pub adjacent to the original site and, of course, on the Monopoly board.

Elephant & Castle

Whole essays have been written on how this inner London hub got its unusual name. The commonest claim is that it is a mis-hearing of 'Infanta de Castile', a title associated with Spanish royalty, some of whom married into the English royal family. The most likely, and sadly most boring, solution is that an elephant with a castle on top was a common motif in medieval days – it was, and remains, part of the emblem of the Cutlers Company, for example.

A tavern called the Elephant and Castle was present at this junction at least 250 years ago. The owner may have chosen the name through some association with the Cutlers, or for purely whimsical reasons.

Whatever the case, the name long predates the opening of the two eponymous stations, which appeared in 1862 (rail) and 1890 (tube). The area is now commonly called Elephant and Castle (or just The Elephant), but it was also traditionally known as Newington. The Elephant & Castle pub – a 1960s rebuild – had closed down, feared lost, until a local campaign saw it reopen in 2016.

Illustration by TOM WOOLLEY ILLUSTRATION

Maida Vale

This attractive Bakerloo stop and the wider area take their names from the Hero of Maida pub, which stood by the Regent's Canal on Edgware Road from around 1809. Its unusual name commemorates General Sir John Stuart, victor of the Battle of Maida in 1806. It closed in the early 1990s.

Manor House

Perhaps the least guessable of the six. The Manor House inn was a well-known stop along the Green Lanes turnpike, perhaps named after the local manor house of Brownswood. It opened at the start of the 19th century and had a distinguished history. Queen Victoria is thought to have stopped here during a journey in 1843. In the 20th century it became a music venue, hosting the likes of Rod Stewart, Fleetwood Mac and Jimi Hendrix. Today, the building is an organic cafe and supermarket.

The Piccadilly line station opened in 1932, taking its name from the then-thriving pub. One little-known fact about Manor House tube station: in 1933, shortly after the station opened, the Prince of Wales (and future Edward VIII) drove a train for the two miles between this station and Wood Green.

Royal Oak

This relatively quiet tube station north of Bayswater shares its title with one of England's commonest pub names. The original Royal Oak was a tree in Boscobel, Shropshire, which served as a hiding place for the future Charles II while fleeing the Roundheads. After Charles gained the throne, many pubs took on the name of The Royal Oak in commemoration, and it remains the third-most popular appellation in England. The one in northwest London gave its name to the tube station in 1871. It is still going strong, though sadly rebranded as The Porchester.

Swiss Cottage

In 1840, a brief fashion for all things Helvetian saw the building of a Swiss-style inn out in the fields north of London. Known as the Swiss Tavern, it served as a coaching inn on the newly built Finchley Road. It became a well-known landmark, eventually giving its name to a tube station and the wider area. A much-rebuilt version of the tavern still stands as the northernmost Sam Smith's pub in the capital.

And some bonus stations

Bull and Bush on Hampstead Heath would have been the capital's deepest tube station, and seventh to be named after a pub. Although significant work was done at platform level, the Northern line stop was never completed, and it remains one of London's least-known 'ghost stations'. The namesake Old Bull and Bush is still trading, and very pleasant it is too.

New Cross is thought to be named after a coaching inn. The area was formerly known as Hatcham, but slowly changed to New Cross from the 17th century, after the prominent Golden Cross inn (near the site of today's New Cross Inn). While its two eponymous stations were formerly on the tube network, they are now classed as part of the Overground system, so miss out on being in the main list through a technicality.

A RIVERSIDE CRAWL OF THE THAMES

We've drawn from two decades' worth of 'experience' hanging out in riverside pubs for this one. It's a tough job, but someone's got to do it.

Central London has many well-known pubs by the river. Places like The Anchor, the Founders Arms and Doggett's Coat and Badge have their charms, but are well known, and tend towards the over-crowded. To find the best waterside drinking, head out of the centre to the east and west. Here are ten favourites.

The White Swan, Twickenham

Here's a beer garden that's so close to the Thames that it sometimes becomes part of it. The 17th-century White Swan is sensibly raised a few steps above the river path, but its outdoor drinking space is not; during higher tides, the area is completely cut off. If you want to experience a boozy stranding, be sure to time your drinks round well or be prepared to wade through ankle-deep Thames water to reach the bar.
Riverside, TW1 3DN

The London Apprentice, Isleworth

This large venue in Isleworth is often forgotten about in lists of London's oldest pubs, but it does have some claim. Henry VIII supposedly popped by while visiting nearby Syon House. It's been rebuilt since then, but the Georgian brick facades still look suitably historic. The views from the riverside garden are unique. Stand in the right place and you look straight down a long stretch of Thames – this could almost be Coniston Water.
62 Church Street, TW7 6BG

Old Ship, Hammersmith

Hammersmith's waterfront contains the greatest concentration of noteworthy pubs anywhere on the Thames. Dip into any retreat between Hammersmith and Chiswick and you are unlikely to experience disappointment. One of the more polished pubs is the Old Ship. It's a bit of a trek from the tube and the high streets, so offers a more laid-back experience than, say, the Blue Anchor or Rutland Arms. The upstairs dining room commands the best views, but the plentiful outdoor seating is pressed tight against the river. Pretend you're on the decks of an old galley.
25 Upper Mall, W6 9TD

The Dove, Hammersmith

This famous old pub stands on a bend in the Thames, offering exceptional views left towards Bazalgette's bottle-green Hammersmith Bridge, or right towards Chiswick. It's not the largest of spaces, but catch the place at the right time and there are few nicer spots. The inside is impressive, too – all wooden beams and pokey corners to get lost in. The pub even claims the Guinness World Record for smallest bar (see page 178) – though we've never been entirely convinced.
19 Upper Mall, W6 9TA

The Ship, Wandsworth

Built near a sewerage outlet in an old industrial part of Wandsworth, the second Ship in our list might not sound like an attractive proposition. But it is. Very much so. The front room is timewarp pubbery, with browns and creams like your granddad used to know. The larger conservatory room, an extension to the original Georgian building, looks much more modern in marine blues. Out back you'll find one of London's more

1. THE WHITE SWAN
2. THE LONDON APPRENTICE
3. OLD SHIP
4. THE DOVE
5. THE SHIP

idiosyncratic beer gardens, with a red phone box and some kind of ship's wheel-type-thing. You can almost imagine you're on a cruise – but with better food.

41 Jews Row, SW18 1TB

Captain Kidd, Wapping

Perhaps the most controversial entry in our list comes in the swashbuckling shape of the Captain Kidd. Wapping riverside contains two other excellent pubs, the Prospect of Whitby and the Town of Ramsgate. These usually trump the Kidd in lists like this, thanks to their olde worlde charm and authentic history. The new Kidd on the block is lesser-appreciated, but deserves greater attention. The excessively wood interior does have its charms, but the real merit of this place is a simple one: space. You're far more likely to bag a Thames-side table here, either in the adjacent beer yard, from the main bar's bow windows, or upstairs in the restaurant. The only downside is the sheer number of people doing pirate impressions. Yeearrgh!!

108 Wapping High Street, E1W 2NE

The Mayflower, Rotherhithe

Another famous riverside pub we can't leave out, The Mayflower brings plenty of tourists to Rotherhithe, an area that might otherwise be considered 'off the beaten track'. The pub's name comes from the ship of the Pilgrim Fathers, who set sail for America from hereabouts. Expect to overhear US accents in the traditional interior. There's no arguing with the charms of this place. Dark timber beams, dangling mugs, low ceilings and a forest of plants make it hard to describe without slipping in the word 'cosy'. Book a table upstairs to enjoy some of the best food in the area. Or find a nook elsewhere and nibble from a cheeseboard.

117 Rotherhithe Street, SE16 4NF

6 CAPTAIN KIDD
7 THE MAYFLOWER
8 THE GRAPES
9 CUTTY SARK
10 THE GUN

The Grapes, Limehouse

A short stroll downriver brings us to The Grapes. This time capsule of a pub is charm personified, straight out the pages of Dickens – literally, for The Grapes features in *Our Mutual Friend* as the Six Jolly Fellowship Porters (see page 152). It's also noted for its owners, who include Gandalf himself, Sir Ian McKellen. River views are hard won – the rear terrace is tiny – though the persistent jostler will get a glimpse of an Antony Gormley sculpture poking up out of the water.
76 Narrow Street, E14 8BP

Cutty Sark, Greenwich

The Trafalgar pub in Greenwich is better known, and is always a pleasure to visit despite the crowds, but walk a little further downriver and you reach the Cutty Sark; not the museum-ship, but the namesake pub. Here you'll find a riverside beer yard with sweeping views round to north Greenwich or, if it's too chilly for that, a roaring fire inside the quaintly timbered pub. The best way to experience this place is to book into the upstairs dining room and take your time over the skipper's catch.
4–6 Ballast Quay, SE10 9PD

The Gun, Isle of Dogs

Another cuisine-focussed pub nowhere near the tourist trail lurks on the east side of the Isle of Dogs. The Gun's been here for a quarter of a millennium, and the interior manages to look simultaneously ancient and modern (partly thanks to a devastating fire in 2001). The view of the Thames is almost film-set perfect, with the dome of the O2 perfectly framed by the dining terrace windows.
27 Coldharbour Docklands, E14 9NS

Illustration by LOUISE LOCKHART

SEEK OUT A CITY SPEAKEASY

Once only to be sniffed out in the grubby crevices of Prohibition America,
speakeasies have now taken on an altogether more deluxe guise.

Walk through fridges, prison doors and Turkish baths to find the fashionable speakeasies of 21st-century London. The snazzy surroundings and drinks at any of these would knock Al Capone for six.

Evans & Peel Detective Agency, Earls Court

Of all the gin joints in all the boroughs in all of London, Evans & Peel is one of the most playful. Press the buzzer and head down the stairs into a private dick's office to present your case (you really have to present a case). Your reward: a bookshelf swings open (classic), and you're in a drinking den straight out of a Raymond Chandler novel – dim lighting, stiff cocktails and, er, beer poured from a radiator. We recommend the Aviation Rhubarb Remix. Whatever your tipple, stick with it. As the great Bogart said on his deathbed, "I should never have switched from scotch to martinis."
310c Earls Court Road, SW5 9BA

See also: Happy hour at the nearby **Troubadour**. Cocktails are 2-for-1 at this boho hideout, where Joni Mitchell, Elton John and Paul Simon have played.

Trailer Happiness, Notting Hill

What do you get when you cross a 1970s tiki lounge with Del Boy's living room? Something a bit like Trailer Happiness – a no-nonsense Notting Hill dive bar, where they somehow turn 50 shades of brown into the kind of place you'd actually like to hang out for an evening. The rum cocktails certainly help; they make them well and they make them strong. Order a Zombie sharer with your mates, and gradually morph into the living dead.
177 Portobello Road, W11 2DY

See also: Rum not your bag? Pay a visit to **The Distillery** – a 'gin hotel' just down the road. The minibars are better than your average.

Alcotraz, Shoreditch

Only in London would you pay to take your own booze into a bar, spirit it past a prison warden, then neck it from a tin cup... while sat behind bars. While inmates of the infamous Alcatraz braved shark-infested waters to get the hell out, people practically fight to get into its liquory Brick Lane namesake. If that sounds too gimmicky for you, instead order a drink at The Courthouse Hotel off Oxford Street – formerly Marlborough Street Magistrates Court. Mick Jagger, Oscar Wilde and John Lennon were all tried here (not at the same time). So was Christine Keeler: order a Russian vodka in her honour.
212 Brick Lane, E1 6SA

See also: **Moonshine Saloon** – a Wild West-themed hoedown, from the same people.

The Victorian Bath House, Liverpool Street

Surely no speakeasy entrance can trump that of the Victorian Bath House. The turquoise-tiled Moorish gem looks like it's been plucked from Istanbul – taking you aback the first time you find it, dwarfed by the high rises of Bishopsgate. Even more surprising: this is a bona-fide bathhouse, dating back to 1817. You won't find heavily paunched men steaming themselves down here now, although you will discover bottles of wine in a bathtub of ice – a nice nod to its history. This place is exclusive; book ahead.
7–8 Bishopsgate, EC2M 3TJ

Illustration by JOSY BLOGGS

TRAILER HAPPINESS

BELOW & HIDDEN

HAPPINESS FORGETS

ORIOLE BAR

ALCOTRAZ

CELLARDOOR

THE MAYOR OF
SCAREDY TOWN

THRILLS

OPIUM

EVANS & PEEL
DETECTIVE AGENCY

FIRST AID BOX

THE VICTORIAN
BATH HOUSE

See also: The Luggage Room –
another properly decadent speakeasy,
dishing up punches, nogs, cobblers, flips,
juleps – you name it.

CellarDoor, Aldwych

Someone tried to hypnotise us in
CellarDoor once. It didn't seem to work,
although later in the night we ended up
buying them a Rob Roy, so maybe it did.
Speakeasies in former public toilets are
ten-a-penny these days (see page 41),
but CellarDoor did it early, and remains
one of the finest. Descend the covered
steps by the Lyceum Theatre to enter a
mirrored microcosm of burlesque, drag,
and classic cocktails shaken and stirred
by on-the-ball tenders. Don't be alarmed
by the glass toilet cubicle doors; they frost
over when you lock them… hopefully.
Wellington Street, WC2E 7DN

See also: The Candlelight Club – a
pop-up 1920s-style jamboree, with live
jazz. Completely lit by candles.

Oriole, Farringdon

Once upon a time, there was a pub called
The Cock. It was an odd pub – not
because of its name, and not because it
was inside Smithfield Meat Market, but
because of its 'reverse' drinking hours,
which meant it served pints of Guinness
to thirsty blood-stained porters at six
in the morning. The late great Anthony
Bourdain was even filmed demolishing
a fry-up here. The Cock has since
regenerated into another bird – Oriole.
We'd describe it as a hybrid of upmarket
tiki bar, mid-century jazz lounge and the
British Museum. The drinks menu is a
boozy fruit salad of showiness; whatever
you order you'll end up with a bit of
exotic foliage jammed up your nostrils.
East Poultry Avenue, EC1A 9LH

See also: Nightjar, a pint-sized sister
bar in Old Street. Reserve a table by the
band and pore over the menu, categorised
into pre-prohibition, prohibition, post-war
and signatures.

First Aid Box, Herne Hill

'Health, nutrition and doctors' orders' are
the theme of this Herne Hill restaurant,
but don't worry – there's plenty of alcohol
to help it work. Get stuck into a couple of
Who Framed Roger Rabbits? – a reviving
elixir of carrot and celery juice, ginger,
vermouth and gin – and see what it does
for your eyesight. First Aid Box also has
a speakeasy-within-a-speakeasy – a Peaky
Blinders-inspired barn, which opens
weekends. Flat caps optional.
119 Dulwich Road, SE24 0NG

See also: The Beast of Brixton, a dark,
skull-addled place close by, should you
want to turn this into a cocktail crawl.

The Mayor of Scaredy Cat Town, Spitalfields

The internet practically broke when Londoners first discovered a restaurant with a Smeg fridge you could walk through, leading into a subterranean cocktail lair. The whole white-goods-novelty-factor may have worn off, but The Mayor of Scaredy Cat Town stands the test of time, thanks to a coterie of genned-up bartenders mixing derring-do concoctions like the creamy/peachy/winy Peachy Keen.

12–16 Artillery Lane, E1 7LS

See also: **Call Me Mr Lucky** – another Breakfast Club speakeasy offering (this one near London Bridge) and **Callooh Callay**, home of the famous walk-through wardrobe.

Opium, Chinatown

We presume that Opium takes its name from the infamous (and often fictional) smoking dens from Sherlock Holmes, Fu Manchu et al. This is a far classier affair: slink off the hustle and bustle of Chinatown's Gerrard Street and ascend the narrow stairs to multiple flights of lantern-lit bars, serving cherry blossom Vespers, sesame old fashioneds and – if you're feeling virtuous – steaming pots of green tea. You can also fill your belly at the dim sum parlour.

15–16 Gerrard Street, W1D 6JE

See also: **Mark's Bar Soho** – a nearby offering from the Hix Empire, where you can slump in a deep Chesterfield with a happy-hour whisky smash, or pretend you know how to play bar billiards.

Below and Hidden, Clerkenwell

What do you mean you've never had a cocktail inside a 3D tapestry?! Below and Hidden – secreted away in the depths of Clerkenwell's Bourne & Hollingsworth Buildings – appears, at first, to be floor-to-wall faux medieval tapestry. And it's good fun to share an overflowing 'crystal' skull Behemoth cocktail with your mates, while admiring the fair maidens and their obedient pets. As the night wears on, the DJ pipes up and it transpires the tapestry is laced with LED lights… this could turn into a messy one.

42 Northampton Road, EC1R 0HU

See also: **The Brig**, which bills itself as 'London's smallest bar'. True or not, you can only fit yourself and three mates in here. The bartender is all yours.

Happiness Forgets, Hoxton

'Great cocktails, no wallies' is the motto at Happiness Forgets. While plenty of speakeasies – including, let's face it, a few of the above – are a tad precious, this basement bar off Hoxton Square welcomes you to wander in off the street, pull up a chair and order one of the best darn sazeracs you can find in London. So long as you're not a wally.

8–9 Hoxton Square, N1 6NU

See also: **Discount Suit Company** – another unpretentious bar, this one doing forgotten classics in an erstwhile tailor's stockroom in the East End (page 125).

AN OENOPHILE'S ODYSSEY

*(That's wine-lovers, for those of us who
haven't brushed up on our Latin recently.)*

Looking for somewhere special to wet your whistle? Fancy a brush with
London's grape-based history? Allow us to lead you on an oenophile's
odyssey through the city, during which you'll encounter everything from
uncorked bottles that have been gathering dust for centuries, to wine being
made right here, right now, in the capital.

Albertine, Shepherd's Bush
Hailed as the birthplace of *EastEnders*, a visit to Albert Square's namesake
should be a rite of passage for soap opera addicts. Back in the 1980s, writers
from the nearby BBC Television Centre came up with the show's first script
in this snug Shepherd's Bush wine bar. You can't go far wrong with the
impressive list of French wines, and tasty cheeseboards to boot, even if you're
more of a *Corrie* fan.
1 Wood Lane, W12 7DP

Berry Bros. & Rudd, St James's
A secret passage once linked the cellars of London's oldest wine shop and
St James's Palace to facilitate the philandering escapades of merry monarch
Charles II – or so the legend goes. There's still plenty to discover in Berry Bros.
& Rudd's West End premises, which date back to 1689 – and confusingly bear
the sign of a coffee mill (that was their star seller when this place first opened).
Feast your eyes on bottles older than Big Ben and admire a set of scales that
once bore the weight of none other than Lord Byron, one of the shop's most
illustrious patrons. Beneath the shop is a labyrinth of cellars and tasting rooms.
63 Pall Mall, SW1Y 5HZ

Illustration by AMELIA FLOWER

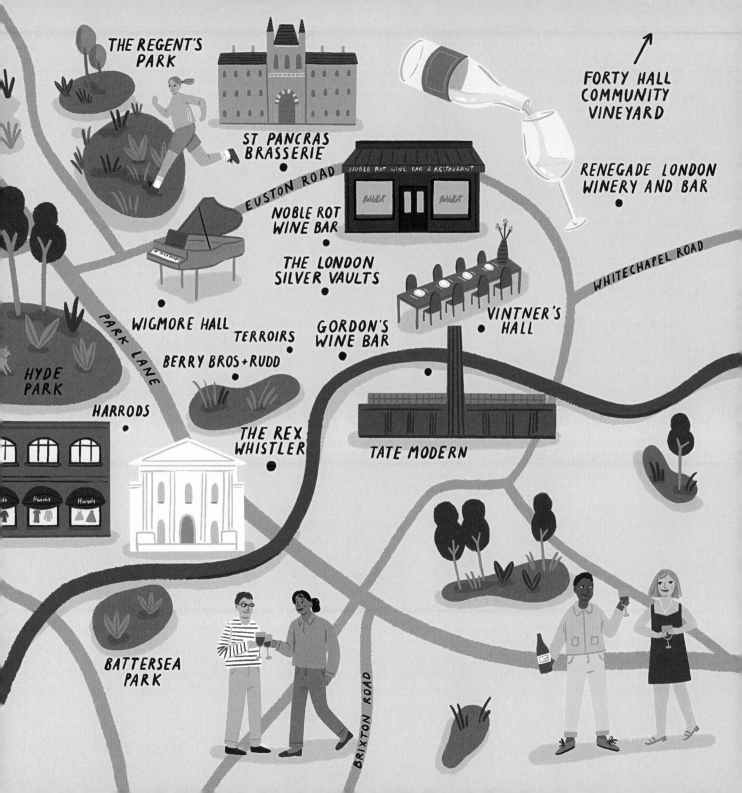

Forty Hall Vineyard, Enfield

Yep, wine is being grown in Enfield – the first commercial-scale vineyard in the capital since the Middle Ages. This organic vineyard launched in 2015, covers 10 acres, and now sells London's first homegrown sparkling wine for centuries. It operates as a social enterprise, and uses modern equipment but traditional methods to get the best tastes out of the grapes. Regular events and tastings take place at the vineyard. You can even volunteer to pick grapes.

EN2 9HA

Gordon's Wine Bar, Charing Cross

Blink and you'll miss this cavernous cellar bar as you're spat out of Embankment station and amble up towards Charing Cross. Established in 1890, Gordon's is thought to be London's oldest wine bar and it's suitably dripping (quite literally – it's dank down here) in atmosphere. Expect pure Dickensian drama – ancient bottles shrouded in dust, rickety wooden tables, and candlelight dancing on the craggy, cave-like walls of the old stone vaults. If that's not enticing enough, both Samuel Pepys and Rudyard Kipling once called the Villiers Street building home.

47 Villiers Street, WC2N 6NE

Hampton Court Palace

Feeling extra-decadent? Go west for a weekend visit to Henry VIII's palatial playground. In the heart of Hampton Court Palace's Base Court you'll find a working replica of a Tudor wine fountain. That's right: your bog-standard water fountain wasn't quite enough for 16th-century royalty, so this booze-dispensing bronze-and-gold-leaf creation was installed instead. Not all heroes wear capes (then again, these ones might have).

And that's not all: wander into the gardens to find The Great Vine. The 250-year-old plant is the world's largest grape vine and on average yields a 600lb crop of fruit every year.

Molesey, KT8 9AU

Harrods Fine Wine and Spirits Rooms, Knightsbridge

Inside the luxury department store's famous Food Halls, you'll find a glorious set of 1920s-style rooms dedicated to booze. Finished with a shimmering marble floor and limed-oak panelling, it's the kind of full-bodied opulence you'd expect from Harrods. But there's more to the experience than Instagrammable interiors. Watch live streams from vineyards across the globe, explore the character of different grapes at the multi-sensory aroma tables, and even get your bottle of choice engraved.

87–135 Brompton Road, SW1X 7XL

London Cru, Fulham

The capital's first ever winery popped up in an unassuming West Brompton warehouse back in 2013. For all of London's charms, the city isn't exactly renowned for its fertile climate, so London Cru uses grapes from a hand-picked selection of European vineyards to concoct its award-winning small batch wines. Find them in a handful of Michelin-star restaurants, or book a tasting tour of the winery itself.

21–27 Seagrave Road, SW6 1RP

London Silver Vaults, Holborn

Beautiful wine deserves to be decanted into equally ravishing receptacles. The treasures housed in the posh shopping mall that is the London Silver Vaults may be a little out of the average drinker's price range, but the intricate Victorian claret jugs and antique bottle-stoppers will inspire you to up your wine-ware game.

53–64 Chancery Lane, WC2A 1QS

Noble Rot, Holborn

The minds behind massively popular alternative wine magazine Noble Rot launched their own wine bar and restaurant in 2015, and happily, it's stayed true to the publication's philosophy of making the world of wine accessible and fun. The drinks list is truly a thing of beauty: heavy on the unjustly undervalued varietals and rare vintages, and scribbled with irreverent tasting notes for anyone who might feel a bit out of their depth. The food wins rave reviews, too.

51 Lamb's Conduit Street, WC1N 3NB

Renegade Wine London, Bethnal Green

Squeeze past a towering display of secondhand furniture in a narrow alley under Bethnal Green's old railway arches, and you'll find an achingly hip urban winery. True to its name, Renegade isn't beholden to European appellation dogma, and instead makes unusual, minimally manipulated wines for you to quaff at your leisure in the onsite taproom. Sure, thanks to your proximity to fermenting fruit you may have to swat away the odd fly in the summertime – but their characterful libations and undeniable street cred more than makes up for it.
Arch 12, Gales Gardens, E2 0EJ

Rex Whistler Restaurant, Millbank

Tate Britain's restaurant was deemed the 'most amusing room in Europe' due to the unapologetically whimsical mural, *The Expedition in Pursuit of Rare Meats*, by the restaurant's namesake. But it's equally renowned for its incredible wine cellar. After a day spent wandering the galleries, shoot sommelier extraordinaire Gustavo Medina an email: he'll happily decant the liquid ambrosia of your choice prior to your arrival so it gets plenty of time to breathe. How thoughtful.
Tate Britain, SW1P 4JU

Tate Modern, Bankside

And now to another Tate. Ponder upon the art of inebriation at Tate Modern. Gilbert and George's *Balls: The Evening*

Before The Morning After is a 'living sculpture' comprised of photographs taken at the now-defunct Balls Brothers Wine Bar in Bethnal Green. If you've ever wondered what a hangover looks like outside of your head, this is it.
SE1 9TG

St Pancras Champagne Bar, King's Cross

Got time to kill before your train? Sip in style at the longest champagne bar in Europe. Located in the beating heart of St Pancras International station, Searcy's faux art deco bar even comes with a 'press for champagne' button to ensure your flute is always full.
Grand Terrace, St Pancras International Station, N1C 4QL

Terroirs Wine Bar, Charing Cross

Often credited with spearheading London's natural wine scene, this popular bistro's earthy and herbaceous libations are about as far as you can get from your average bottle of supermarket plonk. Rooted in the philosophy that a wine should embody the natural environment within which it was created, tantalising tastes of the Loire Valley, Alicante, and the Tuscan coast await you inside.
5 William IV Street, WC2N 4DN

Vintners' Hall, City of London

This sumptuous Baroque building on Upper Thames Street has been used by The Worshipful Company of Vintners

since 1823, though members of this ancient livery company have congregated on the same site since the 14th century. Nowadays, you can book it for everything from wine tastings to your wedding reception.
68½ Upper Thames Street, EC4V 3BG

Sunday Mornings at Wigmore Hall, Marylebone

Get to bed at a sensible time on Saturday, and you'll make it to one of Wigmore Hall's Sunday morning concerts. How better to stir the senses, than with renditions of Ducros, Debussy and Dvorak in the hall's alabaster and marble surroundings? The free glass of post-performance sherry, of course.
36 Wigmore Street, W1U 2BP

GET QUIZZICAL

Question: Who doesn't love a pub quiz? Answer: Don't know!
Phones off, witty team names at the ready – it's time to visit London's best pub quizzes.

One for the film buffs

"You're gonna need a bigger boat". An epic line from cinema history, and the name of London's best cine-centric quiz. The perfect chance for you and your cast of quizzers to unfurl your reels of knowledge, from *Amélie* to *Zulu*.

Clips from films are projected onto a big screen as you answer questions about actors, plots, soundtracks and everything in between. Prizes include cinema tickets, box-sets and most importantly, cinephile bragging rights.

Bigger Boat bobs about, between The Ritzy in Brixton and O'Neill's Flamingo Room in Soho. It's also had residencies in pubs in Highgate and Brentford. The team behind it make occasional quizzing jaunts to Hollywood – yes, these people really like films.
O'Neill's, 33–37 Wardour Street, W1D 6PU (Soho) and **The Ritzy, Coldharbour Lane, SW12 1JG (Brixton)**

Check film-quiz.com for more details.

One for the party animals

It's the bonus rounds at The Old Queen's Head's quiz that steal the limelight. The one where you try to blow the largest bubble. The one where you have to draw something rude and twisted. The kazoo round. We once saw a man leap from a bar stool and dance 'the worm' on the floor, all the while retaining the kazoo between his lips, and blowing 'Teenage Dirtbag' out of it. For a round of shots.

The quiz itself is great fun, with a bottle of champagne up for grabs. If you need it after all those shots.
The Old Queen's Head, 44 Essex Road, N1 8LN

Takes place every Tuesday night, more details on the website.

One for the brain boxes

Hearts were in mouths in 2018 when we heard the Prince of Wales was coming under new ownership. The pub was shut for weeks, much rejigging going on inside. We didn't care about any of that. All we wanted to know was whether London's hardest pub quiz would return. After what felt like forever, our prayers were answered. It's back.

The Prince of Wales doesn't market itself as London's toughest pub quiz. It lures you in looking like any ordinary pub quiz. There's delicious pub grub to dig into while you're quizzing. Any poor soul would fall for such a cruel trick. Then the questions are unleashed and… you're stumped.

Once, we went along with two experienced quizmasters on our team, plus a man who writes trivia books. We came last. You have been warned.
Prince of Wales, 53 Highgate High Street, N6 5JX

Quiz every Tuesday night

One for the nonchalant

This might sound like heresy to the hardcore quizzer, but not everyone is truly 'in it to win it'. Some people just want a laid-back night to catch up with their mates, occasionally peeking into the crevices of their brain for the odd answer. If that's what you're looking for, The Tufnell Park Tavern will be your bag.

It's a quiz for "enjoyment not bafflement" – pizza and drinks can be won through the night, and it's quite possibly the polar opposite of the Prince of Wales. Don't bother inviting nerdy friends. Instead, here's a chance for us average types to shine and *whisper it* maybe even win.

Tufnell Park Tavern, 162 Tufnell Park Road, N7 0EE

Quiz every Monday from 8pm

One for the musos

In the music round, one person suddenly springs into action – shushing everyone else like their life depends on it. If you're that person, The Lexington's music-only quiz is for you.

Formerly run by that bastion of independent British music, Rough Trade, the quiz retains its appeal for those who are genned-up on their obscure Britpop bands and little-known B-sides. Even if you're not a music-know-it-all, the quiz remains reasonably accessible. Surely you'll be able to recognise some pop hits when they're played on a Bontempi organ? Maybe you'll be too busy laughing your head off.

If music really isn't your strong point, focus on getting the best team name. Prize? A multipack of crisps.

The Lexington, 96–98 Pentonville Road, N1 9JB

Quiz every Monday from 8pm

One for those who want something a bit different

The Elm Park Tavern mixes things up a bit. For example, instead of a bog standard history round, how does a heads or tails round sound? Or a sculpture round, for creative types to flex their muscles? Or a 'Find Ian Beale' round (really a thing)?

Get down early as this one tends to pack out, everyone competing for bottles of wine, free food and most importantly, the mega cash pot. Of note is the Elm Park Tavern's superb drinks selection – nothing like a decent pint of cask to help you locate long-running *EastEnders* characters.

Elm Park Tavern, 76 Elm Park, SW2 2UB

Every Monday from 8pm

DRINK YOUR WAY AROUND THE WORLD

Put that London porter down for a moment, and embrace the best libations hailing from overseas that London has to offer.

Ice-cold Honey Brown lager at the Maple Leaf

Icy Canadian beers – including the copper-hued Honey Brown lager – are poured out alongside poutine and meatloaf at this Covent Garden boozer. Fill your face while watching Canadian hockey players get their teeth smashed out in NHL games broadcast live. Make sure you order plenty of beer if you go for the 2kg portion of chicken wings, doused in 'Suicide Sauce'.
41 Maiden Lane, Covent Garden, WC2E 7LJ

Mojitos at Cubana

Cubana claims to have introduced the mojito to the UK back in the 1990s. Whether or not that's true, it's certainly the best place in London to knock them back. Freshness is the key here: lime juice, raw sugar cane and mint muddled in with quality rum – not to mention live Cuban grooves, cool as you like. This is one London club where the people dance well on a Friday night.
48 Lower Marsh, SE1 7RG and 59–61 Charterhouse Street, EC1M 6HA

Pisco sours at Tierra Peru

So beloved is Peruvian pisco sour in London these days, it has its own dedicated week. At Tierra Peru in Islington you can pucker up and slurp down a pisco sour made with Pico Quebranta, lime juice, sugar syrup, egg white and bitters. Or sample the selection of piscos neat until everything goes a bit misty and you imagine you've wandered upon Machu Picchu. At which point it's time to go home.
164 Essex Road, Islington, N1 8LY

Illustration by LINZIE HUNTER

Mint tea on Edgware Road

The sickly waft of shisha pipes and steaming hot mint tea transports you instantly to Marrakech or Beirut. Except this is Edgware Road, a bustling thoroughfare in the middle of London. Pull up a chair outside one of the many cafes, order a mint tea crammed with fresh mint leaves, and listen in to the Middle-Eastern chit-chat over the roar of traffic. This is one time not to stint on the sugar, btw; you'll require at least five cubes.

Edgware Road, W2

Cidre Breton at The French House

A saucy Soho stalwart, The French House wears its heart on its sleeve – a steaming cassoulet of sozzled bonhomie, complete with Galouises-varnished ceiling and sepia prints of old vaudeville acts and trapeze artists. We've never seen The French House when it's not spilling noisily onto the street, but beware: using your mobile phone is a grande non-non. You may order a bottle of the Canard Duchne champagne, but most patrons get to know one another over a sharing bottle of chilled Breton cider. After a couple of these, you'll be best friends for life.

49 Dean Street, Soho, W1D 5BG

Aperol spritz at Frank's Cafe

You might say the Italians created London when the Romans built Londinium around AD 43 – so it's only right we raise a glass to them with a libation they invented. We can safely say that amphoras of Aperol weren't stashed away on the first ships over, but the spritz has become a staple of summer London boozing. Where better to drink it than the top of a car park in Peckham (see page 104), from where you can survey the city.

7th–10th Floor Multi Storey Car Park, 95a Rye Lane, SE15 4ST

A shot of vodka at Bar Polski

We won't wade into the whole who-invented-vodka debate – but the Polish certainly know how to have fun with the stuff. Pull up a stool and work your way through the panoply of flavoured shots: bison grass, quince, lemon drop, walnut, honey, pineapple. Your mouth will be overwhelmed – so too will your head.

11 Little Turnstile, Holborn, WC1V 7DX

Ethiopian honey wine at Zeret Kitchen

Aside from the humungous discs of sour, spongy injera bread served up with dollops of 'wat' stew, Zeret Kitchen makes its own honey wine. Tej, as it's called, is deceptively drinkable owing to its natural sweetness, and makes watching buses plough up and down Camberwell Road a lot more fun. As for after-dinner coffee at Zeret: that comes as part of an age-old ceremony, in this case interpreted with frankincense and popcorn.

216–18 Camberwell Road, Camberwell, SE5 0ED

Lassi at Shayona

After worshipping at Neasden's BAPS Shri Swaminarayan Mandir, many Hindus cross the road to feast on dishes of paneer and dosa at Shayona. It is, after all, the site of the former temple – replaced in the mid-1990s by the huge marble 3D jigsaw puzzle, which now gleams for miles around. The lassi menu is exceptional, including rose, mango and salted. If you're in a really savoury mood, order the chaas, a sour buttermilk drink flavoured with chilli and speckled with cumin seeds.

54–62 Meadow Garth, Neasden, NW10 8HD

Around the world in 80 cocktails at Mr Fogg's Residence

In the Jules Verne classic *Around the World in 80 Days*, Phileas Fogg sets off from Pall Mall's Reform Club with an impossible adventure in his sights. Fifteen minutes' walk from here in today's London is Mr Fogg's Residence: festooned with hot air balloon baskets and crocodile skins, it pays tribute to Verne's derring-do creation. Here, you can travel around the world without clambering out of your leather armchair – courtesy of a list of 80 exotic potions.

15 Bruton Lane, Mayfair, W1J 6JD

10 OF THE BEST WETHERSPOONS

It's OK to drink in a Wetherspoon pub. Here are 10 of our favourites in London.

Wetherspoons: love them or hate them, you actually love them. Not only does the prodigious pub chain keep many of the city's historic buildings intact, apparently it does cheap drinks too.

The Beehive, Brixton

OK, OK, just let us explain. We submit that The Beehive is neither one of London's most historic, nor modern, nor spacious, nor comely Wetherspoons. Neither is it a waterfront venue (unless someone's doing something they shouldn't be, outside). But the atmosphere's a got a real local's feel – unlike many of the more grandiloquent 'Spoons. "It's a bit like *Cheers*," one drinker told us, "Where everyone knows your name." This is somewhere to order a crafty pint and tune into the surrounding dialogues. You can always call in at the Craft Beer Co. round the corner afterwards. It'll cost you, though.
407–409 Brixton Road, Brixton, SW9 7DG

The Capitol, Forest Hill

No prizes for guessing that The Capitol is a former cinema. Making way for the screen these days is a blockbuster of a bar, selling the usual range of well-kept ales, chilled wines from the tap and so on. OK, so it'd be nicer if this place was restored to an actual cinema (they still have the old seats installed in the higher tier), but this is second best. Wetherspoon have turned a few cinemas into boozers, including The Coronet in Holloway and The Montagu Pyke in Charing Cross. The latter shows major sporting events on a massive projector screen.
11–21 London Road, Forest Hill, SE23 3TW

The Crosse Keys, The City

A flagship Wetherspoon, parping with pomp and circumstance, The Crosse Keys is all marbled columns, coffered ceilings, Victorian Baroque facade and a boozing arena large enough to house a fleet of Routemasters. It's the kind of place you can lord it up with an actually affordable glass of prosecco.

If you're not best pleased with Wetherspoon converting flashy old banks like this into pubs, know that The Crosse Keys was originally a coaching tavern of the same name. During construction of the banking house in 1851, a girder gave way, causing a portion of wall to collapse. Five workers were killed. Next time you're here, raise a toast to their memory.
9 Gracechurch Street, EC3V 0DR

The Ice Wharf, Camden

If you've got a 'thing' about being seen in a Wetherspoon, The Ice Wharf could solve your predicament. Order a drink at the relatively nondescript bar, then distance yourself by perching on a lock outside – and calling out "lovely day for it!" at the narrow boats puttering by.

If you suddenly find you've accidentally had one pint too many, The Ice Wharf is neighbours with one of London's most interesting Starbucks – it's got battlements, and is also a miniature tourist info centre for Camden. How quaint.
Camden Wharf, 28 Jamestown Road, NW1 7AP

The Knights Templar, Chancery Lane

The Knights Templar is named after the Catholic warriors of yore who once hung out in the area, when they weren't busy Crusading in the Middle East. Women get to enjoy the pub's best bit: the ladies toilets are a madly opulent affair, dotted with sofas and statues. It's worth ordering a pint of soda water to force a visit. But back to the main pub: it's another former bank, these days thrumming with barristers, knocking back a stiff one after a hard day at the Royal Courts, and probably the odd defendant celebrating/commiserating their case too.

95 Chancery Lane, WC2A 1DT

The Ledger Building, West India Quay

While Canary Wharf's nightlife is mostly about shiny, identikit entertainment boxes teetering over the docks, The Ledger Building (where the ledgers of the West India Docks were once kept) is a delightful exception to the rule. The best thing about this historical building? Its sizeable cobblestone terrace, overlooking the moored boats – one of which is London's only floating church.

The Ledger Building is next door to the Museum of London Docklands, which has its own 'fake' pub, The Three Mariners, which you'll find nestled in Sailortown. It's BYOB. Just don't tell the staff that's what you're doing.

4 Hertsmere Road, Poplar, E14 4AL (see page 70 also)

The Mossy Well, Muswell Hill

A newer addition to Wetherspoon's London dynasty, The Mossy Well dispels the stereotype of 'interesting' carpets and sticky-icky tables with its exposed-brick walls and great shafts of natural light. The pub actually brings Wetherspoon back to its roots: founder Tim Martin once explained to us that he set up the first Wetherspoon in the 80s, just around the corner from here.

The multi-level garden is home to a huge plastic cow and a milk float converted into a small bar. This isn't random; the building was formerly an Express Dairy. And as for that name 'Mossy Well': not a euphemism, but a nod to the origins of the area's name: Muswell = mossy well.

The Village, 258 Muswell Hill Broadway, N10 3SH

The Rochester Castle, Stoke Newington

Open since 1983, The Rochester Castle is the oldest surviving Wetherspoon pub in London. Although the carpet's been changed a couple of times since then, it's got that 'classic' Wetherspoon vibe (fruit machines, mixed clientele, a homely fusty kind of feel). It's a favourite of the Wetherspoon founder too – so if you fancy having a beer/Brexit debate with him, your luck could be in.

More than anything, The Rochester Castle completes Stokey's holy triumvirate of great Irish pub (The Auld Shillelagh), great craft beer pub (The Jolly Butcher's) and great Wetherspoon. Hallelujah!

145 Stoke Newington High Street, Stoke Newington, N16 0NY

The Rocket, Putney

The Rocket in Putney has an outside terrace overlooking the Thames and – importantly – Putney Bridge. As you absorb your poison of choice, swot up on the crossing's remarkable history, which includes prime minister Robert Walpole demanding the bridge be built after missing a debate in the Houses of Parliament because the ferryman was busy getting sloshed in the local; and the attempted suicide of feminist Mary Wollstonecraft. The bridge also happens to be the starting point for the Boat Races*. If you're banking on a seat, get there about a week early.

A pedant would tell you that the Boat Races actually start marginally further upstream. We are that pedant.

Putney Wharf Tower, Brewhouse Lane, SW15 2JQ

Wetherspoons, Victoria station concourse

If you thought the whole Wetherspoon using the word 'Moon' in its pub names was uninspiring (at one point there were 14 The Moon Under Waters), try this for size. This place is called simply 'Wetherspoons'. By the way, the chain seems to variously be known as Wetherspoon, Wetherspoons, Wetherspoon's and JD Wetherspoon. The name allegedly comes from a hapless schoolteacher that Tim Martin admired.

Anyway, if you're waiting for your train to the Kent coast this Victoria Wetherspoon and its terraces overlooking the platforms are a shoo-in.

Victoria station, Victoria Street, SW1E 5ND

A TALE OF TWO GIN CRAZES

(AND A HAZY BIT IN BETWEEN)

*Gin: it's everywhere these days. But this isn't the first time
London has dabbled in Mother's Ruin.*

In the early 1600s, British soldiers fighting alongside the Dutch noticed that their allies transformed into ferocious, fearless fighters on the battlefield, after taking a swig from their hip flask.

The stuff inside it turned out to be a spirit flavoured with juniper berries – something called 'jenever', or gin. The Brits had had their first taste of – and for – 'Dutch courage'.

Four double gins a day

It wasn't until Dutch prince William of Orange plonked himself on the English throne (by invitation) in 1689, however, that the Brits developed a nationwide thirst for gin. Soon, London – bursting at the seams with spices shuttled in from all over the world – started using these exotic goodies to flavour the spirit of the moment. London became the centre of the gin universe.

By 1740, the city of 630,000 debauched souls was producing 45 million litres of gin each year – that's 71 litres per person, or four double gins per day. It's estimated there were some 17,000 gin shops in London alone, a figure that excludes pubs, taverns, restaurants, grocers, barbers or brothels… all of which also did a roaring gin trade. Today – even with a population 15 times larger – London doesn't have this many licensed venues.

The city was cirrhosing from the inside, and alarm bells began to peal. Almost half of the entire British wheat harvest was being used to make spirits, and – as the death rate outstripped the birth rate for the first time – novelist Henry Fielding argued that soon there would be "few of the common people left to drink it". Infant mortality was worse than it is now in Afghanistan. Something had to be done.

Gin terrorists explode a bomb in Parliament

In 1743, parliament introduced a Gin Act, restricting its sale in an attempt to scythe down rampant consumption. The masses were not happy bunnies – so much so, that 'gin terrorists' managed to smuggle in and detonate a bomb in the Houses of Parliament; something poor Guy Fawkes never pulled off.

Soon after, in 1751, Hogarth produced his famous print, *Gin Lane*. Kindly funded by the beer industry, it was one half of an allegorical double-header depicting the evils of gin consumption versus the merits of beer. Alongside images of cadaverous beings strewn in the street, and a baby plunging to its doom, are the words 'drunk for a penny, dead drunk for twopence, clean straw for nothing'. *Gin Lane* was embellished, but by no means fantastical. London spent a chunk of the 18th century gripped by something equivalent to a crack cocaine epidemic.

Now getting desperate, the government introduced new laws with a 'Tippling Act' to try to dry out the nation. But it wasn't until 1757, after the harvest failed three seasons in a row and with the country facing starvation, that a ban on distillation from grain was introduced and the era of cheap gin was finally over.

This didn't force Mother's Ruin to take a back seat though. In the early 1800s, while adding the finishing touches to an empire on which the sun would never set, British troops forced to take quinine waters to avoid malaria were coerced into drinking the bitter liquid with a spoonful of sugar, and a healthy dash of gin. The spirit was moving from something consumed in straw-lined basements, to a classy tipple sipped in Victorian gin palaces awash with cut glass and velvet drapes. Gin had lost volume, yet gained status.

Winston Churchill once remarked that gin and tonics had saved more lives than all of the world's doctors put together. Yet it was never seriously in vogue during his heyday, and was even bullied out of its sacred martini cocktail by vodka in the 1950s. Bombay Sapphire launched in 1986 – touted at the time as being a vodka drinker's gin, lighter in flavour – but it wasn't till the late 1990s that gin would claw its way back into Londoners' glasses.

A second gin craze (without the dead infants)

London was now a city that worshipped vodka. Every new bar that opened prided itself on how many bottles of the stuff sat behind the countertop – a boozy version of the emperor's new clothes, with drab post-communist chic spattered over the labels. Then, in 1999, Martin Miller's gin appeared. The super-premium London dry gin was made using Icelandic water and cucumber. Could gin be cool again?

Bartenders and bon vivants started paying attention. Hendrick's was launched amid an ingenious marketing campaign, emphasising its use of Bulgarian rose and cucumber. People started garnishing their drinks with this very British vegetable (not so much with Bulgarian roses). And then Sipsmith overturned a 200-year-old act of parliament, opened up in an old workshop in Hammersmith and became London's first new traditional copper gin distillery in decades. By the time the 2012 Olympics arrived, gin had well and truly returned – Londoners were glugging it, while cheering on their athletes. Premium tonic arrived in the nick of time, adding further status.

London's second gin craze is now in full flow. The Gin Bar in Holborn serves more than 500 varieties. There's a gin hotel in Notting Hill, which is a multi-storey fun factory dedicated to juniper juice. You can slurp Old Tom gin from the City of London Distillery, barrel-aged gin from East London Liquor Company, and gin that tastes like Christmas from Beefeater. The latter distillery has been plugging away in the capital since 1876. Something told them it was worth sticking around.

PIMM'S: CREATED IN LONDON AS A LEGAL LOOPHOLE

James Pimm owned a successful chain of oyster houses in mid-19th century London. But there was a problem. He was granted the right to sell alcohol – but only with the proviso that the premises were not to be converted into a gin shop or public house. Pimm had a brainwave, and started flogging a 'medicinal' post-meal concoction made from gin and a secret blend of liqueurs and herbs. Served in a small tankard, it was called 'No. 1 Cup'. Later, someone had the idea of mixing it with lemonade, and so a British icon was born. In 2017, tennis fans consumed 303,277 glasses of this stuff at the Wimbledon Championships alone.

Make the perfect Pimm's

The trick is to shove in as much pre-cut exotic fruit as possible. We'd recommend citrus of some kind, berries, cucumber, slices of apple and fresh mint. Decant the Pimm's into a jar with all the cut fruit the night before, then strain it back into the bottle the next day, and mix this 1 part Pimm's to 3 parts lemonade.

THE DOCKLANDS LIGHT ALE-WAY

The Docklands Light Railway (DLR) opened in 1987, and is now a well-established pillar of London's eastern transport network. It's also a great enabler of pub crawls.

Here we follow one of the early bits of track from Tower Gateway to Canary Wharf.

The Minories, Tower Gateway

If Tower Gateway really were a gateway, then The Minories would be its hinge. The pub is scooped out from rail arches immediately beside the station; its cavernous interior is one of the more atmospheric in a part of town otherwise bereft of characterful boozers. We note that Guinness is listed as a 'craft beer'. Hmm. That said, this place is big, attractive and has two outdoor seating areas. A good pub to start a crawl.
64–73 Minories, EC3N 1JL

Jump on the DLR one stop to Shadwell.

The George Tavern, Shadwell

Just a five-minute hike up to Commercial Road and you can't miss the George, standing proudly, flags flying, on the corner with Jubilee Street. Again, this place is small haven for ale fans: lagers are the order of the day. But the regulars come for the unmatched atmosphere of a genuine East End boozer that has stood the test of time. Centuries, in fact. As befitting a place 'mentioned' by Dickens, Pepys and even Chaucer, the pub doubles as an arts and performance venue. One of the true jewels of the drinkosphere.
373 Commercial Street, E1 0LA

Head back to the DLR and ride one stop.

Craft Beer Co., Limehouse

This easterly stronghold of the beer-lovers' pub chain opened in 2017 in the old Railway Arms building. The bar supports more species of beer than we could reliably count after two pints. The small downstairs area is supplemented with a further drinking lounge upstairs and what the pub bills (in large letters) as a 'secret roof terrace'. It's a tiny but welcome outdoor spot for those lucky enough to bag it.
576 Commercial Road, E14 7JD

Limehouse DLR is next door. Scoot one stop east to Westferry.

The Ledger Building, Westferry

A short walk from the DLR and we're into the Canary Wharf Estate. Its best drinking spot is the Ledger Building, one of Wetherspoon's finest (see page 66). It stands within an old commercial premises and is fronted by an imposing Doric arch. Inside you'll find the usual Wetherspoon tropes of cheap and varied beer, with no music or sport. This is never the quietest place to drink – crammed as it is with City types – but it's got charm.
4 Hertsmere Road, E14 4LA.

The Merchant, West India Quay/Canary Wharf

We finish the evening in this neat corner house from the Fuller's group. Formerly the Tea Merchant, the name is now truncated so as not to confuse potential customers into thinking this is a glorified cafe. In fact, The Merchant is the archetypal modern gastropub – it's smart and snazzy and not like anything else on the pub crawl (while, at the same time, being very much like many other upmarket pubs in commercial centres). The best seats here are on one of the outdoor tables overlooking the quay.
25–27 Fisherman's Walk, E14 4DH

The DLR does, of course, extend further through the Isle of Dogs and on to Greenwich and Lewisham, but we'll stop here. We've probably had enough…

Illustration by MERCEDES LEON ILLUSTRATION

THE GEORGE

CRAFT BEER CO

THE MINORIES

THE MINORIES

THE GEORGE

CRAFT BEER

TOWER
GATEWAY

DLR

LIMEHOUSE

WESTFERRY

SHADWELL

DLR

The Ledger

THE LEDGER

THE MERCHANT

THE DOCKLANDS
LIGHT ALE-WAY

CANARY WHARF

WEST
INDIA
QUAY

DLR

LONDON'S STRANGEST PUB NAMES

Among the Red Lions and White Harts, the city has its fair share of weird pub names.
The strangest of all, the Frog and Radiator in Greenwich, closed some time ago, sadly.
But London still has its nominative treasures. Here are 12 favourites.

The Aeronaut, Acton

This lively circus-themed venue is named after Acton-born George Lee Temple, the first Englishman to fly a plane upside-down. Was he drunk when he did it? Probably not.
264 High Street, W3 9BH

The Camel & Artichoke, Waterloo

A name with two components. Artichokes are not unheard of in pub names, with perhaps a dozen across the UK, including the Queen's Head and Artichoke in Camden. The reasons are obscure, various and disputed, though probably whimsical in most cases. This one's been trading since the late 18th century, originally as 'the Artichoke', and may recall the route of the exotic vegetable to market. At some point, the place changed its name to the Elusive Camel (we honestly don't know why). New management in 2006 merged the two former names.
121 Lower Marsh, SE1 7AE

The Case is Altered, Eastcote

Oddly, this name is not unique. The UK contains at least four, including another nearby, south of Bushey. The name probably reflects a legal dispute over licensing which, when resolved, altered the pub's status or 'case'. The wording was used by noted playwright Ben Johnson in the 16th century and seems to have been a common phrase. Another theory suggests a corruption of the Spanish phrase Casa Alta, meaning house on a hill.
Southill Lane, HA5 2EU

The Defector's Weld, Shepherd's Bush

This mighty Young's pub (see page 112 also) supposedly commemorates the Cold War-era Cambridge Spy Ring, one of whom lived nearby. The 'weld' implies a joining together, so perhaps this is one of the places in which the spies would meet. Who knows? Certainly not the bar staff, who we've interrogated on more than one occasion.
170 Uxbridge Road, W5 3LH

The Job Centre, Deptford

The Job Centre is actually a pub, but based inside an old Job Centre. This novel change-of-use prompted something of a backlash when the pub opened in 2014. Accusations of insulting the misfortunate and 'doing gentrification ironically' flew around social media. The dust has now settled, and we have a fine pub made memorable by its 1970s furniture.

120 Deptford High Street E8 4NP

John the Unicorn, Peckham

Like The Job Centre, this pub is part of the Antic chain – which we'll encounter again thanks to its creative ways with a pub name. This one is named after a childhood toy of the owner's daughter. It's as good a way as any to christen a pub, but we hope it doesn't start a trend. Imagine the Skeletor Arms, the Headless Barbie, and the Fisher-Price Garage With The Broken Lift Mechanism.

157–159 Rye Lane, SE15 4TL

The Mad Bishop & Bear, Paddington

This station pub commemorates two very different local characters. The bear is, of course, Paddington, the marmalade-loving ursine who met the Brown family on the platforms down below. The ecclesiastic half of the name remembers the Bishop of London who sold land here to the railway company. He did this at such low cost that he was deemed 'mad'.

1st Floor, Paddington Station, W2 1HB

Pepper St Ontiod, Millwall

You won't find the word Ontiod in any reputable dictionary. It's a modern coinage by Antic, an abridgement of 'On the Isle of Dogs'. The other bit is merely the location (Pepper Street), though the pub pronounces this for some reason as 'Saint'. All a bit odd.

21 Pepper Street, E14 9RP

Pratts & Payne, Streatham

Sounds a bit like a solicitors' firm or estate agents, doesn't it? Although not outwardly weird, Pratts & Payne gets its name from some unlikely source material. The 'Pratts' bit recalls a defunct department store, while the sequel remembers Ms Cynthia Payne, the celebrated hostess of many a sex party. It's another Antic, of course.

113 Streatham High Road, SW16 1HJ

The Pyrotechnists Arms, Nunhead

Unquestionably a unique pub name, the Pyrotechnists Arms was built on the site of a former fireworks factory. Almost as if to invite disaster, it features an image of the Gunpowder Plot conspirators on its pub sign.

39 Nunhead Green, SE15 3QF

The Ship & Shovell, Charing Cross

Another name and, indeed, pub of two halves: its twin bars are separated by an alleyway. Many pubs reference a ship,

but the Shovell is unique. The inspiration is Sir Cloudesley Shovell. He presided over one of the worst disasters in British maritime history when his fleet struck rocks off Scilly in 1707. Something like 1,500 people lost their lives. A bit odd, don't you think, to associate your pub with a Titanic-scale disaster?

1–3 Craven Passage, WC2N 5PH

The Sylvan Post, Forest Hill

Another Antic pub, this one was built inside a former post office, hence the latter bit. Sylvan means 'of the woods', a reference to the location in Forest Hill. Look out for the many postal gimcracks throughout the pub.

24–28 Dartmouth Road, SE23 3XZ

DRINK IN THE VIEW – BARS WITH STUNNING VISTAS

What's the best bar for views over central London? That'd be a Heathrow-bound BA flight, still serving complimentary miniatures of Jack Daniel's. Otherwise, you'll need to turn your attentions to the city's loftiest buildings for your fix of scenery.

Altitude Sky Bar, Millbank Tower, Pimlico

Such is the allure of Sky Bar London, it offers a special Proposal in the Sky package. If your relationship isn't quite there yet, you'll need to make a booking for a drink in the sky (or afternoon tea in the sky) to gain access to the riverside views. Looking down on the Houses of Parliament is a bit of a kick – or turn the other way to clock Battersea Power Station.

Aptly, the cocktail menu pays homage to the views, each libation named after a London landmark visible from the bar (London Eye, Vauxhall Bridge, Chelsea Art School, to name but a few).

30 Millbank, Westminster, SW1P 4QP

Bōkan, Canary Wharf

You needn't leave your house to experience Bōkan's impressive views, thanks to a highly addictive 24-hour live webcam, broadcasting the views from the 38th-floor Canary Wharf bar. The real thing – sitting atop the Novotel London hotel – is infinitely better, though.

An industrial-chic bar rocks floor-to-ceiling windows, and is as big on craft beer as it is on fancy cocktails and fine wines. Sharing platters and starter-style dishes are available to order, and the cocktail menu takes inspiration from the bar's Docklands setting, with Chaos on the River (Campari, orgeat and lemon) heading up the West India Docks section. The Dark Whale, meanwhile, references the East India Docks' blubber-boiling days.

40 Marsh Wall, Isle of Dogs, E14 9TP

Galvin at Windows, Mayfair

This upmarket French restaurant offers greener views than many of its lofty

counterparts. Galvin at Windows is located on the 28th floor of the Hilton on Park Lane hotel, tantalisingly close to the southeast corner of Hyde Park, with Green Park to the south, and St James's Park beyond that.

Signature cocktails, and low and no-alcohol variations are in the offing, with prices starting at £16, and going up to £1,500 for a bottle of champagne. Whisky and gin are well represented, with myriad incarnations of each available from all over the world. Burgers, salads, soups and olives all feature on the substantial bar menu – in fact, we'd be tempted to blow off the restaurant entirely, plumping for a cocktail and burger, and watching Mayfair stretched out like a toy town below.

22 Park Lane, W1K 1BE

Gōng at The Shard, London Bridge

If it's views you're after, the tallest building in the UK is an obvious starter for 10. And provided your wallet can cope with sky high prices, The Shard won't disappoint.

Gōng, part of the Shangri La Hotel, is located on level 52 and claims to be the highest hotel bar in Western Europe, gazing out for miles over west, north and east London. It's still not as high as The Shard's tourist viewing platform, but then you won't get a glass of fizz up there.

Pick from the Champagne Bar, Cocktail Bar or Sky Pool areas (you have to be staying here to take a dip), and get stuck into your poison. Oodles of thought goes into an ever-changing cocktail menu; we once had a James Bond-themed drink, with a bullet frozen in time halfway through the glass. Whatever you order, press your face against the glass and watch the trains shuttle in and out of London Bridge below. They're positively Hornby-esque from up here.

31 St Thomas Street, SE1 9QU

Other bars at The Shard
Down on level 32, Oblix East offers views towards Tower Bridge and Canary Wharf. Try one of their twists on a classic – rhubarb and bubblegum martini anyone, or how about a banana old fashioned? –

while you wait for Tower Bridge to open up. Aqua Shard sits one level lower (which for most bars, is still pretty high) and its generous windows allow you to feel like a giant, towering over everything from the BT Tower to St Paul's. Even the views from the urinals are stunning.

31 St Thomas Street, SE1 9RY

The Heights Bar at St George's Hotel, Marylebone
Something of a lesser-known option is this stalwart, just north of Oxford Circus, where visitors go nose-to-spire with All Saints Langham Place church. If you don't mind your decor a little dated, you can get yourself a drink at The Heights Bar – perched on the 15th floor of the St George's Hotel – at a snip of the cost of other skyline venues, and still see for miles in a predominantly northwest direction.

Otherwise, bag a window overlooking the BBC's Broadcasting House, which

throbs with electric blue light at night. The Heights has long been a setting for boozy Beeb meetings: eavesdrop on some conversations and see if anyone mentions monkey tennis.

Langham Place, W1B 2QS

Bars in the Heron Tower, Bishopsgate
The Heron Tower (no, we're not calling it the Salesforce Tower and you can't make us) hosts two venues which mainly function as restaurants, but come with a decent bar menu. Duck & Waffle on level 40 is famously open 24 hours a day (see page 177), meaning you can imbibe everything from your early morning coffee through to late night cocktails at the 24-seat bar. (For a lazy and pricey bar crawl, install yourself for a whole day, occupying each seat for an hour at a time.)

A couple of floors down, Japanese-Peruvian-Brazilian fusion restaurant

Sushi Samba proffers a hefty 'Beverage Book' to those in need of refreshment, largely dominated by Japanese sake, Brazilian cachaça and Peruvian pisco.

110 Bishopsgate, EC2N 4AY

Iris at The Gherkin, St Mary Axe

Cast your eyes to this bar's ceiling and you'll find yourself beneath an iris-shaped dome, which gives this place its name. Until 2018, views from the top of The Gherkin were reserved for those frequenting the private members' bar – not any more. We recommend visiting soon though; as more and more new skyscrapers cluster around The Gherkin, vistas from within are becoming restricted.

30 St Mary Axe, EC3A 8EP

Restaurant at Tate Modern, Bankside

Tate Modern is all about the visuals – and that includes the views from its 9th-floor restaurant. Though food is its bread and butter, it's open to non-diners after refreshment in liquid form: coffee, beer, wine and stronger elixirs – including an extensive range of gins. Whatever you order, it's served up with views northwards to St Paul's and east towards The Shard.

Bankside, SE1 9TG

Sky Pod Bar at the Walkie Talkie, Fenchurch Street

Sure, you could visit London's Sky Garden for free and release your inner tourist. Or, you could book yourself a table at the Sky Pod Bar, like a Londoner. All the classic cocktails are available, along with a seasonally shifting menu of other serves, including cockle-warming cocktails in the winter. The Shard may be higher, but in our opinion, you get better views of the Thames from over here. There's also the chance you'll see window cleaners squeegeeing their way past your window.

1 Sky Garden Walk, EC3M 8AF

Vertigo 42 at Tower 42, Bishopsgate

Once a year, Vertigo 42 becomes the finish line for Vertical Rush, a sprint up the 932 steps of Tower 42 in aid of charity. But you needn't ruin your calves to get a tipple up here. Although focus is on champagne, wine and cocktails are available for supping while perched on a stool or cosied up in a leather armchair at the outwards-facing bar. Views to the southwest round to the north are the best – keep 'em peeled for Tate Modern, London Eye and St George Wharf Tower.

Once upon a time, Tower 42 was the tallest building in the Square Mile, but as new-builds have increasingly swamped it, the crowds have fallen away, making this a solid option for a quietish date night.

25 Old Broad Street, EC2N 1HQ

And now for a totally different point of view...

The Old Orchard at Harefield, Uxbridge

In utter contrast to everything above, here's a bar with a view of lakes and woods and – perhaps uniquely – not a single building or manmade structure (unless you count the lakes, which were dug in Victorian times). It stretches credulity that such a place might exist in London, but The Old Orchard ticks all the boxes. Just. The Greater London boundary is reached at the foot of the hill and the view gazes out over Herts and Bucks.

This is a fine pub on many scores. The view comes from a spacious beer garden, with nooks and crannies and ornamental tractors for the little ones to explore. Inside, expect a fine welcome and a roaring fire in winter. The beer choice is exceptional for somewhere so, well, rural, with eight real ale pumps. It might have a shout as the best pub in London. Just don't expect to stumble back to the nearest tube station – it's more than half an hour's walk away.

Park Lane, Harefield, UB9 6HJ

QUAFF YOUR WAY THROUGH THE KINGS AND QUEENS OF ENGLAND

Where are London's royalist pubs? Everywhere, frankly. From Royal Oaks to White Harts, many of our common pub names have regal inspiration. Plenty are named directly after individual rulers, as shown by this royal flush of monarchical boozers.

Harold II

The only pre-conquest pub we can find is the **King Harold** in, suitably enough, Harold Wood. The Havering suburb is indeed named after the fallen man of Hastings, so it's appropriate that a local pub still honours his name.
51 Station Road, Harold Wood, RM3 0BS

William the Conqueror

Harold's nemesis has settled closer in, half way betwixt Stratford and Ilford. The **William the Conqueror** is a lively, entertainment-led pub with zero traces of Norman heritage.
630 Romford Road, Manor Park, E12 5AQ

Richard I

One of Greenwich's hidden treasures, **Richard I** boasts a magnificent beer garden and dining conservatory. We're not quite sure why this Young's pub is named after the Lionheart, but by the time you've trekked up the significant hill you don't ask needless questions. The delightful Greenwich Union is next door if you fancy an effortless pub crawl.
52–54 Royal Hill, Greenwich, SE10 8RT

Richard II

Richard II doesn't have his own dedicated London pub. He did, however, inspire one of the commonest pub names in Britain. Anything called the **White Hart** has a Ricardian influence, for this was the king's personal device. London has about a dozen. Our favourite is the Stoke Newington version, which hides the largest beer garden in the area.
69 Stoke Newington High Street, N16 8EL

Henry VII

It's a similar story with the debut Tudor. Henry does not lend his name directly to a pub, but his personal device of a rose is often cited as the inspiration behind the common pub name **The Rose and Crown**. The connection is by no means certain, so we'll not list out all the examples.

Henry VIII

No pub in London is directly named after England's most famous king. However, numerous pubs around town decorate their hanging signs with his portly, menacing face – particularly those with the popular name 'The King's Head'. You'll find examples from Bexley to Barnet, but the best drinking experience is to be had in the **Kings Head**, Tooting. This sprawling Victorian pub is a delight to explore.
84 Upper Tooting Road, SW17 7PB

Henry's elder brother Arthur, who should have been king but died aged 15, is remembered in the names of several pubs, including the **Prince Arthur** near Euston station.

Elizabeth I

At least two pubs in London take their name from Good Queen Bess. **The Queen Elizabeth** in Walworth displays the last Tudor's likeness on a prominent roundel. Meanwhile, **The Queen Elizabeth** in Chingford stands not far from the 16th-century Queen Elizabeth Hunting Lodge. Be sure to order a Bloody Mary, the tomato-based cocktail supposedly named after Liz's half-sister and predecessor, Mary I.

42 Merrow Street, Walworth, SE17 2NH
95 Forest Side, Chingford, E4 6BA

James I

The first Stuart to take the English throne, the scholar king gave us the King James Bible, presided over the British colonisation of America, and made a memorable appearance in *Doctor Who*. Sadly, he didn't give us many pubs. That said, you could do a lot worse than the **King and Tinker** in Enfield. This ancient, almost-rural pub on the northern fringes

of London recalls an old legend involving James. The king became separated from his entourage while out hunting on Enfield Chase one day. He took shelter in this pub, where he befriended a local tinker. The tradesman only clocked the identity of his interlocutor when the king's groupies caught up. James liked the fellow so much, he had him knighted.
Whitewebbs Lane, Enfield, EN2 9HJ

Charles I

Charles is well remembered thanks to his rapid loss of height in January 1649, courtesy of the executioner's blade. Just one London pub remembers his name, and it's a cracker. The **King Charles I** in King's Cross is one of those tiny backstreet gems that, once discovered, becomes a lifetime favourite. Oddly, it carries a stained glass window to

another king, Elvis Presley. (The two also share real estate on the hanging sign of the **Famous Three Kings** in West Kensington, with Henry VIII making up the unlikely trio.)
55–57 Northdown Street, King's Cross, N1 9BL

Illustration by AMY BLACKWELL

Charles II

Charles's son and heir and namesake lacks any pub of his own in London, but the Merry Monarch can indirectly live up to his nickname, thanks to the many pubs called **The Royal Oak**. The name recalls the tree in Boscobel, Shropshire, where Charles supposedly hid from Roundhead troops during the English Civil War. It is the third-commonest pub name in the country, and London has more than 20 – plus the **Penderel's Oak** in Holborn, which also commemorates the royal game of hide-and-seek. Of all the Oaks, the Harvey's house in Southwark is perhaps the most cherished among beer fans. Its hanging sign shows the young Charles looking down on his pursuers.

44 Tabard Street, SE1 4JU

Anne

The last of the Stuarts is another monarch with no directly named pub. However, the **Queen's Head** in Pinner – a 16th-century building of remarkable antiquity, with 17th-century panelling and cellars that may date to the 12th century – features a prominent portrait of the queen on its gibbet-like hanging sign. Formerly The Crown, it was

renamed the Queen's Head in 1715, the year after Anne's death.
31 High Street, Pinner, HA5 5PJ

George I

1714 saw the House of Hanover take the crown of the recently created Kingdom of Great Britain, in the person of George I. To show allegiance to the new regime, many pubs adopted the sign of the white horse, symbol (or sigil if you're a *Game of Thrones* nut) of the House of Hanover. So the story goes. The common pub name **The White Horse** probably has multiple origins. London has around 20. The most notable – for its extensive craft beer range (see page 169) and nickname of the Sloany Pony – is the prominent corner house in Parsons Green.
2 Parsons Green, SW6 4TN

George II

Until 2018, the most forgettable of the four Georgian Georges had his own pub in Hornchurch. It's since changed to a non-regal name. His son and (predeceased) heir Prince Frederick is, however, commemorated in Bromley's **Prince Frederick**.
31 Nichol Lane, Bromley, BR1 4DE

George III

London has no pub called The George III, though the famously 'mad' king is hinted at throughout the pubosphere. His countenance crops up on many a pub sign, while the **Kings Arms** on Newcomen Street (Borough) carries his coat of arms, rescued from Old London Bridge. The most curious link can be found in Bloomsbury, at **The Queens Larder**. The cellar of this pub was supposedly used as a food store by Queen Charlotte while she was nursing her husband at a nearby doctor's house – hence the pub's name.

1 Queen's Square, WC1N 3AR

George IV

The fourth George was deeply unpopular with the public. Odd to report, then, that he has more pubs to his name than any previous monarch. **George IV**s can be found in Marylebone High Street, Kentish Town, Portugal Street, Woolwich and Chiswick, among others. During the long, afflicted reign of his father, George went by the title **Prince Regent** (you may recall the character played by Hugh Laurie in *Blackadder III*). This title is all over town: Regent Street, Regent Square, Regent's Park, Regent's Canal… Pubs of this name are also common throughout London and the wider kingdom.

William IV

Perhaps even more surprising than the preponderance of George IVs is the ubiquity of his immediate successor, William IV. Old Bill is the forgotten monarch of the 19th century, overshadowed by the Georges and, of course, his niece Victoria. He only reigned for seven years, yet has almost as many London pubs. Find them in the Harrow Road, Hampstead, Shepherdess Walk, West Drayton and Grosvenor Road. Our pick of the bunch is the **William IV** in Leyton – a charming Brodie's pub with an old-school interior that might have been fitted in William's day.

816 High Road, Leyton, E10 6AE

Victoria

The long-serving queen very nearly has more pubs devoted to her name than all the rest put together. You'll find pubs called **The Victoria** or **Queen Victoria** in (deep breath): Barking, Belgravia, Belvedere, Bermondsey (x2), East Sheen, Globe Town, Hackney, Isleworth, Lancaster Gate, Marylebone (with Albert), Peckham, Richmond, Romford, Surbiton and Walthamstow. Not to mention a couple of **Princess Victoria**s, and the famous fictional pub from *EastEnders* (actually on a film set in Hertfordshire). Victoria reigns supreme. Several of her offspring are commemorated with their own pubs, including the famous **Princess Louise** in Holborn, while consort **Prince Albert** is also well represented.

Edward VII

The Edwardian era was ushered in by Victoria's son **Edward VII**. His sole London pub can be found in Stratford. It's a dependable, well-run place, highly prized in a part of town that changes beyond recognition every time we visit. The fellow also crops up on several hanging signs, including the **Prince Edward** in Princes Square, Bayswater.

47 Broadway, E15 4BQ

George V

471 playing fields were posthumously named after the present Queen's grandfather, but very few pubs. The exception is the **George V** in Ilford (645 Cranbrook Road, Ilford, IG2 6SX). Otherwise, George may be the inspiration behind several other 'The George' pubs – it's often hard to tell, with six monarchs and a patron saint. His image appears on the sign of the **George Inn**, Morden, for example.

George VI

The Queen's dad is also bereft of pubs, but one venue in Stepney remembers his wife Queen Elizabeth the Queen Mother with fondness. You may not have visited the **Queen's Head** in York Square, but you've almost certainly seen a photograph of its interior. This is the place where, in 1987, her late majesty was photographed pulling and enjoying a pint. She featured on the hanging sign for a while, but a recent refit seems to have banished her likeness from the outside. Gawd rest 'er soul.

8 Flamborough Street, E14 7LS

THE FATAL LONDON BEER FLOOD

'Drowning in a tsunami of beer' sounds like a suggestion from one of those flippant pub conversations about supposedly good ways to die. Yet this very scenario claimed the lives of at least eight Londoners back in 1814.

The location is a familiar one: the Dominion Theatre at the crossroads of Tottenham Court Road and Oxford Street. The theatre is built on a site that was previously the Horse Shoe brewery, run by Meux and Co.

On 17 October 1814, an iron hoop, one of several holding together a seven-metre-tall vat of beer, gave way. The huge tank burst, upending another nearby vessel. The equivalent of 2.5 million pints, mostly London porter, rushed out of the building with fatal consequences.

The wave of booze smashed through one of the brewery walls, killing a teenage servant in the adjoining Tavistock Arms pub. From here, the brown tide spilled out onto Great Russell Street and the surrounding rookeries of St Giles, filling basements and destroying homes.

The remaining victims were all killed on New Street, a small but densely packed alley behind the brewery. They ranged in age from three to 63. In one case, a mother and daughter were taking tea. "The mother was washed out of the window," noted the *Scots Magazine*, "and the daughter was swept away by the current through a partition and dashed to pieces."

The *Morning Post* described the disaster scene as an "immense mass of ruins… the surrounding scene of desolation presents a most awful and terrific appearance, equal to that which fire or earthquake may be supposed to occasion".

The inundation of one of London's poorest areas with unfathomable quantities of alcohol had other effects, no doubt. Secondary accounts talk of locals lapping up the free beer with gusto, and one man is said to have died of alcohol poisoning – though no evidence for this can be found in the newspapers of the time, nor the coroner's report of the incident.

At the subsequent investigation, the jury verdict was that the unfortunate neighbours had met their deaths "casually, accidentally and by misfortune". In short, this was deemed an act of God for which nobody was to blame.

Meux and Co. suffered great financial loss from the tragedy. An estimated £23,000 of beer (more than £1.5 million in today's money) had gone to waste. However, the company successfully claimed back a third of this in excise duty on the lost beer, which had already been paid. Nothing could reimburse those who had lost their homes and loved ones in this bizarre disaster.

The brewery continued trading for more than a century. The curtain finally fell in 1921, when it made way for the Dominion Theatre.

A SWIFT ONE
IN LONDON'S HOTEL BARS

Hotel bars: a bona fide excuse for hanging out in the hotels you might never have need (or funds) to stay at otherwise. We've gathered up London's best, from edgy basement bars to traditionally la-de-da cocktail lounges.

The American Bar at the Stafford Hotel

American-style bars started sprouting up around London and Paris in the late-19th century, and are credited with introducing cocktail culture to the up-till-then wayward, ale-steeped Brits. A hardy few of the original bars are still hanging in there. (See also: American Bar at The Savoy.)

Ironically, it's now thought that London may have invented the cocktail in a roundabout way (see page 17). But there's no doubt The American Bar at the Stafford Hotel is a spiffing place to steep yourself in history, while soaking up a champagne fizz or two. It's all heavy furniture, clubhouse vibes and decades of US sporting memorabilia hanging from the ceiling. Start with a

White Mouse – that was the codename of World War II servicewoman, Nancy Wake. Elusive as, well, a mouse, she was the Gestapo's most-wanted person. Clearly they didn't think to look in this bar, where she was often to be found.
16–18 St James's Place, St James's, SW1A 1PE

The Coral Room at The Bloomsbury Hotel

The Bloomsbury Hotel opened this bright-walled bar in 2017, back when the craze for coral-hued everything was just a twinkle in Pantone's eye. And a seat at their gleaming bar counter's been in increasingly high demand since the paint corp announced it as its 2019 Colour Of The Year.

If we're honest, under the warm chandelier lighting this place looks distinctly more pillarbox red than Instagram-courting coral. But who cares? The cocktails are elegant without being frilly, service is flawless without being stiff – and there's a high-ceilinged,

palm-fronded glamour to the room. Surely one of the best places in London to be living that #livingcoral life.
16–22 Great Russell Street, Bloomsbury, WC1B 3NN

DUKES at Dukes Hotel

James Bond author Ian Fleming was a regular at DUKES, which gives you an idea of this Mayfair bar's target demographic: eminence over celebrity, classic over fashionable, and martinis above everything (see page 43). Said martinis are served from a special rosewood trolley that's been in action for more than 100 years.

There's a 'smart, casual' dress code, which under a microscope looks a lot like: just smart. This is a hotel bar in the old-fashioned mould, for when you want to sink a Vesper like Bond of yesteryear. Though they're certainly not cheap, the martinis pack the punch of a Walther PPK.

35 St James's Pl, St. James's, SW1A 1NY

George's Bar at the Gilbert Scott at St Pancras Renaissance Hotel

The name's a tribute to the original architect of St Pancras Renaissance Hotel, Sir George Gilbert Scott. And so's the bar itself, really. While it does a pitch-perfect line in cocktails, the real reason to visit is the 19th-century magnificence of the room. It's a profusion of columns, burnished gold, dark wood and decorated ceilings. As ornate as many of London's galleries and museums, think of the steep price of a drink at the Gilbert Scott bar as an entrance charge for a museum or National Trust estate, and settle in to nurse your whisky and steep yourself in the historic grandeur for hours. What to order? They do a posh negroni called… The Londonist.

Euston Road, King's Cross, NW1 2AR

Gin Bar at Holborn Dining Room at Rosewood London

Copper-topped, art deco embellished… and crammed with gins, Rosewood London's resident gin bar isn't doing anything by halves, with more than 500 varieties of the stuff. And 30 tonics.

That's already 15,000 possible G&T combinations/reasons to visit Holborn Dining Room's bar, by our count. But one of the most important things they have to offer isn't gin-based at all: it's pies. Close proximity to Holborn Dining Room chef Calum Franklin's pies, to be precise. Works of ornate-latticed, burnished-crusted art, they are stomach-lining for emperors. Prepare for your visit to the Gin Bar with pies. Hell, bracket your visit to the Gin Bar with pies.

252 High Holborn, Holborn, WC1V 7EN

Miranda at Ace Hotel

The basement bar at Ace Hotel's not all that striking at first glance: moodily lit and with a stripped-back design, in a bit of town where that's the default look for a bar.

But above anything, Miranda is a performance space, and the events programming is a work of art. While other hotel bars are trading off their exclusivity or looks, Ace is making sure you have something more interesting to do than Instagramming your evening, with a mix of gigs, club nights, curated arts, documentary screenings and book

launches. And yoga. And live grime acts. And burlesque. Not a lot of that going on at The Dorchester.

100 Shoreditch High Street, Hackney, E1 6JQ

Devil's Darling / SACK / Black Rock at The Napoleon Hotel

This one's a hat-trick of distinctly different bars, all under the same roof. At the top, Devil's Darling, a cocktail bar with classic allure and good views. Ground floor: SACK, a sherry bar that's all sun-bleached barrel-top tables and faded posters. To get to the third bar, you'll have to take the drastic step of leaving the building – but only for about five steps, and it's worth it. Black Rock's basement spot is dominated by a long table made from a halved tree trunk: trenches are carved out and filled with whisky, which you can decant directly from taps embedded into the trunk.

Not only is this possibly London's most hyper-efficient bar crawl, it's possibly London's smallest hotel. One suite, at the top of the building. That's it. Perfect for an equally efficient stagger up to bed.

9 Christopher Street, Finsbury, EC2A 2BS

The Punch Room at the London EDITION

If the Punch Room, hidden at the back of the London EDITION hotel weren't this great, nobody would ever make it there. You'd be sidetracked by the Lobby Bar, with its velvety green sofas and pool table, or by Berners Tavern with its enormous chandeliers and its menus that read like comfort food for emperors.

But this glossy, dark bar still lures people in, riffing on London's 19th-century punch culture with a mix of oak-panelling, candlelit warmth and trademark punch bowls. The original mixed drink, punch bowls are all about sharing – which is lucky, because despite the elegant ceremony they're served with here, the drinks list still packs a serious… um… punch.

10 Berners Street, Fitzrovia, W1T 3NP

The Warrington

This is arguably cheating: the Warrington's really a pub with a handful of lovely hotel rooms rather than a hotel with a bar. But we're including it on the grounds that the pub's utter, lunatic grandeur makes the building as impressive as the bars at most of London's big, historic hotels – and a lot more welcoming than many.

It's a dazzling sprawl of marble and mosaics, curving staircases (made from an old ship, apparently), columns and hanging lamps – and the buzz and crowds are a welcome alternative to the statelier, hushed formality you find at some of London's other hotel watering holes. Come here on a Lord's match day, and prepare to be asked about your opinion on things like dibbly dobblys.

93 Warrington Cres, Little Venice, W9 1EH

THE COCKTAIL WITH ITS OWN POEM

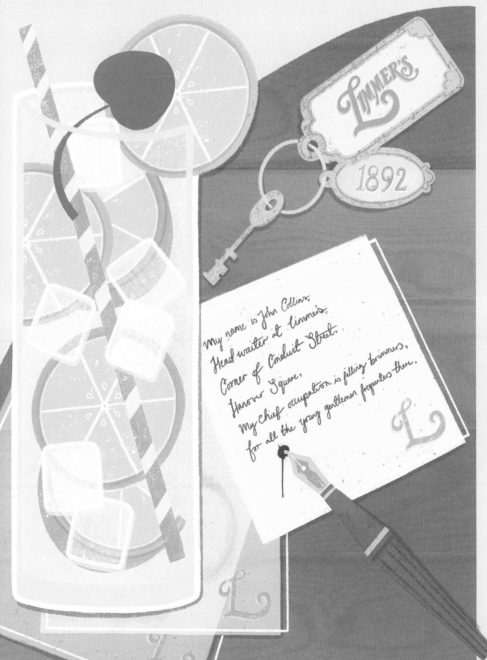

Multiple theories circulate as to the origin of the Collins, an easy-drinking cocktail based on gin and lemon. The most likely leads back to the mid-19th century and a hotel in Mayfair. John Collins was a bartender working at a bar called The Coffee House, set within Limmer's Hotel on Conduit Street – a hotel noted at the time for being 'one of the dirtiest in London'. The drink was immortalised in a poem in a 1892 book titled *Drinks of the World*:

My name is John Collins,
Head waiter at Limmer's,
Corner of Conduit Street,
Hanover Square,
My chief occupation is filling brimmers
For all the young gentlemen frequenters
there.

Make a Collins

Combine 50ml of gin, 25ml of fresh lemon juice, 10ml measure of sugar syrup and shake (or mix) together
Top-up with soda water.
Write a poem about it.

A HISTORY OF DRINKING CHOCOLATE IN LONDON

Londoners can gorge on chocolate in all manner of toothsome emporiums.
Prestat on Piccadilly is widely believed to be Roald Dahl's inspiration for Willy Wonka,
while Mayfair's Charbonnel et Walker is the capital's oldest chocolate shop. But long before
Londoners were nibbling on champagne truffles, they were glugging chocolate.

In the 17th and 18th centuries, hot chocolate was a luxury item for London's wealthy, consumed in chocolate houses where they gathered to socialise and get slightly fatter. Prepared with spices and exotic flavours, this was a richer experience than today's hot chocolates – but also sweeter than the original hot chocolate invented by the Mayans, thanks to the addition of sugar. It was an expensive commodity, and chocolate houses often charged an entry fee as well as for the product.

One of the first written records of chocolate is in Samuel Pepys' diary, the day after the coronation of King Charles II in 1661. He used it as stomach settler for the effects of "last night's drink".

Drinking chocolate was also available in the new-fangled coffee houses (coffee only arrived in London around five years previously; see page 126), but this was often an inferior, watered-down version. Plus, most coffee house visitors were there for the caffeine, which cocoa didn't offer in such quantities.

London's first chocolate house

Despite the later cocoa cluster around St James's, London's first chocolate house was in Queen's Head Alley near Bishopsgate in the City of London. In 1657, a Frenchman opened the premises, luring Londoners in with the promise of an "excellent West India drink". And so, London's hot chocolate craze began.

The chocolate houses of St James's

Given that hot chocolate was initially a drink for the well-off, it's no surprise that St James's was the epicentre of its popularity. One such chocolate house was White's on St James's Street – established as a chocolate house in 1693 and still existing today, as a private members' club (see page 97). In the early days, it had a reputation as something of a raucous establishment, with huge amounts of money gambled over cups of hot chocolate. It's depicted in the sixth episode of Hogarth's *A Rake's Progress*. So important was White's to the history of chocolate that its facade is recreated at Cadbury World in Bournville.

White's wasn't alone in serving hot chocolate to the well-heeled of St James's. Ozdina's on St James's Street was popular with King Charles II (and his mistresses, apparently). The building no longer exists. The Cocoa Tree on Pall Mall, another chocolate house, doubled up as informal Tory headquarters in the 18th century.

Sir Hans Sloane – inventor of chocolate milk

This chap has given his name to large swathes of Chelsea (Sloane Square, Sloane Street, Sloane Gardens, Hans Place, Hans Crescent...) but his link to liquid

Illustration by Lauren Rebbeck Illustration

chocolate comes from further afield. He's credited (and disputed) as the first major proponent of milk-based chocolate drinks, having travelled to Jamaica in 1687 and witnessed locals there mixing chocolate with spice, eggs, sugar and milk to create a beverage. Cadbury later sold a product called 'Sir Hans Sloane's Milk Chocolate'. Prior to this, London chocolate houses would have served cocoa mixed with water and spices, so this brought hot chocolate a step closer to how we know it today. Thank Sloane by raising a takeaway cup to his statue in Chelsea.

Hampton Court Palace chocolate kitchen

As the popularity of drinking chocolate grew, some of London's wealthier residents had dedicated chocolate kitchens installed in their houses (and palaces). Hampton Court Palace is one such building, with chocolate kitchens designed by Sir Christopher Wren in around 1690, just as the choco-craze was taking off. With this kitchen came staff dedicated to the production of chocolate.

Many royals would enjoy chocolate as a morning drink at breakfast, although William III was particularly fond of the stuff, and requested it throughout the day.

Visitors to Hampton Court Palace today can see inside the chocolate kitchens – the only surviving one in the country – and learn about the ingredients used to make these royal drinks.

Tosier's Chocolate House, Greenwich

Thomas Tosier was chocolate maker to King George I, employed at Hampton Court Palace from 1717. It was a job more privileged than most servants, as he worked with expensive, exotic ingredients, and had access to the king's bedchamber to serve him his morning drink of chocolate. Prior to his royal appointment, he ran his own business, Tosier's Chocolate House in Greenwich (no longer there). It was in an area originally known as Chocolate Row, close to what is now West Grove, off Blackheath Hill.

Tosier's wife, Grace, kept the Greenwich business running while he was working at Hampton Court, and clearly made a good job of it; Tosier still exists as a chocolate making company – focusing more on the solid than the liquid form – with stockists around the country, including in Spitalfields and at Mare Street Market in Hackney.

Drinking chocolate in London today

21st-century hot chocolate is a very different beast to its predecessors. With sugar more freely at our disposal – not to mention multifarious syrups and toppings – 17th-century Londoners would barely recognise the drink. You'd struggle to find a cafe or restaurant that doesn't serve it, but for top quality stuff, we recommend the following:

Café Godiva, Harrods: Up on the third floor of the world-famous department store, chocolatiers Godiva offer a menu of luxurious melted chocolate ganache-based hot chocolates.

Hotel Chocolat and Rabot 1745: Several branches of this high-street chocolate shop have cafes attached, which serve a lovely hot chocolate. For an even more chocolatey experience try the brand's restaurant, Rabot 1746 in Borough Market.

Fortnum & Mason: If you like a bit of decadence, the Hot Chocolate Bar at Fortnum & Mason is the way to go. Drinks are completely customisable, so replace the spices of yesteryear with biscuits, marshmallows, toppings and even booze of your choice.

It's not just traditional hot chocolate that Londoners are drinking. Hackney-based brewery Howling Hops – established right here in the capital in 2011 – makes a chocolate stout, a dark and rich drink with coffee notes layered over a hint of cocoa.

Chocolate in its other liquid forms

With 13 million chocolate digestives produced every year at the McVitie's factory in Harlesden, someone – or some*thing* – has the job of covering them in chocolate. That thing is the enrober – a chocolate river/waterfall which coats the top of the biscuits in sweet, chocolate goodness. The McVitie's factory is off-limits to the public, but you can see a chocolate waterfall in action at the Krispy Kreme factory in New Malden. Peer through the window, and try not to drool down it.

THE PUB: ALL THINGS TO ALL PEOPLE

The pub is not just for boozing. Over the centuries, it has served as a centre of the community, bringing people together for sport, hobby, business, transport and even prosecution.

Pub justice

Today we think of pubs as jolly places for relaxing and socialising. But head back a few centuries and the gaiety was tempered with more sombre activities.

Before the rise of police courts, pubs and inns were a traditional place for the dispensation of justice. Magistrates would preside over 'petty sessions' courts within the back or upstairs rooms (today's

ORDER! ORDER!

'function rooms'), while the drinky bit of the pub remained open. Cases of minor theft, assault and, ironically, drunkenness were dealt with in this way.

Pubs were also used for coroner's inquests. These sessions probed sudden or suspicious deaths, often in lurid detail. The practice died out in the mid-19th century as dedicated buildings became the norm.

Animal fighting

Before the invention of fruit machines and Sky Sports, pub-goers got their gambling fix from an altogether bloodier diversion. Many London pubs maintained fighting rings where animals were forced to square-off against one another.

One of the commonest was cock fighting – rooster versus rooster, their legs weaponised with metal spurs. We get the word 'cockpit' from these pub fights. Cockfights were last held in the early 20th century, but the bantam menace is still part of our culture. At least 14 London pubs namecheck the sport, from the Famous Cock Tavern in Islington to the

Fighting Cocks in Kingston. Tottenham Hotspur's crest, meanwhile, features a fighting cockerel with a prominent spur.

Other venues favoured canine brutality. Rat-baiting was perhaps the most popular of all the blood sports. Here, a specially trained dog would take on dozens of rats at a time, with wagers placed on the number and speed of the kills. One black and tan bull terrier named Jacko became famous for dispatching 60 rats in under three minutes. The Dog and Duck in Soho had an aquatic, and horrific, variation. Ducks were released onto an adjacent pond, with their wings tied to prevent flight. A dog was then sent into the pond to join battle. It did not end well for the ducks.

Coach stations

Before the Georgian era, getting around the country was a real pain in the buttocks. Literally. Decent roads could be counted on one finger, and travel was limited to horseback or crude, bumpy wagons. Rides improved during the 18th century with the advent of the first stagecoach routes, but the golden age came in the first third of the 19th century. Better roads and better vehicles made it possible to travel from London to Cambridge in seven hours, where a generation before it would have taken two days.

At the heart of this busy transport network was the coaching inn. These pimped-up pubs popped up every few miles along busy routes, offering accommodation, cheap grub, a change of horses, and that all-important pint of ale to make the onward journey more bearable.

London was the centre of the coaching trade. Its legendary inns, such as the Bell Savage (Ludgate), Bull and Mouth (London Wall) and Golden Cross (Charing Cross) are still marked today with plaques. Dozens of old coaching inns survive on the city's periphery – look for any pub on a main road with an old stable yard (now most likely a beer garden). Few survive near the centre of town. The most famous is the George on Borough High Street (see page 160, and a couple of other mentions elsewhere in this book), which uniquely retains its accommodation galleries. The coming of the railways from the 1830s gradually put paid to the coaching trade, and the pubs of London ceased to double as departure lounges.

Meet-up groups

Londoners have always gathered in pubs to discuss shared interests. Political movements, dining societies, local history clubs – all gravitate towards the pub as a cheap, convivial meeting space. But the internet has opened up all kinds of possibilities for finding kindred spirits, and not just within the dating scene. Rather than socialise with workmates and generic friends, we can now spend our evenings with folk who share our interests, no matter how niche. This is the world of the pub meetup group.

'Room reserved for the London Sci-Fi and Fantasy Group'

'This way to the Geocaching Meetup'

'7pm: The London Machine Learning Group'

Such signs now commonly decorate the door of the pub function room. Every interest is catered for. Thousands of meetup groups operate in the London area, from post-apocalyptic book aficionados to polyamory networks, to Perl coders. And that's just within the letter P. The pub has become the go-to arena for those wishing to meet others who share a passion.

DRINK YOUR WAY THROUGH THE RAINBOW

Richard Of York Got Blotto In Vauxhall, as the saying definitely doesn't go.

RED

Old Red Cow, Smithfield

It would be all too easy to start our bibochromatic journey with a Red Lion. London has at least 26 (see page 32). But let's take our first sip of the rainbow in one of central London's finest pubs, the Old Red Cow in Smithfield. The moo-some name recalls the famous cattle market that traded in Smithfield for centuries.

The ORC is a tiny place, often full to capacity. Catch it at a quiet time, however, and you'll enjoy one of London's most convivial drinking spaces, with the best real ale and craft beer selection in Smithfield. Once the Elizabeth line opens this place will find itself heavily oversubscribed, so get a table while you can.

71–72 Long Lane, EC1A 9EJ

ORANGE

The Orange Tree, Totteridge

London contains a small crop of Orange Tree pubs, with zesty locals in Winchmore Hill and Richmond, among others. Pimlico even has a straightforward The Orange. Pick of the bunch though, surely, is this delightful countryside inn in the ancient and picturesque village of Totteridge. It has a sleepy, bucolic feel, a world away from the busier areas of Finchley and Barnet between which it is sandwiched. The focus is on dining – with pub grub of the quality you'd expect in a village whose residents have included Roger Moore, Cliff Richard and Arsene Wenger – but drinkers are also very welcome. The Orange Tree is a little out of the way, and most people are either local or drive (or both). However, the 251 and 326 buses stop right outside.

7 Totteridge Village, N20 8NX

YELLOW

The Lemon Tree, Covent Garden

We can't quite hit the jackpot with yellow. The closest thing is the Yellow House in Surrey Quays – well thought of, but more of a bar/restaurant than a traditional pub. Meanwhile, Camden Irish-pub Quinn's has been painted a lurid shade of yellow for as long as we can remember but nothing in its name suggests our colour. Instead we're going to plump for a Covent Garden stalwart in the shape of the Lemon Tree (lemon also being a shade of yellow). This small boozer on Bedfordbury is just about hidden enough to miss out on the tourist footfall, which means it's a good bet if you're after a peaceful pint in this part of the West End.

4 Bedfordbury, WC2N 4BP

Illustration overleaf by BEK CRUDDACE

DRINK YOUR WAY THROUGH THE RAINBOW

SOMEWHERE OVER THE RAINBOW

THE ORANGE TREE

THE ORANGE TREE

WESTWAY

WESTWAY

MARYLEBONE ROAD

EDGWARE RD.

LADBROKE GROVE

BAYSWATER ROAD

HOLLAND PARK AVE.

BLUE ANCHOR

BLUE ANCHOR

HOTEL INDIGO

BROMPTON RD

SLOANE STREET

WARWICK RD

TALGARTH RD.

KINGS ROAD

GREEN

Green Man, Fitzrovia

The Green Man is another common pub name. London has at least nine Green Men, three of which are within a very short walk of one another in Soho and Fitzrovia. We're plumping for the Riding House Street venue. For one thing, it's painted green inside and out. For another, the place – pretty much unchanged in the two decades we've known it – has always felt extremely welcoming. The upstairs function room is also worth knowing; it's the perfect size for a birthday bash or office party.
36 Riding House Street, W1W 7EP

BLUE

Blue Anchor, Hammersmith

Central London contains numerous Blue Posts. You'll find The Blue Eyed Maid in Borough (see page 173), the Old Blue Last in Shoreditch (owned by edgy publication Vice) and a Blue Lion on Gray's Inn Road. But blue is the colour of water, and so we turn to the Thames for our azure entry. Among Hammersmith's many fine water-side drinking holes, the Blue Anchor feels the most nautical. It could be the location, on the apex of the river curve, or perhaps the ubiquitous

paddles that decorate the panelled walls. Rain or shine, this is a shipshape pub from which to watch the Thames flow by. And, every spring, the Boat Races too.
13 Lower Mall, W6 9DJ

INDIGO

Hotel Indigo, Leicester Square

Indigo is a colour favoured by bars rather than pubs. The most central – and about as central as you can get – resides at Hotel Indigo in Leicester Square. The bar itself – ersatz art deco – is fine, but nothing you can't find in any number of central hotel bars. Its big draw, though, is the view. The rooftop terrace offers excellent sight lines over the West End. That includes a bird's eye peek at the Square's famous Odeon, which is itself lit up in indigo at night.
1 Leicester Square, WC2H 7NA

VIOLET

Mulberry Bush, South Bank

With the closure of the swanky Purple Bar at Fitzrovia's Sanderson Hotel, drinking dens of this hue are hard to come by. Fortunately, the Mulberry Bush on the South Bank saves our rainbow. This comfortable Young's pub is an excellent place to dine, just a couple of hundred metres from the riverfront yet hidden from the masses. Unless, that is, something's filming at the nearby ITV studios – in which case it can get very busy with audience members.
89 Upper Ground, SE1 9PP

Now we've reached the end of the rainbow, you can find the Crock of Gold by seeking out the pubs of that name in Wembley or Ruislip.

THE CURIOUS WORLD OF LONDON'S GENTLEMEN'S CLUBS

London's most exclusive bars are worlds unto themselves, with peculiar rules and oddball traditions.

Whether we're marvelling at the latest architectural addition to the City's skyline, mourning the closure of a treasured tapas joint, or steeling ourselves for whatever unbearably quirky pop-up may be next on the horizon, change is part and parcel of urban living. But within many of the grand Georgian buildings that flank St James's Square and line Pall Mall and Piccadilly, time seems to stand still.

Welcome to clubland. Here you'll find the centuries-old playgrounds of royals, politicians, and all manner of newly minted entrepreneurs. Inside, it's all gilt-framed oil paintings, stuffy smoking rooms, and bottles of champagne resting in silver buckets. In short, the upper crust of the 18th century would probably feel right at home.

The first gentlemen's clubs were established in the 1700s as places for the blue-blooded to let off some steam, away from the city's increasingly filthy and overcrowded streets and outside the ostensibly more feminine domain of the home. But these were always more than places to tell dirty jokes in frock coats while knocking back a brandy or two:

membership was a way to exert one's ample social and economic capital.

While a few of the surviving clubs have relaxed their terms of membership, allowing women and well-heeled commoners to join their enclaves of old world glamour, they nevertheless maintain a mahogany veneer of exclusivity. As well as stumping up often eye-watering membership fees, hopefuls must satisfy all sorts of requirements – including simply waiting until a hefty number of existing members have kicked the bucket – before they can enter the fold. Assuming you've got the patience, inclination, and requisite anatomy to apply, here's a handful of the most esteemed and intriguing for your consideration.

White's:
The club that's fit for a prince

Who would have thought that a hot chocolate emporium founded by an Italian immigrant in 1693 (see page 88) would eventually become the drinking den of choice for two future kings? White's, London's oldest club, today counts both Prince Charles and the Duke of Cambridge as members (the

heir apparent even had his stag do here). Good luck getting behind its Grade I listed doors, though – you must win the support of 36 members in order to be granted membership, and the waiting list is supposedly years long. Women are permitted as guests only, a policy that led former prime minister David Cameron to tear up his membership back in 2005.

Garrick Club:
The artist's Eden

Located on the outskirts of clubland in the West End, Garrick Club is one for the thespians. Founded as a place for the aristocracy to mingle with actors, it has since attracted all sorts of artsy folk: its past members list reads as a who's-who of London literati throughout the ages. When Charles Dickens published remarks made by William Makepeace Thackeray there – a cardinal sin in clubland, apparently – a bitter feud that became known as the Garrick Affair ensued between these two distinguished members. Since then, the likes of T S Eliot, Laurence Olivier and Rex Harrison have walked its jewel-toned halls.

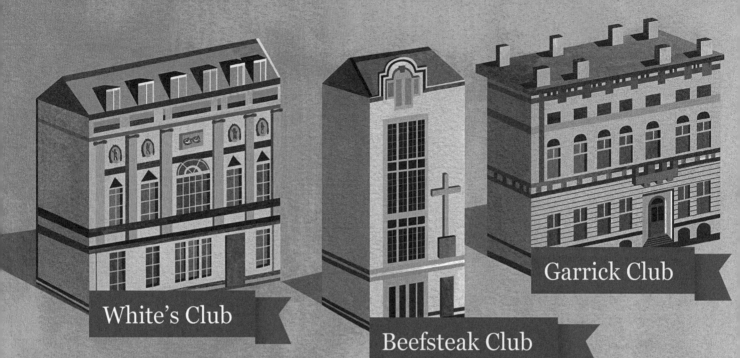

White's Club

Beefsteak Club

Garrick Club

Reform Club

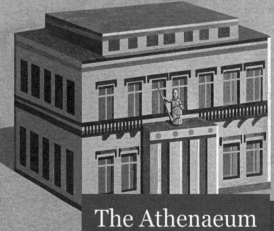

The Athenaeum

Reform Club:
One for the radicals (sort of)

After the enactment of The Reform Act 1832, the Whigs – the political party that spearheaded this package of electoral reforms – wanted a new hub for discussing radical ideas. And boy, did architect Charles Barry deliver. The result is an Italian palazzo-style clubhouse complete with Corinthian columns, flamboyant decor and a glass ceiling, which was proverbially smashed in 1981 when The Reform became one of the first clubs of its kind to admit women. The club has long ceased to have any political function, and nowadays claims to attract members from all sorts of backgrounds. That said, its members list includes a fair few baronesses and knights, including Sir David Attenborough.

The Athenaeum:
Olympius-level opulence

What better mascot for a club that London's intelligentsia flocks to than Athena, the ancient Greek goddess of wisdom? Her gold statue looms over the portico of the ridiculously palatial Athenaeum clubhouse on Pall Mall. When John Wilson Croker proposed a club "for Literary and Scientific men and followers of the Fine Arts" in 1823, he certainly wasn't messing around: to date, 52 members have bagged themselves a Nobel Prize. If you fancy following in these boffins' footsteps, the club is an excellent place to start swotting up. Some 80,000 works are housed floor-to-ceiling across three spectacular libraries. Once you've found your tome of choice, head to the smoking room, curl up in an armchair by the fire and have the barkeep fix you a whisky. No cigars though – it's a fume-free zone.

Beefsteak Club:
The club for carnivores

Unless you're vegetarian, you're probably partial to a nice, juicy steak. But do you like it enough to join a club dedicated solely to a shared love of beef? There have been many beefsteak clubs since the 1700s but the best-known is the Sublime Society of the Beefsteaks. These guys got so into things that they created badges emblazoned with a gridiron and the motto 'Beef and liberty'. Because nothing says freedom like chowing down on a prime cut of dead cow. The original Society folded in 1867, but a successor, called simply The Beefsteak Club popped up the same year. It was at this resurrected club that *Dracula* author Bram Stoker purportedly first heard the tale of Vlad the Impaler… possibly while sinking his teeth into something medium rare.

Illustration by HAYDN SYMONS

The changing face of clubland

The anachronistic quirks that characterise today's surviving gentleman's clubs are, it seems, integral to their enduring appeal. But in recent decades a new breed of private members' clubs that cater to more contemporary values have cropped up. Take the Soho House clubs for instance, where suits are banned and so-called 'creative souls' – of any gender – are favoured over 'wealth and status'. And 2018 notably saw the launch of The Allbright, a women-only members' club, hailed as a hub for empowerment for female entrepreneurs that sticks two fingers up at the old boy's network. But while The Allbright's membership is not dependent on who you know, with a waiting list running into the thousands and a joining fee of £300 it can hardly be considered truly egalitarian.

Perhaps that's asking too much, though. Exclusivity is what defines a members' club, after all. The boundaries of clubland may have become blurry, but for better or worse, its core function – to communicate wealth and prestige – remains firmly intact.

DESERTER DO THE OLIVER REED PUB CRAWL

Londonist's drinking buddies, Deserter, have selflessly devoted their lives to a never-ending pub crawl in South London. Here, we follow them as they stagger in the footsteps of Wimbledon's legendary boozehound, Oliver Reed.

On a recent trip to Valletta, I found myself inexorably drawn to a place known only as The Pub.

The walls of this cosy Malta boozer are bedecked with pictures of Oliver Reed, who died in this very bar during a break from filming *Gladiator,* after taking on the Royal Navy at drinking. The Pub plies a morbid trade in t-shirts commemorating his death. On the front it says 'Ollie's Last Bar' and on the back, '8 Pints of Lager, 12 Double Rums, 14 Whiskeys – Legend'.

It hit me, then, that I must reprise Reed's 'Wimbledon Run' – a pub crawl devised by the man being applauded for drinking himself to death. Half-life came along as my wingman to make sure I didn't do anything silly, "Like shandy".

Rose & Crown

The Rose & Crown is smart, old and handsome – like Ollie in his earlier days. A hotel pub, with a stone floor, decent beer and an inviting ambience, it's a fine start. This is where the competitors would gather.

Yes, competitors, because it was a sort of race. Ollie's gang (once, apparently, including Steve McQueen) would meet here and have a pint in each of the then-eight pubs (the King of Denmark and the Brewery Tap have since gone) before returning to the Rose. Whoever was last had to get the final round, which could be pretty hefty, despite losing a few contestants along the way.

Why make drinking a competition, I wondered? Why sully one of life's great and simple pleasures with the stink of rivalry, opposition, victory and defeat?

"Well, it's obvious, Dirts," said Half-life. "Free ninth pint, innit? That's just maths."
55 High Street Wimbledon, SW19 5BA

Dog & Fox

From the Dog & Fox you can see all the Union Jacks that adorn the shops and cafes of the village, like we're in Jubileeland. Luckily, for crawl purposes, the Dog & Fox is only a two-minute walk – or run if you're doing it properly. Running was the least of it with Reed. He'd often challenge people to fist fights or arm wrestling (see: how he died), or order everyone to march around a lake then swim across it, in tedious shows of machismo.

"What's wrong with just drinking?" said Half-life.

Reed did more than enough of that, going on extraordinary benders, notoriously drinking 100 pints in 24 hours. "The thing is," said Half-life, "Once you get past 20, you're not even enjoying it."

Reed was also fond of childish pranks, throwing chairs and smashing up bars, but not at the Dog & Fox, where the landlady, Joyce, simply wouldn't put up with his bullshit.
24 High Street Wimbledon, SW19 5EA

Illustration by KATE ROCHESTER ILLUSTRATION

Fire Stables (née The Castle)

Strong women were not a type that Reed favoured. He and South London's Glenda Jackson – an actor and former MP who would hate to be called a legend – found themselves mutually repellent. There can't be any doubt that he was an unbearable misogynist. A handsome and charismatic f**ker, though, he was dearly loved by those who could put up with him.

Fire Stables is also only a couple of minutes from the previous pub and is a bit more gastro and a bit less… pub. The third Young's pub in a row, thankfully they all seem to serve ale from the Wimbledon Brewery too.

"I don't mind Young's," said Half-life. "I mean, if you can't have variety at least have lots of it."

27–29 Church Road, SW19 5DQ

The Swan

I was quite glad of a 10-minute walk after the third pint, but definitely wasn't going to break out into a trot. Some think it's sad that Reed is remembered more for his drunken escapades than his work as an actor. Maybe, but whose fault is that?

He was, however, a quite brilliant film actor, who, despite being untrained, brought something special to the screen. He was always the consummate pro on set, even if kick-off was at 7am and he was out till 6. Perhaps it was this that gave rise to the theory that he only ever played the drunk. In which case, he deserves another Oscar (he won one posthumously for *Gladiator*).

We had a nice pint of Common before heading to the Common where our last two pubs waited for us, like loved ones.

89 Ridgway, SW19 4SU

Hand in Hand

A cosy, charming, even quaint little pub with a nice outside space, the Hand in Hand had the best-kept beer, with the most variety, plus you can take drinks out onto the green opposite.

In the olden days when pubs closed after lunch, Reed and his pals would get some bottles and go on a 'pissnic' on the Common till they opened again.

By all accounts Ollie was a gentle, sensitive and even shy man when sober. Then, between pints one and eight he could be loquacious, funny and gregarious. After that – and there would still be a long, long time to go – he would become an utter arsehole, a bully and a bore.

Half-life had some sympathy here. "I'm very shy in the morning," he claimed.

"More like shy of the morning," I said.

6 Crooked Billet, SW19 4RQ

Crooked Billet

Not more than 50 yards away was the final pub of the tour, another cracker that overlooks the green. Indeed, the Crooked Billet provides deckchairs for customers to sit out and sup in. A brief walk along the south side of the Common would take you directly back to the Rose & Crown. I had to admire the genius of the Wimbledon Run.

As his film career faded, Reed became notorious for his talk show appearances, where he would show up drunk, rambling and incoherent in an early example of car crash TV.

"I met him once," said Half-life, surprising me, seeing as we'd been talking about him all day. "Can't remember much about it though."

Despite shambolic appearances on *Aspel, The Word* and *Late Night with David Letterman,* he was invited to appear on *After Dark,* Channel 4's high-brow live talk show that saw thinkers, politicians and characters from the fringes of the arts discuss thorny subjects. Reed was due to appear to talk about men and violence.

"The producer knew me from the poetry circuit and was worried Ollie would turn up too fucked to go on, so he called me to play back-up. I left early and all to make sure I didn't mess up me big chance. Unfortunately I had a few liveners on the way. When the police dropped me off at the studio they decided Ollie was the safe bet."

As we sat in the Billet, under Reed's giant shadow, it was easy to recall his extravagant talent and constitution; to remember he was dearly loved by many in these parts, especially for his generosity. But I couldn't escape the thought that he was also a bit of a tit.

I suppose a t-shirt reading: '8 Pints of Lager, 12 Double Rums, 14 Whiskeys – Bit of a Tit'. wouldn't have sold as many units as the 'Legend' one.

14–15 Crooked Billet, SW19 4RQ

HIGHBALLS ON HIGH BUILDINGS: LONDON'S BEST ROOFTOP BARS

From spring's first rays, through to summer's dying embers that fade into autumn, Londoners will find any excuse to head up high for a rooftop bar and a libation to raise your spirits.

When winter rolls around, we chuck on a couple of extra layers, offer up a quick prayer to the gods of patio heaters, and do it all again, switching Aperol for mulled wine.

London's rooftop bars know that we love them, and they fully play up to it, serving a permanent rotation of menus and themes – even igloos – dotted across London's skyline.

Coq d'Argent, Bank

Some people call it a banker's haunt. We call it the Bagpuss building, on account of its pink stripes. Either way, Coq d'Argent is a surprisingly large venue, the restaurant mainly tucked away inside, serving up contemporary French cuisine.

Outside on the rooftop terrace, meals from the grill menu are served at lunchtime, but in the evening focus is firmly on spirits and cocktails, with bar snacks offered as a stomach-lining option. If you happen to be a banker who's just got a bonus, order a £985 bottle of the 1988 Salon.

The space is a variety of covered and open-air, with various pop-ups throughout the year, including the annual winter Lodge d'Argent, dressed to look like a ski lodge. Heaters and blankets are plentiful, but Coq d'Argent's terrace comes into its own in the summer, when those luscious (fake, we assume) green lawns give way to sunkissed views of the City skyline.

1 Poultry, EC2R 8EJ

The Culpeper, Whitechapel

Ascend numerous flights of creaky stairs to find the Culpeper's crown – a small rooftop, half of which is a greenhouse. The planters of homegrown veg add to the feeling that this is more like a private garden than a pub. Actually, you can stay the night here – they've got a handful of rooms. The Culpeper in question is the 17th-century herbalist Nicholas, who died nearby in 1654. There's also a bijou distillery named after him in Gatwick Airport.

40 Commercial Street, E1 6LP

Frank's Café, Peckham

If you told someone 15 years ago you were opening a Campari bar on top of a multi-storey car park in Peckham, they'd have assumed you were insane. Now, the annual opening of Frank's Café beckons sunseekers far and wide to order their Italian-style spritzes (see page 64), lie out on the warm concrete, and muse over whichever artworks have been installed up there (we were particularly impressed by the Trafalgar Square lions, made from crepe paper). The view of the City from here is a peach too.

Multi Storey Car Park, 95a Rye Lane, SE15 4ST

The Loft at The Alexandra, Wimbledon

Rooftop bars aren't as big a deal in west London as they are in east. But The Loft is a self-professed fan, claiming to be "the best of Shoreditch meets Wimbledon. #poshcool". Certainly, the exposed brick walls slathered in neon graffiti, and the selection of craft beers and gins scream 'hipster paradise'. Order a Milanese G&T (it's got Campari added) and make a toast to the other side of the city.

33 Wimbledon Hill Road, SW19 7NE

Madison, St Paul's

For the WOW factor, head up to Madison. It's located on the eighth floor, above One New Change shopping centre and offices. This might not sound all that romantic, but the views will make your jaw drop. Up here, you're practically nose to nose with the dome of St Paul's. You're not just gazing out at the London skyline… you're IN it.

The vibe is chilled; the comfy sofas and low tables wouldn't look out of place in an Ibiza beach bar. The bar and seating area is covered, but the terrace area with the best views is open to the elements, making summer the optimum time to visit. In peak months, you'll be queueing even to get in the lift.

Rooftop Terrace, One New Change, EC4M 9AF

Netil360, Hackney

Gasholders and cranes litter the skyline of the sizeable rooftop bar at Netil360. If you've an eye for industrial chic, this is for you. Strung up fairy lights glimmer as the sun sets, and you launch into your third can of Beavertown. It's not all about the drink though; more righteous Londoners can come up here bright and early for a yoga sesh.

1 Westgate Street, E8 3RL

Oxo Tower, Bankside

It's cheating slightly calling the Oxo Tower venue a 'rooftop bar', as it's not strictly on the building's roof. What it is is a restaurant, bar and brasserie rolled into one, 10 floors above the South Bank, with a terrace that offers views all the way along the river, and over towards St Paul's and beyond.

Even in dodgy weather, it's a decent option for after-work drinks or a pre-theatre meal – provided you've booked a table. They do an afternoon tea, and a curiously named 'Not Afternoon Tea'. Oxo Tower comes into its own when the sun is beaming and those floor-to-ceiling glass doors are wedged open, giving the entire venue the feeling of being outdoors.

Barge House Street, South Bank, SE1 9PH

Queen of Hoxton, Shoreditch

A veritable playground for adults, Queen of Hoxton might teeter on the edge of the Square Mile, but its heart and soul are firmly in Shoreditch.

The rooftop transforms into a new theme every season, although the cosy, carpet-strewn wigwam is a permanent fixture. In recent years, Moulin Rouge, Dr Strangelove and Valhalla have come and gone, each incarnation bringing with it themed cocktails (cocktail slurped from a Viking horn, anyone?) and utterly Instagrammable decor.

The rooftop has limited eyeline, thanks to its lofty Broadgate neighbours. But, there's usually so much going on – think life drawing classes, drag bingo, hip hop karaoke – you barely care.

1 Curtain Road, EC2A 3JX

Radio Rooftop at ME London, Strand

Glance east to the skyscrapers of the City, west to central London… or down for views straight into the courtyard of Somerset House. Radio Rooftop, above the ME London hotel, has undergone several transformations in recent years, but it's finally found its mojo as a hip year-round hangout.

These days, food is as much of a priority as drinks are, with an impressive menu running through breakfast, brunch, afternoon tea and all-day dining. Dress code is 'smart and glamorous', and the drinks menu depends on what the current pop-up is.

336–337 Strand, WC2R 1HA

The Tankard, Kennington

It's said that a young Charlie Chaplin sometimes darted into The Tankard to pick up bottles of soda. The (often-sozzled) characters he ran into here would later go on to inspire his clowning. We doubt the pub had a pretty roof terrace back then, nor a comprehensive craft beer selection showcasing local brewers including Fourpure, Redchurch and Five Points. If Chaplin could see some of the prices, he'd undoubtedly collapse laughing.

111 Kennington Road, SE11 6SF

The Trafalgar St James, Trafalgar Square

See eye-to-eye with Nelson (well, almost), at what must be London's most central rooftop bar.

The Rooftop at The Trafalgar St James offers both covered and open-air seating areas, and we'd recommend braving the elements for the best view of the masses snapping selfies in Trafalgar Square below. Fear not, blankets and heaters are provided in the chillier months.

The signature cocktails reference some of the places you can see from up here (Soho Sunset, Gunpowder Plot).

2 Spring Gardens, SW1A 2TS

WHERE'S MY TAP WATER FROM?

Of all the drinks featured in this book, there is only one that unites every Londoner: tap water. Where does it come from, and how does it reach your glass? Let us paddle back through the waters of time for a little context, before diving into currents more current.

A hint of poo

The River Thames and its tributaries have always been London's chief source of drinking water. You can imagine what a joy that must have been in the 19th century, when the run-offs from a thousand factories commingled with barely treated sewage. The 'Great Stink' of 1858 was caused by a river so repugnant that the House of Commons was abandoned. Those who drank from water pumps faced their own hazards; many perished from cholera in the mid-19th century, victims of a feculent tryst between cesspit and water supply.

The situation improved dramatically with the construction of Joseph Bazalgette's interceptor sewers in the 1860s. Around the same time, the tidal Thames was shunned by water companies in favour of upstream sources. Cholera cases diminished and the Thames got a whole lot cleaner, if still far from wholesome.

Where does today's water come from?

Every day, Thames Water pumps around 2.6 billion litres into London's water supply. This unimaginable volume is still drawn largely from the rivers. About 65% of our water is taken from the Thames and the Lea, then stored in reservoirs to await treatment. You can't miss the great blue oblongs to the north and west of the Greater London map. The remaining 35% is drawn by borehole from aquifers (natural reservoirs) beneath London. This water has its origins in rainfall that has seeped down through the soil.

Once collected, the water undergoes a complicated process of filtration and purification. It then enters the London Ring Main – a 50-mile pipeline that engirdles the capital. From here, the water is distributed into storage reservoirs and the wider mains, and thence into the pipes that rove toward your kitchen.

Will there always be enough?

Turn on the tap and water comes out. Never fails. But the reliable supply cannot be taken for granted. In Thames Water's own words, London is 'seriously water-stressed', meaning that a high percentage of our environmental water is already part of the supply network. Mix in climate change and London's ever-growing population and water shortages become a real threat.

The water companies have plans in place that go beyond fixing leaky pipes and declaring hosepipe bans. Under northeast London lies Britain's only artificially recharged aquifer used for public water supply: the North London Artificial Recharge Scheme (NLARS). Water is saved up during happy, wet months, then released in times of drought. It can provide enough daily water for about 1.2 million Londoners. Thames Water has also built a desalination plant at Beckton, which can strip the salt from river water, to provide daily supply for almost a million people.

London's tap water might not be as deliciously soft and pristine as, say Iceland's or Denmark's. But believe us, it's been a hell of a lot worse. Now someone pass us that Brita filter.

DRINK YOUR WAY AROUND LONDON LIKE CHARLES DICKENS

In the early pages of Oliver Twist, *we learn that 'every other house' in Barnet is a pub of some kind.* The Pickwick Papers, *meanwhile, is one magnificent pub crawl masquerading as literature. The novels of Charles Dickens are steeped in booze. But which pubs should you visit to best channel the great author?*

Pubs mentioned by Dickens

Dickens was a discerning fellow when it came to his settings. Not once, in any of his novels, does he mention a London train station by name. Buckingham Palace gets no acknowledgement. None of his characters visit the South Bank or Bankside. Most of them *do* visit the pub at some point.

Mr Pickwick and his friends are seldom out of their cups. Many of the hostelries are outside London. Others, such as the Golden Cross in Charing Cross or

THE ARTFUL DODGER

the White Hart in Borough are long gone. One place you can still visit, however, is the **George and Vulture** (3 Castle Court, EC3V 9DL) – or the George and Wulture, as the Wellers call it. This ancient City pub, now a chop room, has origins in the 13th century, and was a favourite of Dickens. Mr Pickwick and Sam Weller stayed in rooms above the pub throughout much of the second half of the novel.

The Pickwickians also pay a visit to the **Spaniard's Inn** (see page 123), north of Hampstead. This historic pub, with a spurious connection to Dick Turpin, still harbours one of London's finest beer gardens, though be prepared for a bit of a trek from Hampstead tube.

The best known pub in Dickens is perhaps **The Grapes** in Limehouse (see page 50). Large sections of Our Mutual Friend take place at this riverside pub, thinly disguised as the Six Jolly Fellowship Porters (see page 152). It retains its olde worlde feel. The long, narrow bar with

almost zero natural lighting can feel like a time machine in the depths of winter.

The Boot (116 Cromer Street, WC1H 8BS), south of King's Cross, is the chief assembly point for the anti-Catholic Gordon rioters in *Barnaby Rudge*. Dickens describes the agitators waking up in the fields around the pub with killer hangovers. It still trades as The Boot today, and is a characterful Irish bar.

Finally, the **George Inn** in Borough (see page 160) is affectionately known as Shakespeare's local, but it also has Dickensian connections. The famed coaching inn gets a brief mention in *Little Dorrit*, when Mr Tip pops in to write a begging letter. The pub today is a fine old congeries of wonky rooms, though its inclusion in every tourist guidebook can make for a cramped experience.

Pubs inspired by Dickens

Until recently, London had two pubs named directly after the master. The rather good Charles Dickens pub on Union Street, Southwark is now a nouveau-Irish bar, leaving just the **Dickens Inn** at St Katharine Docks (Marble Quay, E1W 1UH). This huge wood-framed boozer looks like it's been serving pints for centuries. While the building is 18th-century, it's a modern conversion. Dickens would not have been able to drink here unless he'd broken into a warehouse with a hip flask.

A handful of pubs have appropriated the names of Dickens characters. We're rather fond of the **Betsey Trotwood** (see page 8). This live music venue, named after David Copperfield's great aunt, has a cosy, intimate feel to it. We have no idea why it adopted this name; the redoubtable Ms Trotwood has no links to the area. **The Artful Dodger** (again, see page 8) is a proper East End boozer, with impressive bay windows and a traditional carpeted interior. The famous pickpocket from *Oliver Twist* never

BETSEY TROTWOOD

visits the area, though the tragic Nancy had lodgings in nearby Ratcliffe. The pub name would better suit the One Tun on Saffron Hill, on the site of Fagin's den.

Finally, head to Stroud Green for a pint at the **Nicholas Nickleby** (6–8 Ferme Park Road, N4 4ED), which Google Maps describes as 'enduring old-school local pub with darts'.

Please Sir, I want some more...

Dickens and booze are intimately linked. Every hoary pub in central London claims his custom, and who could prove them wrong? He certainly supped at the George, and the George and Vulture. Several other pubs have strong claims. Strung together, they would make a very handsome pub crawl.

The most 'Dickensian' of all pubs is surely **Ye Olde Cheshire Cheese** (see page 132). This warren of a building is so well known as to hardly need an introduction. Expect panelled rooms, roaring fires, traditional English fare (including great wedges of pork pie) and a complete dearth of natural light.

Another charming pub, habitually described as 'Dickensian' though Elizabethan in origin, is **Ye Olde Mitre**

(1 Ely Court, EC1N 6SJ). Guide books will tell you that this is the most difficult-to-find pub – it lurks down an alley through a narrow arch. In reality, it's well signposted and well frequented.

Bloomsbury's **The Lamb** (94 Lamb's Conduit Street, WC1N 3LZ) has a classic Victorian interior of dark wood and etched-glass panels. A recent refurbishment has perhaps erased a little of the old-world charm, but not fatally so. Dickens would surely have visited while living round the corner on Doughty Street.

Dickens is claimed by another ovine pub, the **Lamb and Flag** (see page 131) in Covent Garden. The author cut his teeth as a journalist working nearby. Much of the Victorian interior survives, enlivened by some rather strange modern murals on the stairs.

THE CELEBRATORY DRINK WITH A MOURNFUL BIRTH

Chances are you'll know this heady mix of champagne and the Black Stuff from St Patrick's Day celebrations – but its origins are sombre. The Black Velvet is thought to have been created in 1861 at Brooks's Club, St James's Street. Queen Victoria's husband, Prince Albert had died only weeks earlier of typhoid fever, triggering a period of mourning throughout Britain; this cocktail was the bar's own way of showing respect to Vicky and Bert.

Make a Black Velvet

Simply half-fill a flute with champagne or sparkling wine and slowly pour Guinness on top. It will float slightly, showing off the colour differentiation. If you want to go hardcore, make it in a pint glass. Or order one at Brooks's – it still exists.

A CIRCLE LINE PUB CRAWL

Over three years, Londonist's friend Sam Cullen went on the hunt for the best pub in the immediate area of each of the 270 London Underground stations. He thinks doing the Circle line in a day is just about possible.

At 28 stops, this crawl was already long enough, before TfL extended the Circle line down to Hammersmith in December 2009. That brings it up to 35 in total. Gulp.

The pubs we've chosen for each station are either the closest or within a five-minute walk. Oh, and by the way, *Londonist* urges you NOT to binge drink. Plenty of tap water on your way round, OK?

Hammersmith – The Hop Poles

A Long Island iced tea is among the cocktails on offer at The Hop Poles, but for goodness' sake, don't. This is all about pacing yourself. There are craft beers aplenty too – settle for one of these and climb to the spacious roof garden, where you can muse over the huge undertaking you've just embarked on.

17–19 King Street, Hammersmith, W6 9HR

Goldhawk Road – BrewDog Shepherd's Bush

BrewDog is in the process of invading London one pub at a time with their trademark exposed brickwork and strong as heck beers. Generously, this place also serves boozy elixirs from London breweries like Gipsy Hill and Partizan. The five pinball tables – including an AC/DC one – won us over.

15 Goldhawk Road, Hammersmith, W12 8QQ

Illustration by OLIVIA WHITWORTH ILLUSTRATION

A pub crawl OF THE CIRCLE LINE consisting OF THIRTY·FIVE·STOPS

Shepherd's Bush Market – Defector's Weld

The Defector's Weld (see also page 72) is a sprawling place, with big windows looking out over Shepherd's Bush Green. A very decent spot for people watching, while you sup on your half pint of Young's. On Friday and Saturday nights, DJs play till 2am. But we can't afford to hang around that long. Drink up.

170 Uxbridge Road, Shepherd's Bush, W12 8AA

Wood Lane – The Allis

Once the BBC studios where greats from Parky to French and Saunders filmed, The Allis is now a swanky bar. An artwork, depicting the spooky girl/clown testcard, reminds you of the building's former use. We'll have to admit, we spent our entire time here imagining it was the BBC canteen where Alan Partridge attacked Tony Hayers with some cheese. Sadly there's no Blue Nun on the menu.

101 Wood Lane, Shepherd's Bush, W12 7FA

Latimer Road – The Garden Bar

Relax on a lounger in The Garden Bar's enchanting oasis, and when it inevitably rains, retreat to one of the wooden grottos. On a curious tangent, we think The Garden Bar might be the only licensed wedding venue on the crawl. On the off-chance you've already met someone nice by this stage.

41 Bramley Road, Notting Hill, W10 6SZ

Ladbroke Grove – The Elgin

With its stonking great mirrors, stained glass windows, glazed tiling and etched glasswork, The Elgin could almost be a museum. Fortunately, it's very much a living, breathing boozer. Maybe you'll be lucky enough to catch some live music while you get in a swift one here.

96 Ladbroke Grove, Notting Hill, W11 1PY

Westbourne Park – Union Tavern

The main selling point of this pub is its setting by the Union Canal. An expansive garden backs onto the waterway, from where you can watch the occasional narrowboat drift by. It's not exactly idyllic though – there's a gritty, industrial vibe, what with the urban hum of the Westway, and the bus station's barbed-wire fencing. Some people go for that kind of thing.

45 Woodfield Road, Maida Hill, W9 2BA

Royal Oak – The Porchester

This was the pub which gave Royal Oak station its name. Sadly it was renamed many years ago. Raise a glass to its former moniker, and move swiftly on.

88 Bishop's Bridge Road, Bayswater, W2 5AA

Paddington – Fountains Abbey

The grand name belies an average, slightly tired Greene King offering. Still, it's right opposite St Mary's Hospital, where Alexander Fleming discovered penicillin. It's also one of the few pubs on the crawl to have Sky/BT Sports. On a previous visit we watched some very vocal Italian tourists go from ecstasy to agony when Juventus got back to 3-3 with Real Madrid in the Champions League, only to concede a last-minute penalty scored by Ronaldo. At least he plays for Juventus now…

109 Praed Street, Paddington, W2 1RL

Edgware Road – The Chapel

Two semi-interesting facts about this place: it was formerly called Pontefract Castle. And it's in the shape of a triangle (inside, rather than out). Happy? Onwards we go…

48 Chapel Street, Marylebone, NW1 5DP

Baker Street – The Metropolitan Bar

This grand Wetherspoons is located inside the building above Baker Street tube that used to be HQ of the Metropolitan Railway – owners of the first stretch of London's underground network. They've not missed the opportunity to scatter tube memorabilia liberally about the place.

7 Station Approach, Marylebone Road, Marylebone, NW1 5LA

Great Portland Street – The Albany

The gargantuan windows at The Albany make it a neat spot for watching the world going by, if only there was the time to do it on an epic pub crawl like this. If you do decide to stick around, treat yourself to an entire baked camembert from the bar menu. Surely that won't end in tears.

240 Great Portland Street, Fitzrovia, W1W 5QU

Euston Square – Euston Tap

Located within one of the few remaining parts of old Euston station (see page 158), the Euston Tap is a beer-lover's dream. For one thing, the selection of brews will knock you for six. For another, it's two pubs in one, occupying adjacent gatehouses. Together, they offer almost 50 different draft beers on tap (see page 166). If you start seeing four Euston Taps, you might want to have a Coke.

190 Euston Road, Euston, NW1 2EF

King's Cross St Pancras – The Parcel Yard

Dodge the hordes of wand-wavers at Platform 9¾, and ascend to this railway-themed station pub, adorned with images of old steam trains. You can see their contemporary replacements if you sit by the windows looking onto the platforms. It's also one of the few pubs in England we've visited which has a lift up to it – handy if you're already feeling a bit knackered. See page 159 also.

King's Cross Station, King's Cross, N1C 4AH

Farringdon – The Castle

In many ways The Castle is your standard, bustling central London pub. But one eyecatching bit of decor reveals the most interesting feature: a painting depicts King George IV applying for a loan from the then-landlord to service gambling debts from a nearby cockfight. In return, George granted the pub a pawnbroker's licence, which it still holds and explains why there is a pawnbroker's sign outside. Thankfully the pints here aren't so expensive that you need to pawn your possessions.

34–35 Cowcross Street, Farringdon, EC1M 6DB

Barbican – The Shakespeare

Flat-roofed pubs have acquired a bad reputation over the years, but The Shakespeare doesn't conform to this stereotype. It's a welcoming watering hole; comfy leather armchairs give the place a homely feel, which you aren't expecting given the brutalist exterior. Food tip: get stuck into the expansive pizza menu.

2 Goswell Road, Golden Lane Estate, EC1M 7AA

Moorgate – The Globe

Nicholson's pubs can be found on City street corners almost as ubiquitously as City suits themselves. The Globe is the first of several on the crawl. Vintage lamps glow on the walls, illuminating the obligatory pictures of 'historic London'. Eschew your traditional warm pint, for a glass of refreshing Pilsner Urquell.

83 Moorgate, Finsbury, EC2M 6SA

Liverpool Street – Hamilton Hall

Hamilton Hall is such a looker of a pub, you scarcely care how noisy it gets. It trades from the former ballroom of the Great Eastern Hotel – one of those palatial Victorian railway hotels. Tilt your head to admire the golden chandeliers and rococo flourishes while you sup on your drink. This is living. See page 159 also.

Liverpool Street Station, Liverpool Street, EC2M 7PY

Aldgate – Hoop & Grapes

This characterful place survived the Great Fire of London by a matter of yards, surely making it the oldest pub on the crawl (see page 132). It's also the only timber-framed building in the City – they were banned after the fire. While it might look poky from the outside, it extends back a long way. This is a place where pub crawls collide: you may well run into people on the Monopoly trail, dressed up in top hats (or, less likely, irons).

47 Aldgate High Street, Aldgate, EC3N 1AL

Tower Hill – The Hung, Drawn and Quartered

Fuller's turned this former bank into a pub in 1995, naming it after a line from Samuel Pepys' diary. The walls are decorated with pictures of various historic figures including Oliver Cromwell, Henry VIII and at least a couple of his six wives. They've also got the text of the Treason Act 1351, which we assume allowed for the punishment of being Hung, Drawn and Quartered.

26–27 Great Tower Street, City of London, EC3R 5AQ

Monument – The Crosse Keys

With its marble pillars and domed skylights, The Crosse Keys is a cut above your usual 'Spoons (see page 65 also). Thankfully the circular bar here is also huge, which helps to deal with the thirsty hordes. They had 21 ales on tap on our visit – the list displayed on a TV screen above the bar, like an airport departures board. Chocks away!

9 Gracechurch Street, City of London, EC3V 0DR

Cannon Street – The Cannick Tapps

The only subterranean boozer on the crawl. The Cannick Tapps has gone for what we'd call a purposively scrappy vibe – half-painted walls, ripped posters and the like. They've also got lightbulbs in what look like egg whisks. Excitingly, they have a Mini SNES. Sadly, some old gent was on it during our visit.

109 Cannon Street, City of London, EC4N 5AD

Mansion House – Ye Olde Watling

Ye Olde Watling's dark timbered rooms lend it a historical atmosphere, though it's not as old as you might think. Originally built in 1667, it was subsequently rebuilt in 1901 and again in 1947 after the Blitz. It was absolutely rammed when we dropped by – but it spills out into an alley, where punters congregate in vast numbers.

29 Watling Street, City of London, EC4M 9BR

Blackfriars – The Blackfriar

The Blackfriar's wedge-like shape reminds us of New York's Flatiron building – and is one of the most fascinating pubs on this crawl to boot. Art nouveau friezes of jolly monks line the walls inside and out – many of them getting up to no good. You'll be tempted to stay for a few here, but onwards! See pages 30 and 156 also.

174 Queen Victoria Street, Blackfriars, EC4V 4EG

Temple – The Edgar Wallace

The Edgar Wallace is named after a prolific crime novelist of the early 20th century – apt for a pub in London's legal district. (Wallace also created *King Kong*.) The ceiling is plastered with hundreds of beermats, while the walls have old cigarette adverts for brands like Rothmans and Old

Holborn. On the stairs are photos of Cliff Richard and Bruce Forsyth – previous winners of 'Glove Wearer of the Year'.

40 Essex Street, Strand, WC2R 3JE
(Note: this pub is closed at weekends, but it's such a fun place we couldn't not include it.)

Embankment – The Princess of Wales

The final Nicholsons pub on the crawl and probably the most generic. On a more positive note, it did have seven ales on tap plus various lagers when we visited. We'll excuse you if you decide to shuffle a few doors down for a sherry at Gordon's Wine Bar though (see page 58 for that one).

27 Villiers Street, Charing Cross, WC2N 6ND

Westminster – The Red Lion

The Red Lion is packed with politicos during the week, no surprise given its Westminster location. At least one of the TVs here has BBC Parliament on, for those who want to at least pretend they are trying to keep up with whatever's going on across the road.

48 Parliament Street, Westminster, SW1A 2NH

St James's Park – Buckingham Arms

A two-minute walk from Buckingham Palace, this cosy Young's pub is the refuge of many an exhausted tourist. You can also watch them trudge by through the pub's glorious windows. But don't get too comfortable – like a Marathon sprinter on

the Mall, you're on the home straight of this pub crawl now…
62 Petty France, Westminster, SW1H 9EU

Victoria – Windsor Castle

This civil servants' favourite is the only Sam Smith's pub on the crawl. Its thrifty drinks will no doubt be welcome, as your wallet will have taken a right hammering by this point. Enjoy your cheapo pint while admiring the cut-glass gin-palace partitions.
23 Francis Street, Westminster, SW1P 1DN

Sloane Square – The Antelope

Our favourite touch in The Antelope is the red curtains, adding a dramatic, theatrical flourish. The snug area to the side of the main bar sports wallpaper that's a map of London in 1832. It's amazing how similar the city looks to today's, bar one major thing – no railway stations (which means no Circle line pub crawl…)
22 Eaton Terrace, Belgravia, SW1W 8EZ

South Kensington – Zetland Arms

We'll be honest. The Zetland is one of those very dull Greene King pubs, peddling generic 'ye olde fish and chips' to Albertopolis tourists. The dullest pub of the crawl – knock back a tap water, use the toilets and be on your way.

2 Bute Street, South Kensington, SW7 3EX

Gloucester Road – The Hereford Arms

Head to a wall at the back of the The Hereford Arms, and you'll find it plastered with posters from Alfred Hitchcock films. He lived nearby, and used the Royal Albert Hall for shooting two versions of his film, *The Man Who Knew Too Much*.
127 Gloucester Road, Kensington, SW7 4TE

High Street Kensington – Britannia

The Britannia sits on the site of the Britannia Brewery, which opened in 1834. It's been serving drinks to punters ever since; unfortunately it no longer brews its own ale, so you'll have to settle for a Young's bitter or Peroni. The jazz soundtrack playing on our visit here helped keep us moving.
1 Allen Street, Kensington, W8 6UX

Notting Hill – The Churchill Arms

And now for something completely different. Visit The Churchill Arms in summer, and you'll find it blanketed in hanging baskets and flowers (see page 30). At Christmas, it glitters with 90 Christmas trees festooned with 11,500 lights. The Winston-themed trinkets and Union Flags inside are no less impressive. Also look out for the cricket bat on the wall; the pub staff play an annual match against The Antelope from Sloane Square. This was also apparently the first pub in London to have a Thai kitchen. What a place.
119 Kensington Church Street, Kensington, W8 7LN

Bayswater – Prince Alfred

A former Canadian soldier here once asked us where the best place in London was 'to meet broads'. The Prince Alfred is a touristy pub alright – maybe you can escape to the sometimes-open roof terrace and crack open a bottle of fizz to celebrate completing the Circle line pub crawl. But let's face it, the last thing you'll want right now is another drink. You might find them selling flowers out the front of the pub. If so, buy a bunch to help explain to your loved one what you've been up to.
112 Queensway, Bayswater, W2 3RR

CATCH A THEATRE SHOW...
IN THE PUB

London is a goldmine of quality theatre – and we're not just talking about the glittering (and often exorbitantly priced) West End.

Here's our rundown of every pub theatre worth knowing about in London. Cheaper than those fancy-schmancy Theatreland productions, most of these places have a superior beer selection for interval drinks too.

Note the ring of pubs formed around the City and the West End – an invisible boundary, reasonably neatly denoting what people consider 'central London'. There was a similar pattern in Shakespeare's day – a time when booze and theatre went hand-in-hand, and such premises were banned from the centre of London. But as we all know, there's often more fun to be found on the fringes.

Here are some of the London pub theatres' star players.

Etcetera Theatre, Camden Town

Above an Irish boozer – The Oxford Arms – on the unfathomably busy Camden High Street might seem like an odd location for a pub theatre. However, Etcetera makes it work, and has now hosted more than 2,500 productions. Like many other pub theatres, it's a popular comedic haunt, but puts on a variety of stage shows too – from bi-lingual surrealist pieces about gods, to horror-action-comedies about an outbreak at the monster institute. It's especially buzzing during Camden Fringe, which takes over for the majority of August.
265 Camden High Street, NW1 7BU

Finborough Theatre, West Brompton

West Brompton's pea-green Finborough Theatre is one of the most beloved pub theatres among London's dramatic community. So much so that plays regularly sell out – if you want to see a production here, booking in advance is recommended. If you didn't get a ticket in time, this place is still worth popping into. Console yourself with the selection of craft beers downstairs.
118 Finborough Road, SW10 9ED

The Gate, Notting Hill

A space that transforms with each production, except one thing stays the same: it's always above the Prince Albert pub in Notting Hill Gate.

The theatre brings ground-breaking international plays to a London audience. One to visit for an evening when you've got your thinking cap on.
11 Pembridge Road, W11 3HQ

Upstairs at the Gatehouse, Highgate

The Gatehouse stands formidably at the top of Highgate Hill, looking down at the rest of the village. And looking down on the Gatehouse is Upstairs at the Gatehouse. The highly versatile space has seen hundreds of shows since its inception in 1985. Of particular interest are the Ovation Theatres productions – who also run the theatre. They nearly always put a classic Broadway musical during the winter months. Nothing like jazz hands to warm you up.
Highgate West Hill, N6 4BD

Katzpace, Borough

This newbie isn't the best established theatre on this list; nor does it have the biggest productions. We've included

Illustration by LISA BERKSHIRE

it because of two curiosities. One, its pertinently central location – just moments from London Bridge – makes it stand out. Secondly, it isn't connected to a pub per se; instead German *bierkeller*, Katzenjammers. Fill up your stein, then head to the intimate 50-seat theatre to watch some fresh voices in the theatre world.

24 Southwark Street, SE1 1TY

Old Red Lion Theatre Pub, Islington

If there's a pub theatre equivalent to the West End, it's Angel. Four high-quality pub theatres dwell here, each worth its salt. If we have to whittle it down to one, it'd have to be the Old Red Lion (see page 132 also). It's got a cavernous pub downstairs and a wooden-pewed theatre above, making it feel like you've stumbled into a hidden chapel. In recent years, it debuted the riotously successful *The Play That Goes Wrong*, which now lives on in the West End.

418 St John Street, EC1V 4NJ

Royal Vauxhall Tavern, Vauxhall

Royal Vauxhall Tavern is one of London's premiere – and oldest – LGBTQ venues. Drag shows and cabaret, both of which present a rollicking good time, are on the menu here. These shows feel no need to play it safe; you might be watching Drag Kings one night – H P Loveshaft anyone? – and a Madonna-themed variety show the next. And there's always the annual Christmas Panto, where things get a little more adult than your usual community theatre offering. Lashings of innuendo? Oh yes there is!

372 Kennington Lane, SE11 5HY

Tabard Theatre, Chiswick

In leafy Chiswick lies one of London's most stunning pubs, The Tabard. It hangs out over the pavement in a medieval style, and the inside is just as remarkable – with tiling depicting bucolic nature by William Morris' mate William De Morgan. We recommend the pub's cuisine before you head upstairs for the theatre. There's a diverse range of shows on here, from plays aimed at younger audiences to more serious fare, and big names from the world of comedy like Al Murray and Richard Herring.

2 Bath Road, W4 1LW

Theatre503, Battersea

Situated on 503 Battersea Park Road, above The Latchmere pub, Theatre503 makes the bold claim of staging more work by first-time writers than any other theatre in the country. It's nearly impossible to prove whether this is true or not, but a glance at the programming makes it look exceptionally believable. The theatre stages the first productions of writers who've gone on to scoop up plenty of industry awards. Attend a play here and remember the playwright's name – they might just be tomorrow's superstar.

503 Battersea Park Road, SW11 3BW

STRANGE BREWS: LONDON'S WEIRDEST DRINKS

If there's one thing London is really great at, it's taking something perfectly normal and making it… well… weird.

In 2015, the Wonkaesque duo Sam Bompas and Harry Parr unveiled a walk-in alcoholic weather system – a giant breathable cocktail cloud – at Borough Market. This collision of meteorology and mixology allegedly referenced the mists of time – it also proved just how off-the-wall London's drinking scene had become.

Beer made from old bread

Alright, so it's not the kookiest brew ever made in London. That honour goes to a one-off batch, made by Dalston's **40ft Brewery**, which used yeast from Roald Dahl's writing chair. Still – beer made from old bread? Pretty kooky.

Toast Ale uses surplus bread – including unsold loaves from London's bakeries – at its Southwark brewery. Hops, yeast and water are added in a swoop of booze-addled witchcraft (if you insist on science: the bread's carbohydrates are broken down to sugar by amylase in the barley, and the yeast converts the sugars to alcohol). Hey presto! Pale ales, lagers and IPAs galore. All profits go to charity to end food waste.

So the more you drink, the more good you're doing.

Cray cray cocktails

Once upon a time, London's idea of a cocktail was a G&T with an umbrella plonked in it. Now, they glow, flame, bubble and smoke.

Don a hazmat suit to 'cook up' a *Breaking Bad* cocktail, à la Walter White, in the back of an old RV at **ABQ London**.

The Deep in the Sea cocktail at King's Cross' **GNH Bar** is made with salmon and dill-infused vodka. We've tried it and hated it, but apparently others love it. That's what the barman told us.

Dare to accept the 'grasshopper challenge' at **Burlock** in Marylebone – a bar decked out like a Havana barbershop? Munch a grasshopper, then chase it with a shot of rum and a beer. Your prize? You get to ring a bell.

Shoreditch's **London Cocktail Club** will do you a bacon-and-egg martini, garnished with an actual rasher of crispy bacon…

…and, for dessert: **Cocktail Trading Co**'s American Pie literally comes sealed in a pastry lid.

Artesian – often trumpeted as one of the world's best cocktail joints – is consistently inventive with its cocktail menus. Last time we were there, we drank/ate a cocktail/dish of embryonic-looking 'eggs', injected with apricot eau de vie, and sprinkled with flowers and herbs. It was inspired by birth. It was an acquired taste.

Speaking of semi-solid cocktails, **69 Colebrooke Row**'s Prairie Oyster looks just like a mollusc, but is in fact a deconstructed Bloody Mary. A tomato yolk explodes on the tongue, unleashing a torrent of horseradish vodka, oloroso sherry, celery juice, Worcestershire sauce, homemade pepper sauce and white wine vinegar. Well worth shelling out on.

Freakshakes in London

Towers of cream, mountains of doughnuts, slabs of brownie – and that's all before you get to the milkshake. Freakshakes are a sight to behold, a meal within a drink, a sugar buzz that'll have you bouncing off the walls for days.

Maxwells in Covent Garden first started serving freakshakes in 2015, and now refers to itself as "the home of the freakshake". Our advice? Avoid the famous 'Unicorn' freakshake. It looks good on the 'Gram, but a chemically flavour leaves a bitter aftertaste. Go for the Salted Caramel Donut option instead.

If you demand unicorn, head to Forest Gate's **Candy Floss Crêperie**, which does a bright-blue beast that promises

e-numbers by the bucketload, topped off with a candyfloss cloud and a giant lolly. Bethnal Green's **Canvas Cafe**, meanwhile, is credited with whipping up London's first vegan freakshakes.

Burger chains **BRGR CO**, **Byron** and **TGI Fridays** are in on the action too; the latter's Birthday Cake Shake is topped with a whole slice of birthday cake. We're not ashamed to admit we've had one. It wasn't even our birthday.

Drinking Kombucha in London

Kombucha – not to be confused with London Zoo's Ribena-swilling silverback gorilla Kumbuka – is a fermented black or green tea drink, available in various fruity flavours, and usually drunk cold. It's very slightly alcoholic, and has been filtering its way into the London mainstream drinking scene in recent years. It's regularly used in cocktails and mocktails in the capital's bars too.

It's also being made here. Tottenham-based **Wild Fizz Kombucha** brews it on a houseboat and Hackney Wick's **Jarr Kombucha** is Europe's first kombucha taproom.

Eat Drink your cereal at Cereal Killer Café

We are strongly – STRONGLY – of the opinion that cereal is to be eaten, and not drunk (tipping up the bowl to swallow the dregs doesn't count). So you can imagine our wariness about **Cereal Killer Café**'s cereal-laced beverages.

Start your day with a coffee made with milk flavoured by either Coco Pops or Frosties – the soggy cereal itself is strained off, thank goodness. Move onto the 'stacked hot chocolate' and 'cereal chillers' (milkshake) section of the menu for drinks topped with cream, sauce and cereal, including Lucky Charms and Froot Loops.

If you're visiting after 11am, indulge in cereal-based cocktails, including the Drunk Leprechaun (vodka, cream soda, marshmallow syrup and Lucky Charms) or the Apple Jack (Jack Daniels, Apple Fanta, ground cinnamon and, unsurprisingly, Apple Jacks).

EL&N Café in Mayfair is also in on the cereal coffee game, with a Lucky Charms latte offered at all its branches.

MOST HAUNTED PUBS

If you like your pint with a spirit or your gastro grub with a ghoul,
then these nine pubs will be right up your street.

The Bow Bells, Bow

A ghost with a penchant for toilet humour is believed to be in residence at this Mile End boozer. He or she makes themselves known by flushing the toilet in the women's loo when someone is on it. The prankster has apparently struck on many occasions from the 70s right up to the present day. At the height of the problem in 1974 the pub's then-landlord attempted to rid the ghost with a séance. At the point when the spirit was asked to show itself, the door of the women's toilets swung open with such force that it smashed a pane of glass. No one knows who the perpetrator is or why they are there, but for ladies in need, it's certainly a bit of a bummer.
116 Bow Road, E3 3AA

The Flask, Highgate

This tree-flanked Fuller's pub next to Highgate Cemetery is not as peaceful as it might look. One spirit who likes to make herself known from time-to-time is reputedly the ghost of a Spanish barmaid who hanged herself in the pub's cellar – where you can now sit – over a failed romance with the publican of the time. She's been known to move glasses and blow down the backs of customers' necks, while the pub's lights have also been seen to sway and temperatures noticeably drop when she's around. As if that's not enough, a man in Cavalier dress may also be glimpsed crossing the room and disappearing into a pillar.
77 Highgate W Hill, N6 6BU

The George, Temple

A ghostly Cavalier has also been repeatedly seen in the basement of this pub opposite the Royal Courts of Justice. Although the current building – complete with black and white timber frontage – dates back only as far as the 1930s, its foundations are much older, which may explain the association. The most publicised sighting of this unknown cavalier came in the 70s when painters and decorators were carrying out refurbishment work. After seeing the figure, one decorator fled upstairs and appealed to the landlord. The latter told the painter: "I shouldn't worry about him… my wife sees him all the time".
213 Strand, WC2R 1AP

The Grenadier, Belgravia

This quaint-looking pub just off Hyde Park Corner roundabout dates back to 1720. It was originally built to house the First Royal Regiment of Foot Guards, later known as the Grenadier Guards, for the heroism they showed fighting off the French Grenadiers at the Battle of Waterloo in 1815. While the upper floors of the building were used as an Officer's Mess and frequented by King George IV, the cellar was used as a place to drink and gamble for the lower-ranking soldiers.

The story goes that one of these soldiers – now affectionately known as Cedric – was caught cheating at cards by his comrades. His punishment was a beating so aggressive that he died, and many believe he haunts the pub to this day. Many objects in the pub have been said to either disappear or move without explanation, while punters have reported long-lasting icy chills. Both drinkers and landlords have heard footsteps wandering around empty rooms, and pained moans coming from the cellar. In one instance it is said that a chief superintendent from New Scotland Yard was having a drink in the pub when he noticed smoke start to waft around him. As he reached into the smoke, he shouted in pain and withdrew his hand, now marked with the burn of an invisible cigarillo. The pub's ceiling is covered with banknotes, put there by

visitors hoping to rid the ghost by paying off Cedric's cards debt (see page 147).
18 Wilton Row, SW1X 7NR

The Old Bull & Bush, Golders Green

A farmhouse was built on the site of this Hampstead Heath-side pub in 1645, and it gained a licence to sell ale in 1721. For centuries there has been local talk of hauntings. Strange bangs and bumps surprise visitors, and a shrouded Victorian-style figure moves across the bar area. A potential explanation was uncovered during refurbishment in the 1980s: behind one of the cellar walls, a skeleton was found surrounded by Victorian surgical equipment. The skeleton has now been buried, but the haunting is said to remain.
North End Way, NW3 7HE

Rising Sun, Smithfield

Legend has it that this Sam Smith's pub set next to St Bartholomew's Hospital was, in the early 19th century, the preying ground of a particularly brutal form of body snatcher. These gangs would drug drinkers at the pub and later murder them to sell their bodies to the hospital for medical research. This grisly past has seemingly left its mark. Two barmaids who lived above the pub in 1989 claimed they were often woken in the night by a presence that would sit on the end of their beds and slowly pull the duvet off

Illustration by Stephanie Hofmann Illustration

them. Many others have heard footsteps in the upstairs bar while cleaning away downstairs late at night. In 1990, the then-landlady was showering in the staff bathroom when she heard the door open and close again. She then saw the shower curtain pulled to one side and felt an icy-cold hand run down her back – again, there was no one to be seen.
38 Cloth Fair, EC1A 7JQ

The Spaniards Inn, Hampstead

Spirits come in triple measures at this pub by the Heath. The first is Dick Turpin, infamous for highway robbery, whose father is often cited as the pub's landlord during the 18th century (he wasn't). The highwayman's spirit is said to roam the upstairs rooms, causing intermittent bangs and clangs. Downstairs, a moneylender by the name of Black Dick, who was run over by a horse and cart outside the pub, presides over the bar area and has frequently been felt pulling on the sleeves of drinkers. Outside, Dick Turpin's faithful horse – affectionately known as Black Bess – apparently haunts the car park. Neighs and hooves have been heard by many over the years. See page 132 also.
Spaniards Road, NW3 7JJ

The Viaduct Tavern, St Paul's

This Fuller's pub opposite the Old Bailey dates back to 1875 and occupies the site of a former jail. The Viaduct was previously a thriving gin palace, and is the last example within the City boundaries. Aside from knocks, footsteps and the odd shiver,

two particular stories cement its haunted reputation. In 1996, a manager was tidying the cellar when the door suddenly slammed shut and the lights went out. After feeling his way to the door, he found that no matter how hard he tried, it refused to open. Hearing his cries for help, his wife came and opened the door, claiming it was unlocked and easy to move. On another occasion in 1999, two electricians were working in one of the pub's upstairs rooms. They had rolled the carpet up to get to the floorboards when one worker felt a couple of taps on his shoulder; shortly afterwards, both men apparently saw the rolled-up carpet lifted and then heavily dropped back onto the floor.
126 Newgate Street, EC1A 7AA

The Volunteer, Baker Street

This pub close to Regent's Park was a recruiting station during World War II, but its haunted history goes much further back. It is built on the site of a large 17th-century house which belonged to the wealthy Neville family. When it caught fire in 1654 it burned to the ground, taking the entire family with it. A well-dressed man in surcoat and breeches now wanders through the pub's cellar – believed to be former man of the house, Rupert Neville. Footsteps have also been heard, and on occasion the pub's lights have mysteriously flickered on and off. The pub's cellar is believed to be from the original house, the only part of it which remained after the fire.
245–7 Baker Street, NW1 6XE

BARS BENEATH YOUR FEET

Ignore all those people urging you to 'look up'.
Many of London's best drinks are being served beneath your feet.

214 Bermondsey, Bermondsey

If gin's your tipple, head to 214 Bermondsey (nestled beneath restaurant Antico). 100 varieties of Mother's Ruin line the shelves, waiting to be mixed with the bar's own hand-crafted tonic water. Themed tasting flights allow you to discover your gin of choice: pick from The Great British Gin-Off and Tour of London, each offering three related drinks for £18 – plus tasting notes for gin geeks to pore over with glee.
214 Bermondsey Street, SE1 3TQ

Basement Sate, Soho

The one thing that can make a great cocktail bar even better? Combining the libations with gorgeous puddings, of course. Founded on the same kind of ingenuity that gave us the cronut, this Soho spot has hit on one killer USP. From tonka bean chocolate lava cake to marshmallow and ginger-curd crumble, there are some impressive flavour combinations here for those with sweet teeth.

The sugar rush continues on the drinks menu, with such intriguing options as The Jessica Rabbit (gin, carrot juice, golden syrup and elderflower) and Not a Pornstar (Bourbon, Aperol, passion fruit, vanilla syrup and egg white). If you're dining out in Soho, skip dessert and come here.
8 Broadwick Street, W1 AHN

Bounce, Farringdon

London's original ping pong bar has it all: booze, wood-fired pizzas, and high-octane tabletop sport. Though Bounce accepts walk-ins, it's worth rallying at least five of your most competitive mates and making an advance booking if you're planning a game during peak hours. If you're up for something a little more high-tech, show off your backhand over a round of Wonderball, which uses snazzy projection mapping to turn the table into a giant, neon-hued computer game.
121 Holborn, Farringdon EC1N 2TD

B.Y.O.C. City, Aldgate

In most bars, you'd be shown the door for trying to smuggle in your own bottle of vodka, but B.Y.O.C. isn't your average neighbourhood watering hole. Here, you're encouraged, nay, compelled to bring the booze. Select the spirits you like best, stump up the £30 entrance fee on the door, and hand over your liquor to one of B.Y.O.C.'s more than capable bartenders, who'll use it to create the cocktail of your dreams (with a little help from their ample selection of juices, syrups, and bitters). Find it under James Cochran's Barullo restaurant.
19 Bevis Marks, EC3A JA

Cahoots, Soho

An ersatz abandoned Underground station reinvented as a 1940s-themed cocktail bar, Cahoots is inspired by its history as a World War II air raid shelter. Everything about this venue has been carefully chosen to transport drinkers back in time; swish wooden escalators lead down to a tube carriage bar where guests perch on moquette and sip carrot juice cocktails from wartime-thrift hip flasks, old milk bottles and tins. Swing dancing and sing-a-longs around the piano come as standard.
Kingly Court, 13 Kingly Street, W1B 5PG

Discount Suit Company, Spitalfields

Moody lighting? Check. Wood panels and exposed brickwork? Double check. This tailors' stockroom-turned-cocktail-joint off Petticoat Lane ticks all the usual boxes for a cosy yet stylish basement bar. What sets it apart – aside from its intriguing East End heritage – is a short but oh-so-sweet list of forgotten classic cocktails that your bartender will whip up with lightning speed. The Neal's Yard cheese boards make for an unbeatable bar snack, and someone's usually spinning ultra-hip choons on vinyl.

29a Wentworth Street, Spitalfields E1 7TB

Freud, Covent Garden

The bohemian charm of Freud is no coincidence. It's the brainchild of Courtauld Institute of Art alum David Freud, who sought to recreate the spirit of the Viennese coffee bars which inspired his artist father, Lucian (yep, that Lucian). The no-frills cellar bar boasts some of the best-value cocktails in central London (ours is a Moscow mule, thanks). Despite having stuck around since 1986, Freud's chalkboard menu and rickety furniture make it look like it was cobbled together hours before you arrived.

198 Shaftesbury Avenue, WC2H 8JL

Merchant House, City of London

Embrace your inner Bertie Wooster at Merchant House, a swish bar where the drinks are themed around British history. Found underneath a hidden courtyard near Cheapside, this oak-panelled hideaway oozes old world class, without feeling elitist.

The menu is set out like a book with beautiful illustrations of each potion, alongside intriguing titles such as 'Tarred and Feathered' (rum and salt) and 'Fields of Gold' (poitin, oat milk, house orgeat, buttered genever and malt). Such finesse extends to the bar snacks, which include oysters and game terrine pot. La-de-da.

13 Well Court, EC4M 9DN

Oliver's Jazz Bar, Greenwich

A narrow set of stairs lead you down to London's homiest jazz club – its look completed with a kitchen range that belongs in a 19th-century cottage (still works in the winter, too). Order a large brandy, pull up a chair, and lose yourself in the noodling of a jam session. Bonus tip: the nearby Fan Museum does an excellent, and excellently priced, afternoon tea in its orangery.

9 Nevada Street, SE10 9JL

Original Sin, Stoke Newington

The younger sibling of Hoxton's Happiness Forgets (see page 55) oozes the same playful, low-key glamour as its East End counterpart. Think chocolate leather booths behind wrought-iron railings, art deco-style sconces shaped like pineapples, and a mustard-yellow pool table that's free to use. The menu is short but perfectly formed, sporting classic cocktails with a contemporary twist. Try the rose negroni or sherry-spiked daquiri.

129 Stoke Newington High Street, N16 0PH

Reverend JW Simpson, Fitzrovia

A scattering of candles on the pavement and an exquisite stained glass window are two clues that Reverend JW Simpson occupies the site of an old rectory. Another, of course, is the name. The bar plumps for an aesthetic that's more shabby chic than sacrilege. That said, its disciples' (that's what they call the bartenders) devotion to crafting divine drinks is practically evangelical. Congregate for luscious libations like the sinfully rich Cygnet: a rum and coffee-liqueur concoction featuring homemade muscavado-and-black-pepper syrup, and artisan Irish-whisky cream. For something educational, attend one of the Reverend's 'Spirited Sermons', a cocktail masterclass themed around one particular liquor.

32 Goodge Street, W1T 2QL

HOW LONDON BECAME UTTERLY ADDICTED TO COFFEE

At a time when confusion over the name scribbled on the side of a cup is the limit of conversation between strangers in cafes, it's hard to imagine that London's coffee houses were once considered the height of civility. But when coffee first arrived in London, it was the drink of the intellectuals.

Coffee comes to London

The advent of coffee in the capital is harder to trace than that of tea, although we do know that coffee arrived earlier, thanks to Londoners travelling to and from the Ottoman Empire. The Levant Trading Company, and later the British and Dutch East India companies, were among early importers of coffee to England. When it arrived, it was stored in warehouses such as those in Shad Thames and at Hay's Galleria.

The first coffee was a rudimentary drink, made well in advance and reheated when served. This was long before the days of filtering, and the niceties of milk and sugar weren't added until much later. Coffee wasn't much enjoyed by people at the time, who slurped it for its stimulant qualities rather than its taste. Adverts and posters of questionable scientific basis were published by proprietors of early coffee houses to get people hooked on the drink. You'll find one such piece of propaganda the British Museum, entitled 'The Vertue of the Coffee Drink'.

It encourages people to take their coffee "as hot as can possibly be endured", so long as it doesn't take the skin off your mouth, or give you blisters.

London's first coffee houses

The grand lantern of Cornhill's Jamaica Wine House screams 'history'. But wine is a mere descendant of the site's beverage history. The modern-day watering hole sits on the site of London's first coffee house – a rather grand description for what was effectively a shed serving up a bitter liquid.

As a blue plaque informs 21st-century passers-by, Pasqua Rosée opened a coffee house here in 1652. Although the premises bore Rosée's name and picture, a Daniel Edwards was the driving force behind it. A member of the Levant Company and a Turkish goods trader, Edwards employed Rosée as a servant. It's thought that Edwards' visitors enjoyed coffee so much he employed Rosée to flog it to the public, although an alternative story is that the two had a falling out and Rosée set up the business alone, having

been introduced to coffee by Edwards. Either way, it was a popular venture, reportedly selling 600 servings of coffee every day. Samuel Pepys mentions a visit in his diary in December 1660 – a big year for Pepys, as he also discovered tea.

Over to the west, Oxford was ahead of the game. The scholarly city was home to 'penny universities' (named for the penny entry fee and academic conversation of coffee houses) before London got its first whiff of a coffee shop. In fact, it may be due to their success in Oxford that they came to London at all. Pasqua Rosée actually opened a coffee house in Oxford in 1651 before bringing it to London a year later – and his wasn't the only coffee house operating in Oxford at the time.

You might not be surprised to learn that women were banned from coffee houses (although some had female staff members). Male writers, politicians, journalists, poets and other members of the educated classes would gather to discuss the issues of the day. Different venues had different focuses – political chat was much rifer in the coffee houses of Westminster, while theatrical reviews were offered freely by patrons in the West End.

Tavern owners saw Rosée's enterprise as something of a threat to their custom, but that didn't stop several other coffee houses popping up in subsequent years. Rosée himself apparently had plans to open a second branch nearby – London's first mini-chain, perhaps? – but this never came to pass.

Button's Coffee House, Russell Street

Another establishment of note is Button's Coffee House, which opened in Covent Garden's Russell Street in 1712 and functioned as the unofficial offices of a newspaper named *The Guardian* (nothing to do with the modern newspaper). So persistent was the presence of *Guardian* writers in Button's that a letterbox in the shape of a lion's head was installed on the exterior of the building, for the public to submit news for publication. The paper lasted barely seven months, but the lion can be seen at Woburn Abbey today.

Lloyd's Coffee House

Modern insurance market Lloyd's of London – famous for its Lutine Bell, still pealed after maritime disasters – exists today thanks to a 17th–18th-century business called Lloyd's Coffee House. A popular meeting place for sailors, merchants and shipowners, relationships forged here led to the establishment of Lloyd's of London, and several other businesses of seafaring matters.

Tom King's Coffee House, Covent Garden

Not all early coffee houses were high-brow. Tom King's Coffee House – later known as Moll King's Coffee House – in Covent Garden was a mid-18th century venue of ill repute. It opened at the time the local taverns shut, and remained so until dawn. Coffee was reportedly an afterthought; alcohol was served, and the business functioned primarily as a brothel of sorts. To satisfy a legal loophole, there were no beds on the premises bar the Kings' own. Instead, introductions between prostitutes and customers were made, before going elsewhere to get down to business. King's Coffee House features in Hogarth's *Morning*, showing two men pawing at girls in Covent Garden Piazza in the early hours.

Bar Italia, Soho

Soho's Bar Italia is not one of London's earliest coffee shops by any stretch, but

its 1949 birth date makes it London's longest-running. It's served the likes of Jimi Hendrix and the Rolling Stones in its time – and presumably Jarvis Cocker, seeing as Pulp wrote a song about it. Its impressive tenure is nonetheless obliterated by Oxford's Queen's Lane Coffee House, which has been operating continuously since 1654.

Nearby, Algerian Coffee Stores has been around since 1887. It specialises in tea and coffee blends, plus the equipment you need for brewing your own. These days, you can get a takeaway coffee too.

Coffee houses under threat

Traditional taverns and ale houses weren't the only ones threatened by these new-fangled coffee houses. Charles II tried to ban coffee establishments in 1675. The official line was that they disturbed the peace and promoted idleness, but Charlie was no doubt fearful that they provided the ideal environment for rebellious meetings and the plotting of treason.

Unfortunately for the king, several of his minsters were coffee lovers and opposed the ban. It was abolished before it even took effect, and London's caffeine takeover continued apace.

Arrival of the coffee giants

Whatever your opinion of the quality of their coffee, there's no denying that chain coffee shops have made their mark on London. But when did these modern-day incarnations emerge?

The capital's first Starbucks opened on Chelsea's King's Road in 1998, a BBC report at the time stating that it "intended to be the first of 500 stores in Europe." 20 years later, London alone often feels like it's close to that number. You can still grab a latte on 123 King's Road.

Pret A Manger predates Starbucks, opening its first branch in Hampstead in 1983, although as its name suggests, the focus was more on the food than the takeaway coffee. Despite its Italian-sounding moniker, Costa was established here in London, beginning as a coffee roastery in 1971 before opening its own store in Vauxhall Bridge Road in 1978.

Coffee ghost signs

Ghosts of the London coffee industry can still be seen around town. Squint up at the house by bus stop KC on Kennington Lane for a nod to the building's past as Albion Coffee House, apparently a regular haunt of Charlie Chaplin's father.

Harder to spot is an old advertisement for 'The Royal Coffee & Dining Rooms', located on Holloway Road, overlooking St Mary Magdalene Garden.

'James Ashby & Sons Ltd Embassy Tea & Coffee' can be made out on the side of 195–205 Union Street in Southwark. Although the building was under threat in 2008, it's still standing – and the sign still mostly visible – today.

Keep your eyes peeled in the vicinity of Tooley Street and Hay's Galleria for old signposts to the Bramah Tea and Coffee Museum. Alas, the museum closed in 2008 following the death of its founder, Edward Bramah. But for a few years it was a fascinating snapshot of the history of the tea and coffee trades in the capital.

London's most unusual coffees and coffee houses

As with most things, London has taken coffee, run with it, and made it weird. These days, rainbow lattes and themed coffees aren't uncommon, but perhaps the oddest – and certainly the most expensive – coffee sold in London was Kopi Luwak, which went on sale in the capital in 2011 at £70 a cup. It's made using the droppings of Luwaks (civets) in Sumatra, who eat coffee cherries and excrete the beans. The controversial harvesting method has faced criticism from animal rights groups, with Harrods calling for tougher regulations of the production process, and the man responsible for first bringing the coffee to London regretting the move.

As for unusual coffee houses, we offer you the tale of the 'fellatio cafe'. There were once plans to open a 'blowjob cafe' in Paddington, where customers would drink their brew while receiving a blowjob from an escort. Unsurprisingly, the venture never took off. Surprisingly, the plans appeared in 2016, rather than the 17th century, as you might expect.

Another odd historical coffee house was in (the extant) St John's Gate, where the proprietor insisted you speak Latin, or get out. He was William Hogarth's dad.

Roasteries in London today

Today, coffee's not only served in London, the beans are roasted here too. Caffè Nero prepares its special coffee blend in its Battersea-based Roastery, before shipping it to branches all over London and beyond to go into your morning latte. The coffee sold in cafes at Tate art galleries, meanwhile, is produced inside a World War II bunker in the grounds of Tate Britain. It roasts a whopping 22,000 kilos of coffee every year.

Both of these are off-limits to the public, but if you want to watch your coffee being freshly roasted before it's served, head to The Roastery and Bake Hall in Harrods, where beans are prepared in-house, allowing Harrods control over the quality. Sit back at the marble bar counter in the art deco hall and listen out for the bell, which rings every 15 minutes to announce that freshly baked bread is ready.

It's funny how things have come full circle. Thinkers of the day would meet at coffee houses to share the news of the day and discuss it, pontificate and write about it. In today's freelance economy, a large number of the articles you read online everyday are probably written in coffee shops, by journalists poring over iPads and Mac Books. Their immediate audience is much smaller, but their worldwide audience is much, much wider. All powered by a good old cup of coffee.

A COCKTAIL TO 'WAKE YOU UP AND F**K YOU UP'

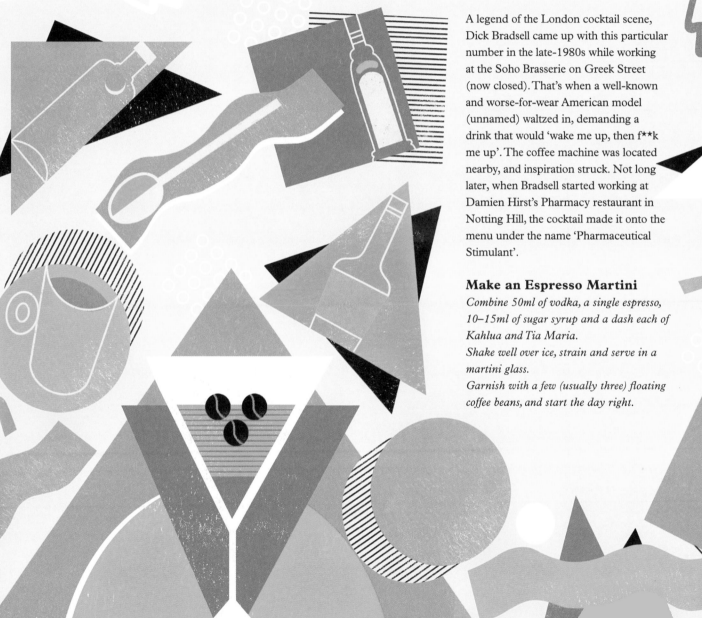

A legend of the London cocktail scene, Dick Bradsell came up with this particular number in the late-1980s while working at the Soho Brasserie on Greek Street (now closed). That's when a well-known and worse-for-wear American model (unnamed) waltzed in, demanding a drink that would 'wake me up, then f**k me up'. The coffee machine was located nearby, and inspiration struck. Not long later, when Bradsell started working at Damien Hirst's Pharmacy restaurant in Notting Hill, the cocktail made it onto the menu under the name 'Pharmaceutical Stimulant'.

Make an Espresso Martini

Combine 50ml of vodka, a single espresso, 10–15ml of sugar syrup and a dash each of Kahlua and Tia Maria.
Shake well over ice, strain and serve in a martini glass.
Garnish with a few (usually three) floating coffee beans, and start the day right.

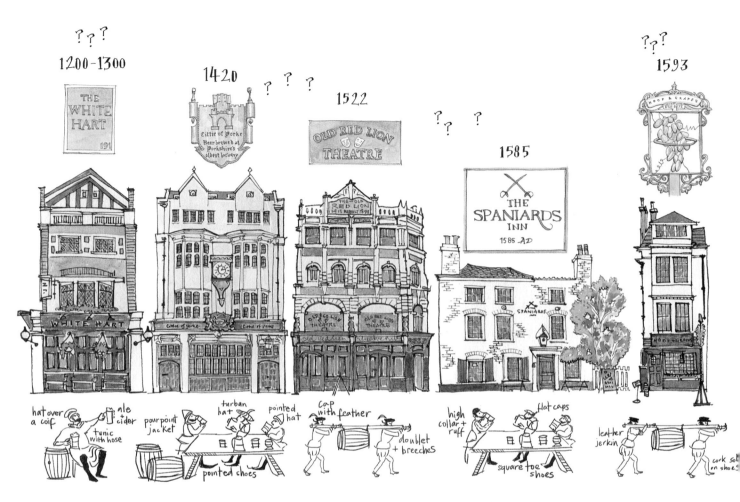

WHICH IS LONDON'S OLDEST PUB?

You could spend an interesting day running round London, trying to answer this question by visiting every claimant to the title. However, by the end you'd be so drunk you wouldn't be able to remember your name, let alone your mission.

That's because there are almost as many ways to define the answer as there are pubs with 'Ye Olde' in their name. Is it the oldest pub by name, by location, by age of building or of interior, by length of licence – or some magical combination of the lot?

Dubious claimants

This is complex stuff, worth exploring in more detail. To take a couple of examples, High Holborn's Cittie Of York has fine

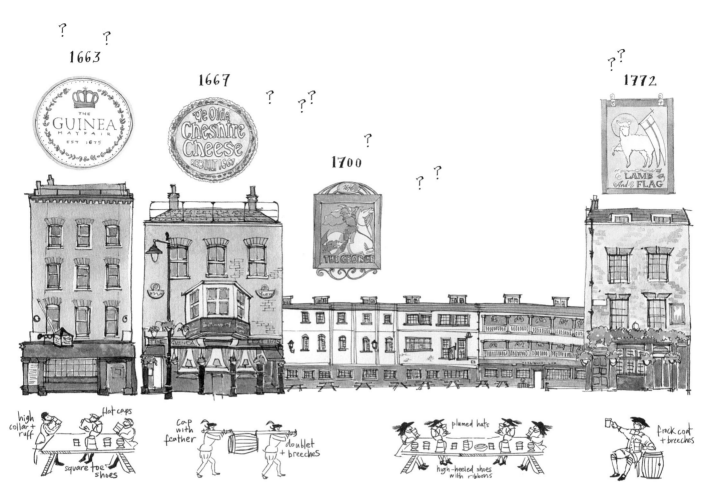

credentials, occupying the site of an inn since 1420. However, the building itself dates only to the 1920s, while its name was pinched from an older tavern that used to sit across the road. Or take Mayfair's The Guinea, which has been a pub since 1423 but took its current name in 1663 and occupies a building that dates from around 1720. For almost every promising, illustrious or celebrated candidate from the Wapping's Prospect

of Whitby to Twickenham's White Swan there are caveats that create confusion.

West End watering holes

This is an arena in which appearances and folklore can be deceptive. The Lamb and Flag in Covent Garden (see page 108) looks as if it is about to fall over and sometimes claims Tudor origins, but has in fact only been a licensed premises since 1772 when it was called The Cooper's

Arms. It only became the Lamb and Flag in 1833. Some of the interior is Victorian while that ancient-looking frontage dates all the way back to… the 1950s.

At the other end of the scale is the nearby White Hart, a fairly unassuming pub on Drury Lane. This newish-looking boozer claims to be London's oldest licensed pub; it was mentioned in Old

Illustration by Rebecca Lea Williams

Bailey records as far back as the 13th century. While that seems compelling, the claim has problems.

The original White Hart was not only in a different building – it was in a completely different location. The current version was built in the 1800s on land that didn't even belong to the medieval inn. That's not to say the White Hart doesn't have genuine history of its own – for one, it was the location of Communist Club meetings from 1846, and in 1847 Karl Marx addressed a meeting of the German Workers' Educational Society held in its "large and splendid" upstairs room. But is it old? Not really. At least not in London terms.

An Islington candidate

Over in Islington, the Old Red Lion is a promising candidate. This St John Street mainstay claims to hark back to 1415, a date quoted by several Victorian sources one of which notes it has "a greater claim to antiquity than any other hostelry in the metropolis if we except perhaps the (since-demolished) Talbot or Tabard in Borough".

The oldest written evidence records a Red Lion on this site in 1522. Several famous names are connected to the pub, including William Hogarth, Thomas Paine and Samuel Johnson. It's a fine claim, although it should be said that the Red Lion briefly changed its name and has also been rebuilt several times. The current building dates from 1899 – see page 118 also.

A famous quartet

Complexity upon complexity. What does one do about Ye Olde Cheshire Cheese? It certainly feels old and the building dates back to 1667 – a familiar post-fire date for so many City pubs. Particularly intriguing are the cellars, said to have once been part of a 13th century monastery, while the pub also has what CAMRA (Campaign for Real Ale) believes to be among the oldest surviving original woodwork in London. Indeed, CAMRA argues that there is no complete surviving pub interior in London from before the mid-19th century, but points out both the Cheshire and the George in Borough (see page 160) have ancient parts – bits of the George may even predate 1700.

One of the oldest exteriors is that of The Spaniards Inn, built in 1585, although not a pub until some 150 years later. Clientele is famously said to include Dick Turpin, as well as Keats, Dickens, Byron, Constable, Hogarth and more – this one is part pub, part time capsule.

Less illustrious but almost as old is the Hoop & Grapes in Aldgate (see page 113), built in 1593 and housed in one of the few timber-framed buildings to survive the three London horsemen of the Great Fire, the Blitz and 21st-century property developers. There are older pub buildings, there are older pub names, there are older pub interiors, there are older pub licences, but few that feel quite as authentically venerable as this place, so it seems a fitting end to the quest.

AN ODE TO THE MILK ROUND

In 2016, we woke up uncommonly early, caught the first tube to Walthamstow Central, and hopped aboard Colin Chesnaye's milk float, motoring around the near-deserted streets of northeast London, and talking to him about his milk round.

"It's like a car. If you want an Audi you pay the price. If you want a Nissan you pay a little bit less. We're the BMWs."

Milkman Colin Chesnaye has been doing his milk round in east London for 39 years, and is adamant that 76p buys you much more than just a pint of red top in a glass bottle. For a few extra quid a week than you'd pay at the supermarket, you're getting a personal delivery service who whistles while he works, trusts you to settle up at the end of the month, and will fight through hell, high water – and plenty of drizzle – to get your milk to you.

"Rain, shine or snow, the milkman will show," laughs Colin.

"If people want milk earlier I go out of my way, because if they've got to go to work, leaving the milk on the doorstep advertises that they're out. So I try to go round there and put myself out, so the milk's on the doorstep before you go out."

Colin – who's owned his milk round since 1996, and now works through Parker Dairies, knows his customers so well that although he has a thick handwritten ledger filled with orders and addresses, he rarely checks it.

Starting in Whipps Cross each morning he covers 45-odd streets between here and Walthamstow; the round is more spread out and patchy than it would have been 30 years ago, but there's still a community feeling.

As we zip around the residential streets of E17 at 7am on a mild spring morning – bottles of red, green, blue and gold top clinking in the back of his float – people call out to Colin in the street. It's not unusual for Parker Dairies milkmen to get invites to family events and weddings. You wonder how many Ocado delivery drivers can say the same.

In a strange paradox, because so many of Colin's customers are still in bed, there's a clandestine nature to the operation; milk, eggs and bacon are hidden behind flower pots and gnomes; the favour is returned with cash and cheques stashed under mats or behind the dahlias.

Keeping the float afloat

Our mode of transport today is hardly the subtlest of vehicles; the cream and powder blue Smiths Elizabethan Cabac, manufactured in the mid-1980s, runs off a motor powered by 36 batteries, and makes one hell of a racket when you're sat in the cab.

"When we finish the round, normally we go back to the depot and put it on charge for 10, 12 hours," says Colin, "It's like a mobile phone."

That's if you make it back. Plucky though the floats are, they're liable to suffer a dead cell, conk out and start smoking. That's when you call for Bernard and Jim – Parker Dairy's semi-resident float fixers. They'll do anything, from removing nails from tyres to sloshing another coat of paint on. Duct tape is also invaluable in this business.

Bernard, who's been fixing floats for 45 years, recalls a time when one skidded on an icy hill, went through a hedge, tipped over, and landed on a customer's doorstep. She opened the door, saw the crashed vehicle and collapsed from shock.

Says Colin, "If they have a float that's no good anymore they won't scrap it, they'll take all the parts off it, put it into a corner, and use it for another float. Nine times out of 10 we get by."

"Hipsters love milk in bottles"

The make-do-and-mend attitude and green credentials (electric vehicles, recycled glass) has always been a part of the milk industry. Now this approach is back in vogue with Londoners, who are falling in love with the milk round all over again.

Parker Dairies depot manager Paul Lough recalls: "The first day I walked into the yard, the yardman come up and said 'I don't know why you're bothering son, it's got five years in it'. And that was 29 years ago.

"Now in London having your milk delivered has become cool and trendy. All the hipsters love having their milk delivered in glass bottles.

"We've gone through 20 years of supermarkets and multiples selling milk cheaper – and us losing customers – and now we've just started to turn the corner."

Parker Dairies – established in 1989 by John Parker, with a single round in Dalston – now serves 12,000 customers and 80,000 pints of milk weekly with 28 rounds reaching from Romford to Westminster.

While milk magnates such as Unigate, Co-op, Dairy Crest and Express Dairies have evaporated, due in part to rounds growing bigger and bigger and service suffering as a consequence, independent companies like Parker played the long game.

"Everyone knows you can buy milk cheaper elsewhere," says Paul. "We realised we can't compete on price. We've lost that battle. But what the supermarkets will never have on us is our service."

These days that includes reaching out to younger punters; Parker Dairies now has a website where you can order milk and groceries, as well as a Twitter account, where the dairy's customers tweet pictures of their cornflakes and vintage wire baskets they've found for storing their milk. The best tweets are printed out and are stuck in the office corridor.

£2,000–£2,500 of parking tickets

Though many of the milkmen – and it is all men at Parker – commute from places like Basildon, Southend, Canvey Island and Braintree, there's an air of camaraderie in the yard. As floats pull in at the end of a shift, roundsmen chat with one another, swap stories from the week. Often these stories involve traffic wardens.

"We're having to start earlier and earlier to just get in front of the traffic and the lovely traffic wardens that give us tickets," laughs Paul, "there's no room for common sense with the traffic wardens. Obviously you can't just park your car where you want to in London. But we get out, walk 30ft to the doorstep, drop off two pints of milk and walk back.

"Last year we were probably getting £2,000–£2,500 worth of tickets."

There have been one or two problems with employees in the past, too. Someone in the office recalls being sent out to look for a new milkman who'd disappeared on his first round. They found his float in the middle of an estate, and soon after discovered their man lying on the roof of a nearby van, sunbathing. When they woke him up, he complained "I'm catching some rays, man!"

That was his first and last round. Paul's got a story of his own: "A relief chap was covering for this guy. He got to the door and there was this note in the bottle: 'To my darling Dave, if you can meet me tonight, leave the empties, if not, can you take them away.'"

So the rumours about milkmen are true then?

Paul chuckles. "Have you not seen how many ugly children there are in Waltham Forest?!"

BARS THAT FLOAT

Looking for a night out that'll really float your boat? London's bobbing with bars, pubs and cafes on boats, ships and barges, dotted along the River Thames and the city's canals.

Alfred Le Roy, Hackney Wick

When it's not cruising the River Lee Navigation and east London canals, you'll find *Alfred Le Roy* moored up alongside Crate Brewery in Hackney Wick. The cocktail bar is a versatile space, its retractable roof kept firmly on in winter to create a cosy bar vibe, and whipped off in the summer, magicking up an outside drinking area. If you want to see it in action, book onto a food and drink cruise and feel the wind in your hair as you chug up and down the canals.

Alfred Le Roy features on the Club Soda Guide – which helps mindful drinkers seek out low- and no-alcohol drinks in London – for its top-notch mocktails (see page 138 for others).
Canalside Mooring 7, Queens Yard, White Post Lane, E9 5EN

Bar & Co, Temple Pier

This vessel practically rocks when FC Barcelona are playing – it's the official home of Penya Blaugrana London, the London outpost of Barca's supporters club. Tennis, rugby and basketball are also screened regularly.

Beyond sport, *Bar & Co* is something of a party boat, with a bar, restaurant and nightclub packed into one boat-shaped fun house, moored at Temple Pier. There's a small bar on deck, but most of the action takes place down below, where up to 130 people can be found boogying at once.
Temple Pier, Victoria Embankment, WC2R 2PN

Barge East, Hackney Wick

Its elegant shape and fabric, sail-style signs always put us in mind of a pirate ship when we catch a glimpse of *Barge East*. In reality, it's an old Dutch barge, but you get the feeling that magical things could happen on board.

The excellent East London Liquor Co's products are used in the cocktails, while Truman's brews appear on the beer list. Even the tea is sourced from the London Tea Co. Local bevvies are intermingled with Dutch offerings – a nod to the vessel's heritage.

Barge East is a predominantly outdoor affair, the aforementioned sail being erected as a canopy to stave off the London chill. Fairy lights trace the ship's outline, making for romantic reflections in the water on balmy summer nights.
River Lee Sweetwater Mooring, White Post Lane, E9 5EN

Darcie & May Green, Paddington

The ever-expanding Daisy Green chain of Aussie coffee shops took to the water with *Darcie & May Green*, a pair of boats moored in Paddington Basin, overlooking the Grand Union Canal.

The barges are linked up end to end, and easily identifiable by their psychedelic livery, designed by Pop artist Sir Peter Blake. *Darcie's* your lady for all-day dining; *May's* a go-to for coffee and cocktails. You could always do a double-header.
Grand Union Canal, Sheldon Square, Paddington Central, W2 6DS

Feng Shang Princess Chinese restaurant, Regent's Park

Even with its claim to be "the best Chinese restaurant in Primrose Hill", including *Feng Shang Princess* on a list of bars feels a bit cheeky. It is predominantly a restaurant. But if we're talking floating experiences in London, it's got to get a namecheck.

Where *Feng Shang* shines is its cocktail menu, sticking firmly to the classics (think bellini, mojito, kir royale, pina colada). At just shy of £15 a pop, it's not the cheapest, but on a summer's evening, with the red Chinese lanterns swaying in the breeze, it's pretty darn atmospheric.

Southern Star Cumberland Basin, Prince Albert Road, NW1 7SS

The Milk Float, **Hackney Wick**

Moored up at Hackney Wick (yep, the canal's in demand around these parts), where the River Lee Navigation meets the Hertford Union Canal, *The Milk Float* (puntastic name…) is ideally placed for refreshments after a walk through the Olympic Park. It's a cafe and bar, so you'll find Aperol spritz and locally made ginger beer on the menu, alongside knickerbocker glorys. Thursday is tapas night, the barbecue gets fired up in summer, and if you're feeling fired up yourself, you can hire Moo Canoes from the venue and take a paddle up the canal.

River Lee Navigation, E9 5EN

R.S. *Hispaniola*, **Victoria Embankment**

"We drink beer and we drink Cola, all aboard the *Hispaniola!*"

We have no idea what that line is from – it's buried somewhere deep in our childhood, and Google's no help. But it goes through our mind every time we chug past R.S. *Hispaniola* on a Charing Cross train on Hungerford Bridge.

If the weather's decent, head to the *Hispaniola*'s Upper Deck. There's much amusement to be had up here, watching tourists on Hungerford Bridge waving at others on the boats below, and the captains honking their horns to whip their

passengers into a holiday-induced frenzy. In adverse weather, head inside to the Pinkton Parlour, where the rose-tinted decor lives up to its name.

As you can imagine, R.S. *Hispaniola*'s prime position across the river from the London Eye makes it firmly in demand on New Year's Eve. They even do a 'London Eye' cocktail. South Bank Gin can be found in several of the drinks here too, despite the vessel being moored on the North Bank.

Victoria Embankment, WC2N 5DJ

Tamesis Dock, **Lambeth**

More pub than bar, *Tamesis Dock* is a traditional boozer, with the less traditional feature of being plonked on top of the Thames. The converted 1930s Dutch barge has an eclectic collection of benches, tables and bar stools up on deck, from which you can ogle the Houses of Parliament. If the weather's not on your side, the wooden bar inside is trimmed

with everything from nautical bells and navigation maps to disco balls, pop art, and a chandelier fashioned from glass bottles. Descend the colourful stairs to a snug area crammed with charmingly mismatched leather sofas and bar stools. It's like the *Black Pearl*, but run by hipsters.

Booze-wise you're looking at beer and cider rather than margaritas and pina coladas. If you must do spirits, ask them to mix together a brandy and water, and hey presto – grog!

Albert Embankment, Lambeth, SE1 7TP

Tattershall Castle, **Victoria Embankment**

Tattershall Castle is R.S. *Hispaniola*'s raucous neighbour. Its skew-whiff chimney is a beacon to anyone looking for a nautically naughty good time – live comedy, pub quizzes, jazz footie matches (on the TV, not played on deck, unfortunately). You can even get married here. Just go easy on that bouquet throw.

The boat itself was used as a passenger ferry on the Humber Estuary in the 1970s. Its London debut was as a floating art gallery, before realising its true calling in life was serving up booze to all that sail in her. These days, gin is a prominent feature on the drinks menu; there are at least 10 varieties available to mix and match with a selection of tonics. Spritz, spirits, wines, beer, ciders and cocktails also form a compelling reason to delay your return to dry land.

Victoria Embankment, SW1A 2HR

A PUNCH THAT PINES FOR LONDON

In 1694, Admiral Edward Russell was commanded to remain in Spain over winter to trap the French fleet in the Mediterranean. He was less than happy about forfeiting Christmas in London, grumbling: "I am at present under a doubt with myself whether it is not better to die". To make a point, he petulantly threw the grandest party of the time on Westminster's account, the focal point of which was a tiled fountain filled with punch, and a small boy in a boat floating in the middle serving it to his guests.

Make Admiral Edward Russell's Punch

An aptly sized fountain may prove difficult for you to source, so here's a scaled down recipe for one…

Brew some Earl Grey tea; remove the tea bag after a minute or two so it's nice and light.
Mix 4 parts of the tea with 4 parts brandy, 2 parts lemon juice, 1 part sugar syrup and 2 parts of Oloroso sherry.
Grate in nutmeg to taste.
Stir with ice and strain over ice into a short cup, garnish with berries and you're ready to party like an admiral.

WHERE TO DRINK WHEN YOU'RE NOT DRINKING

Staying sober doesn't have to be boring.

"It's Pepsi, is that OK?"

A familiar refrain if you're swerving alcohol (see also: "What, not even beer?" and "Oh, but you will if I slip some vodka into your lemonade"). If you're avoiding booze, be it for health or religious reasons, or simply because *whisper it* you don't like the taste, London can feel a lonely place. A parched wasteland in a sea of craft beers, flavoured gins and ever-more-convoluted cocktails. Even the museums have bars. So what's one to do for a teetotal night out with more than a watered-down OJ for company?

Alcohol-free bars

The obvious answer is to move your date/mates meet-up to an alcohol-free bar. London's not exactly flush with these, perhaps because 'alcohol-free bar' doesn't make for a sensible business plan. The only people we're aware of making it work is Redemption Bar, a mini-chain with branches in Notting Hill, Shoreditch and Covent Garden.

Technically it's a restaurant-bar. The food side of things is vegan, gluten-free and low in unrefined sugars, while the bar doesn't serve a drop of the demon drink. Instead, the menu's heavy in smoothies, alcohol-free wine and beer, and 'fruities', Redemption's own take on the mocktail. Refresh yourself with an apple mockjito – apple presse, fresh mint and lime, and sparkling mineral water – as you wallow in righteousness.

Alcohol-free restaurants

London's home to number of alcohol-free restaurants, and awash with BYOB establishments. If you're not interested in booze – don't bring any. Simple. (Note: scrounging a glass of vino from the couple at the next table halfway through the meal is frowned upon.)

Ace Cafe – limited alcohol

The bikers' haunt on the North Circular near Stonebridge Park (Ace Corner, N Circular Rd, NW10 7UD) isn't completely alcohol-free, but options are limited – which make sense when you think that most of the customers drive (or ride) there. Focus instead on steaming mugs of tea and towering knickerbocker glories, washed down with some 1950s rockabilly.

Bonnington Cafe, Vauxhall – BYO

Kitsch veggie/vegan eatery Bonnington Cafe (11 Vauxhall Grove, SW8 1TD) is an unlicensed premises. It's also a budget-friendly place for dinner, as it's community-focused, with a rotating team of local members chipping in with the cooking. Just don't let them rope you into doing it.

Govinda's, Soho – alcohol-free

Soho's veggie restaurant Govinda's (9–10 Soho St, W1D 3DL) is part of the Radha-Krishna Temple, which belongs to the Hare Krishna spiritual movement. You'll often see/hear them banging their mridanga drums outside. The menu is predominantly Indian (daals, paneers), but other cuisines are available. Drinks are purely hot (try the barley coffee) or soft – no alcohol.

Persepolis, Peckham – BYO

Sally Butcher's legendary Persian cornershop/restaurant Persepolis (28–30 Peckham High St, SE15 5DT) operates a BYO policy. Bevvies on the menu include fragrant Persian tea with cardamom, mango smoothie, and sour cherry juice.

With a selection that tantalising, why bother bringing wine?

Tayyabs, Whitechapel – BYO

BYO curry houses can be sniffed out around town, but if you want some serious quality lamb chops head to Tayyabs (83–89 Fieldgate St, E1 1JU), Whitechapel's famed North Indian restaurant. And order a banana lassi while you're at it.

London's best mocktails and alcohol-free beers and spirits

If you're happy for those around you to carry on making merry while you indulge in non-alcoholic alternatives, seek out London's best mocktails and alcohol-free beers. Most watering holes have a token mocktail or two on the menu, but others go all out in making teetotal customers as welcome as their beer-swigging chums…

Bar Three, Spitalfields

The cocktail menu at this minimal basement bar (65a Brushfield St, E1 6AA) is split into four denominations of booziness – 'free', 'light', 'medium' and 'full'. There are only three drinks in the 'free' section (Spritz, Lemonade, and Sling), but the bartenders know their way around a shaker, and it feels rather fancier than someone throwing some orange juice and lemonade into a glass and charging you £8 for the privilege. The lemonade, for example, blends lemon thyme with elderflower and soda for a tipple that'll have you dreaming of sultry summer days. You won't get that from R. White's.

The Book Club, Shoreditch

With a reputation as a party animals' haunt, The Book Club (100–106 Leonard St, EC2A 4RH) is surprisingly adept at catering to the booze-free. It offers an entire zero proof menu, heavily reliant on Sipmith's range of imitation 'spirits' to add some zing to your night of speed-dating/salsa dancing/life drawing. Alcohol-free versions of a martini and a spritz are available, but for something that'll make your friends go "ooh, what's that?" order a lavender lemonade: apple juice, lavender syrup and soda combine for a refreshing concoction that's happily nothing like your grandma's bath salts.

Cocktail Lounge at Zetter Townhouse, Clerkenwell

This vermillion-painted cocktail bar (49–50 St John's Square, EC1V 4JJ) –

named curiously after a 'Wicked Uncle Seymour' – offers an impressive list of non-alcoholic cocktails. A Virgin Mary (the teetotaller's classic) is available, alongside a fig leaf lemonade, elderflower fizz, and other concoctions that sound infinitely more interesting than a Diet Coke.

The Connaught, Mayfair

The Connaught (Carlos Place, W1K 2AL) boasts its own house-distilled gin, so serious is it about tippling. But patrons wishing to keep a clear head are also catered for. The cocktail menu is divvied into several sections, with at least one alcohol-free option in each. The Glossy comes in a coppery-red hue shade (designed to match the decoration of the bar) and consists of red berry kombucha, milk oolong tea, Amalfi lemon leaf syrup and pink grapefruit juice. The Smooth Mover is a refreshing blend of salted cacao coconut water, eucalyptus syrup and lime juice. Before you go thirstily bounding over there, know that prices average £12 for one of these mocktails.

The Permit Room at Dishoom, Shoreditch

Want to know a dirty little secret? Dishoom's Permit Room (7 Boundary St, E2 7JE). Designed to replicate the 'permit rooms' of prohibition-era Bombay, where only those with a permit were served booze, it focuses on hardcore traditional cocktails – juleps, old fashioneds and the like. So far, so tipsy, but there's an extensive 'Dry Tipples' menu too, offering sober alternatives. Think Sober Martini and Dry Old Fashioned. It's hard to believe there's no alcohol involved, but it's true.

If booze-free beer is more your bag, keep an eye out for products from these companies on your next night out:

Nirvana Brewery
Leyton-based Nirvana Brewery create entirely non-alcoholic beer, inspired by the entirely uninspiring range that was available until recently. Pale ales, lagers, stouts and IPAs are all available in 0% form. No more Beck's Blue for you.

Small Beer Brew Co.
Small Beer Brew Co. specialise in 'small beers' – that's beer with 0.5%–2.8% ABV (and the same kind of beer they were feeding babies with in Shakespeare's day). It's stocked at selected pubs and beer shops. Keep an eye out.

Drink different

If nothing so far floats your boat, don't fret – here are some places with such outstanding non-alcoholic drinks, you'll be glad you're swerving booze.

"Go hard or go home" doesn't just apply to 2am sambuca shots. Milkshakes, freakshakes and smoothies all count as 'upping your drinking game' as far as we're concerned. Load up on sugar and fruit in liquid form at the following venues… just brace yourself for a sugar crash:

Freakshakes at Maxwell's Covent Garden
This American grill (34 King St, WC2E 8JD) has a regularly rotating menu of completely OTT freakshakes. Garishly colourful, drowning in sugar, and towering high with sweet goodies that definitely don't belong in a drink – exactly how a freakshake should be. If you're into American food – juicy burgers, messy ribs, crunchy onion rings – you're in the right place. But be warned: the freakshake is a meal in itself.

American diner milkshakes
We've lost count of the times we've eaten at an American diner with a friend who orders a pretentiously hip imported craft beer, only to catch them enviously ogling our milkshake. Well guess what? *Londonist* doesn't share food. You want your dinner with a side of milkshake? Get your own.

For our money, you'll get some of the best milkshakes at **The Diner** chain. Around nine flavours are usually available (with some vegan options too), but through rigorous tasting, we've reached the conclusion that mint choc chip is the best accompaniment for a carb-heavy meal. For a retro experience, make yours a Coke float.

Tinseltown and **Shake Shack** are also excellent milkshake options.

Juices at Yeotown Kitchen
If you're off booze for health reasons, we salute you. You won't be left wanting for health-focused juice bars in this city, but

one that stands out is Yeotown Kitchen (42 Chiltern St, W1U 7QT) – and not just for some of the names (Medicinal Mushroom Latte, anyone? How about a Sun Warrior Protein?). The Marylebone wellbeing venue offers meditation classes as well as an extensive health food menu. Smoothies, superfood smoothies, 'Yeotinis' and 'adaptogenic lattes' (no, we don't know either) are all alcohol-free. Probably good for you, too.

Bubble tea
Bubble tea is worth trying once, just for the sheer taste, texture and colour pile-up. This Taiwanese invention tends to be sweet, containing grains of tapioca 'bubbles', and is available in countless flavours (mango, rose, honey oolong, Earl Grey – the list goes on). You can usually mix and match your base flavour with your bubble flavour. **Mooboo**, with venues in Camden and Harrow, **Biju** in

South Kensington, Soho and Westfield, and **Bubbleology** (many branches) are all solid – well, liquid – options.

Kombucha

Let's talk about kombucha, shall we? The fermented tea drink has been filtering its way into the London mainstream for a few years now, and while the fermentation process does release a small amount of alcohol, it's negligible, and the drink is often heralded as a booze alternative. It's increasingly being used as a mocktail ingredient too.

Wild Fizz Kombucha is a north-London based kombucha brewer. You can order for home delivery, or get in touch and they'll point you in the direction of your nearest stockist. Alternatively, Europe's first kombucha tap room, **Jarr Kombucha** in Hackney Wick (8a Queen's Yard, E9 5EN), is open to visitors, while Caravan – the coffee connoisseur, found across the city – has earned itself a reputation as one of the best places for chugging kombucha in the capital.

Little Duck Picklery, Soho and Dalston

"Drinking vinegars, elixirs and infused kombuchas" is the way Little Duck Picklery describes the drinks served at its two restaurants, **Ducksoup** in Soho (41 Dean St, W1D 4PY) and **Little Duck** in Dalston (68 Dalston Ln, E8 3AH).

Yes, wine is on the menu too, but let's focus on the other drinks. It's all fermented in-house, and changes seasonally, but an example menu includes pear and celery kombucha, and quince or cranberry drinking vinegars.

Late-night activities that don't involve alcohol

Who says a night out with friends has to revolve around bars and pubs at all? London's got plenty of other venues open all evening, ideal for meeting up for a catch up, or even a date.

Late night coffee shops and bakeries

Some of London's late night coffee shops do serve booze (the Grind chain, for example, as well as legendary venues Bar Italia and Scooter Caffe). So if you want a completely alcohol-free venue, it's worth checking before you go. Your best bet, if you're not too much of a coffee snob, is the large chains. **Starbucks** on Kingsway is open until 10pm, and the Embankment branch stays open until 11pm, with various **Caffe Nero** and **Costa** branches echoing these hours, particularly in central London.

Soho's **Hummingbird Bakery** is open until 8pm six days a week, and we cannot over-exaggerate how much we advocate swapping a post-work pint for a post-work slice of rainbow cake. Fancy cake-and-coffee shop **L'Eto** stays open late (11pm in Soho and Brompton), and cafe-du-jour **EL&N** (239 Brompton Rd, SW3 2EP) is open until midnight, giving you approximately seven hours of post-work coffee-quaffing (and cake-munching) time.

Tea bars

Previously a reserve for Great Aunt Mildred and her chums, tea bars are becoming hip and… no, wait, hear us out. Covent Garden is now home to huge tea emporium, **Mariage Frères** (38 King St, WC2E 8JS), with its own tea salon open until 10pm every night.

For daytime booze-dodging, the **Yumchaa** mini-chain and **Good & Proper** in Clerkenwell (96 Leather Ln, EC1N 7TX) are excellent choices for tea lovers, each offering a dazzling array of leaves, while later into the evening you can pick up dinner and a cuppa at Vauxhall's **Tea House Theatre** (139 Vauxhall Walk, SE11 5HL). Even Whittard is in on the act, its **Covent Garden Tea Bar** (17 The Marketplace, WC2E 8RB) serving up tea and cake until 8pm most nights.

Late night ice cream

At most of London's ice cream bars and gelaterias the closest you'll get to alcohol is a scoop of rum and raisin, and many are open until late, particularly in the summer.

Venetian import **Grom** (16–18 Piccadilly, W1J 0DF) serves until 11pm, and if you take your scoops to go, you might just make it to Green Park before it melts. Similarly, **Gelupo** (7 Archer St, W1D 7AU) near Piccadilly Circus opens until 11pm/midnight depending on the day, with a menu that changes daily and unusual flavours including avocado, and roasted plum.

WORKING MEN'S CLUBS: STILL A THING IN LONDON

The nature of drinking in London has changed radically over time. To many working-class citizens across the city, their regular was a working men's club; pay an annual membership, in return for cheap beer and quality bantz, year-round.

Nowadays these clubs have dwindled in number, thanks in part to the rise of inexpensive supermarket alcohol. But it's also due to the changing demographics in the make-up of London's working class, and gentrification in traditional working-class areas.

Dave's map shows where you can still find working men's clubs in London. Some of these are ex-working men's clubs, turned into regular pubs – but retain that nostalgic working men's club vibe. Others are a very 21st-century take on what a 'working men's' club can be.

Bethnal Green Working Men's Club

Perhaps the best-known of London's working men's clubs, though that name is used loosely. Bethnal Green Working Men's Club hosts everything from *Twin Peaks* fan nights to Disney drag acts. This was once a more traditional working men's club, dating back to 1887 – and though we're not sure how many old-school East End geezers are left, the community spirit lives on. You'll spot the club from the Banksy sprayed on the side.

42–44 Pollard Row, E2 6NB

Illustration by Dave Draws Ltd

Catford Constitutional, Catford

An odd assortment of images pepper the walls at the Catford Constitutional. Churchill and Lenin rub shoulders with vintage *Private Eye* covers, along with someone's personal family photos from the 70s. Yes, this is an Antic conversion so there's a bit of a faux sense of the past at play. However, this was once a real functioning constitutional club, and Antic saved it after it was left derelict for 20 years. Bravo indeed.

Catford Broadway, SE6 4SP

East Finchley Constitutional Club

A club for the community – that's the aim of East Finchley Constitutional Club. The venue hosts music and dance nights, quizzes… and even baby and toddler classes (doubt you'd have got *those* back in the day). Whatever takes your fancy, one thing remains the same; the relaxed atmosphere. Make an afternoon of it by stacking up coins on the side of the snooker table, or leaf through a paper in the spacious garden.

The Walks, N2 8DE

Effra Social, Brixton

Another Antic conversion, the Effra Social dates back to the Victorian era when it was a Conservative club. Apparently Churchill and John Major occasionally drank here (not together). Some might take that to mean that the Effra is posh, but allow us to assure you it's nothing of the sort. It's got that small hall feeling about it and, most importantly, a stage, which is put to good use with regular DJ nights, reggae sets, dances, quizzes and film clubs.

99 Effra Road, SW2 1 DF

Mildmay Club, Stoke Newington

Dating back to 1888, the Mildmay Club takes its history seriously. At the club's peak, it had more than 3,000 members, and is always on the lookout for photographs and memories from the club's past. That's not to say this is a place in decline. It's currently growing and has live entertainment every Saturday night. Warning: joining the club is no easy feat – you must find a member to nominate you and another to second that nomination, the traditional way. See also: our piece on gentlemen's clubs, page 97.

33–34 Newington Green, N16 9PR

MOTH Club, Hackney

MOTH Club is a glittering beacon in Hackney that draws in those east-London types like an eponymous moth to a light. Except that's not what MOTH Club's name is about at all. It actually stands for Memorable Order of Tin Hats – a military veteran's club that originates in South Africa. Nowadays it hosts gigs and club nights from acts who play before a tinsely backdrop. That doesn't mean the venue has shed all its old-school punters; they can still be found in the bar at the front.

MOTH Club, Valette Street, E9 6NU

Norfolk House Constitutional Club, Peckham

Norfolk House is another ex-Conservative club, established in the back garden of a house on Queen's Road, more than 70 years ago. Like many clubs from the time, originally women weren't allowed to be members. That stuff doesn't fly in the 21st century, and Norfolk House is now a welcoming place to all. Among the members is a branch of the Royal Antediluvian Order of Buffaloes, colloquially known as the Buffs – a fraternal organisation a bit like the Masons.

188 Queen's Road, SE15 2HP

Peckham Liberal Club

In a time before gentrification, Peckham was a proper working class area, as demonstrated by working men's club, Peckham Liberal. This place is a rare breed, owing to the fact it's still functioning as such – an annual membership of £25 gets you drinks for prices long-thought outlawed in London. When they're not shooting film scenes, you can come and indulge yourself in the strains of local 'band', the Peckham Chamber Orchestra. Just don't expect to escape Peckham's hipsters. They've cottoned onto this place.

24 Elm Grove, SE15 5DE

Plumstead Radical Club

Plumstead Radical is another club where history intertwines with politics. The Radicals were working class liberals who eventually affiliated to the Labour party. Again, politics have faded, and the club has other priorities nowadays. Like

karaoke and table tennis. Hats off to the plum-coloured insignia across the door.

83–88 Walmer Terrace, SE18 7DZ

Teddington Constitutional Club

An outlier when it comes to these clubs, for two reasons. First, geography – Teddington Constitutional Club is in west London where our map is otherwise rather bare. Secondly, it's an old-school club that serves real ale, whereas other clubs tend to rely on mainstream lager and… well, that's about it.

5 Stanley Road, TW11 8TP

Walthamstow Trades Hall

Like an old-school working men's club, you can buy membership here, earning you massive discounts for events at the club. Said events are massively varied: bingo nights, ceilidh evenings, and plenty of chances to get your boogie on. Said boogying is often to 'Barry's Magic Sounds'.

61–63 Tower Hamlets Road, E17 4RQ

Willesden Working Men's Club

Union Jacks galore. That's the look at Willesden Working Men's Club, the kind of patriotic club that holds a party for the centenary of the end of the World War I. The club's a real community, organising trips away to the seaside and jaunts to the gee-gees. Along with that it's a good spot for lovers of a raffle, shove ha'penny (old skool), and hosts a regular chess club for adults and children. This is the place to break out your Sicilian Defense. It's also the only place on this map to provide a backdrop for a Q-Tip video.

202 Villiers Road, NW2 5PU

Wood Green Social Club

To balance out the number of ex-Conservative clubs on this list, here's one with links to the Labour party. Once upon a time this was a terrible place to get a drink; one of the founding members was a teetotaller and the club was dry for over 25 years. Eventually, that changed, partially to recognise the fact that beer was the drink of the working classes. And you can still get a pint there today, something many choose to do before or after a Spurs game.

3–4 Stuart Crescent, N22 5NJ

BIZARRE AND BEAUTIFUL DRINKING TRADITIONS

Traditions and rituals are an integral part of London's drinking culture. Everything from cosying up in our preferred pub snug, to the splitting of a packet of crisps to share/not actually share with the table.

Another ritual dear to our own heart is disappearing off to the loos when it's our round. Some of London's traditions are downright bonkers though. See for yourself.

The Twelfth Night, Bankside

A blend of ancient midwinter customs and contemporary festivity unfolds each January on Bankside. Things kick off outside Shakespeare's Globe with the arrival of the Holly Man (the winter guise of the Green Man). He comes by rowboat – it was so choppy one year, we wondered if he'd actually make it to shore.

He's decked out in foliage and accompanied by the devil Beelzebub and other eccentrically dressed associates, who join together to Wassail, or toast, the people. There's singing, dancing and a play to enjoy before the crowning of a king and queen for the day, who lead everyone down to the 17th-century George Inn. Once at the pub there's storytelling, more dancing, the Kissing Wishing Tree (your guess is as good as ours…) and, thankfully, gallons of mulled wine.

Where: Outside Shakespeare's Globe and then onto the George Inn (see page 160)
When: Early January

Ceremony of the Widow's Bun, Bow

A tradition birthed by a tragedy. Or a supposed tragedy, because nobody has ever ascertained the veracity of the tale. The story goes that a widow once lived on the site where the pub now stands. Her only son served in the Navy, but every Easter, he'd dutifully return home for one of his mother's (presumably delicious) hot cross buns. One year – possibly during the Napoleonic Wars – he didn't come back. The heartbroken mother continued to bake a bun for him every year.

The house was demolished in 1848 to make way for the pub, and a store comprising dozens of these buns was discovered. The pub landlords decided to continue the widow's tradition, varnishing the old buns and hanging them from a net dangling over the rafters, along with a new one each Good Friday (baked with the date on top). The honour of hanging the new bun now goes to a member of the Navy each year – they're raised aloft by their colleagues. Boxes of freshly baked buns are handed out afterwards.

Where: The Widow's Son, Bow (E3 3PJ)
When: Good Friday

Swearing on the Horns, Highgate

Ever wanted to kick a pig out of a ditch in Highgate? Here's your chance. The Swearing on the Horns is an entirely farcical affair, in which people gain the freedom of Highgate by swearing an oath on a set of horns. Said oath is comprised of absolute gibberish, and the most famous line goes something like this:

"You must not eat brown bread while you can get white, except you like the brown the best."

Get the gist? Good, neither do we. At the end of it all, you're rewarded with the aforementioned pig-kicking-right, if you're in dire need of somewhere to sleep. There are few other bits of nonsense to speak and a few more 'rights' earned by swearing on the 'magical' horns.

Swearing on the Horns dates back hundreds of years, but throughout that time it's always been somewhat slapstick. Nowadays it has a tendency to bounce around a few pubs in Highgate: The Duke's Head, The Wrestlers and The Bull have all held the ceremony in recent years.

Where: Certain Highgate pubs

When: various

The Pineapple's Easter bonnet competition, Kentish Town

This competition launched in 1964 and, despite a few years off here and there, is still going strong today. It's a chance to flex your creative muscles and come up the maddest hats imaginable.

Word of warning: don't try to get away with gluing a few random bits and bobs to a straw hat. People take this thing seriously – a kid once turned up wearing a pterodactyl-inspired creation with a built-in squawking mechanism. Probably didn't even win.

Where: The Pineapple, Kentish Town (NW5 2NX)

When: Easter

The Alexandra's Christmas meal, Wimbledon

For many, Christmas centres around one feeling: loneliness. The Alexandra in Wimbledon wants to change that, and every Christmas Day it lays on a free lunch for those who'd otherwise be spending the day alone. People are seated together in an aim to get them talking and do away with festive loneliness.

Christmas loneliness is often thought of as something that afflicts people in their later years, but The Alex serves anyone who comes through the door solo, no matter their age. In past years that has included a student who missed the last train home, and an unfortunate soul who got dumped on Christmas Eve.

Where: The Alexandra, Wimbledon (see page 104)

When: Christmas Day

The Soho Waiter's Race

Since the 1950s, waiters have dashed through the streets of Soho every year, bubbly teetering on tray, for the Waiter's Race. It's a sprint through one of London's best-known drinking districts in a bid to be the fastest. And, of course, you mustn't spill any of that precious fizz. Back in the day, things were more formal; Google the 1959 footage and you'll see contestants in immaculate tailcoats. The rules state that the race must be run in a waiter's work attire, but these days that often means t-shirts and trainers. Oh, and that bottle of champagne has been downgraded to a bottle of prosecco –

we're not quite as extravagant as our forefathers. Other than that, not much has changed.

Here's the rub: you have to be a waiter in the Soho area to participate. However, everyone is invited to watch. Just be sure to give the waiters as wide a berth as possible – you don't want to ruin their shot at eternal glory. Or get prosecco spilt on you. Or maybe you do.

Where: The streets of Soho

When: Mid-July

The Grenadier's banknotes, Belgravia

Secreted away on a cobbled mews in Belgravia sits The Grenadier. It's home to a tradition that people from all over the world have taken part in, even if they don't all know the reason behind it. The tradition involves sticking signed banknotes to the ceiling.

At first glance, this appears to be a monetary spin on a common tradition – plenty of bars around the world invite tourists to sign their names on cash. However, there's a story behind what happens at the Grenadier that sets this apart: the tradition of pasting up banknotes allegedly started as a way to pay back a debt owed by the pub's resident ghost, Cedric (see page 121 for the whole story), so his soul could move on. Alas, it's never quite enough, and to this day he lingers. Apparently.

Where: The Grenadier

When: Make your contribution to Cedric's debt anytime the pub's open.

A BLUE POSTS
PUB CRAWL

Ever noticed the West End's preponderance of drinking dens called 'The Blue Posts'?
There are three in Soho alone, plus one in St James and one in Fitzrovia.

A sixth on the corner of Tottenham Court Road and Hanway Street closed down in the 1990s. Much further back, a Two Blue Posts pub could be found on Old Bond Street, while an Old Blue Posts, famous for its dining room, closed round the corner in Cork Street in 1911.

Why are there so many pubs called the Blue Posts?

An old legend suggested that blue posts were once used to demarcate the boundary of a royal hunting ground. The theory is alluring – Soho supposedly takes its name from an old hunting cry – but it begins to look a little shaky when the pubs are plotted on a map (see right). This is a somewhat irregular space in which to hunt, and pays no heed to any of the ancient lanes that bordered the area.

The second explanation – backed up, possibly, by hanging signs – has blue posts as the forerunners of taxi ranks. Sedan chairs could be hired from any location sporting an azure bollard. We're slightly skeptical. In the absence of any primary account that mentions such posts (that we're aware of), might these places have taken their names simply as a way of identifying them before the advent of door numbers?

A pub crawl of Blue Posts
Blue Posts, 81 Newman Street

This Blue Posts was once full of blue posties, thanks to its proximity to an old mail depot (since demolished). It's a quaint place, with the usual charm and low prices of the Sam Smith's chain. On our Saturday visit, the place was so empty that the staff were playing darts. In busier times, the burgundy ceiling, cosy seating and wooden panelling offer atmospheric surroundings in which to enjoy a cheap ale. The pub carries an attractive hanging sign, which seems to confirm the meaning of the Blue Posts as a mounting site for sedan chairs.
W1T 3ET

Illustration by JANE SMITH

The Blue Posts, 22 Berwick Street

This tiny pub in the duodenum of Soho is what lazy reviewers might call 'a good-old-fashioned boozer'. Blue number two is pokey, bathed at night in hazy red lighting, and sports a collection of wall-mounted plates from the Sunday supplements. It feels welcoming and local. That's if you make it through the door. With frosted glass all around, the place can look like it's shut during the day.
W1F 0QA

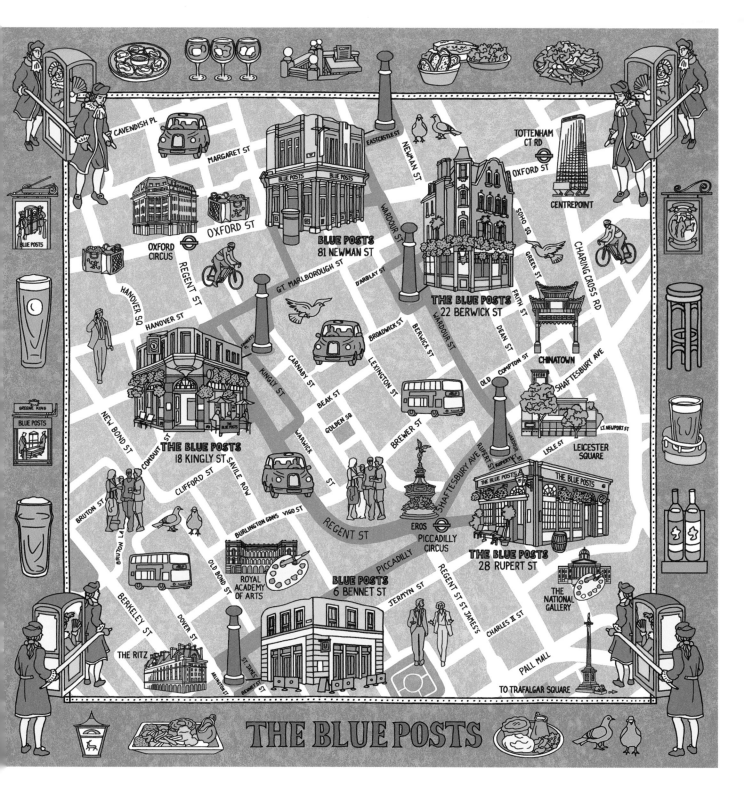

THE BLUE POSTS

The Blue Posts, 18 Kingly Street

Carnaby Street might be world famous, but its parallel sibling is much better-stocked with booze. We've visited this branch of the Blue Posts non-franchise more than any other, and always find a table no matter how bustling the rest of Soho might be. That said, the handsome Victorian exterior does draw its fair share of tourists seeking to experience the authentic British pub. They could do a lot worse than this place, well-stocked for a Greene King pub. Look out for the hanging sign, which again shows two men carrying a lady in a sedan chair.

W1B 5PX

The Blue Posts, 28 Rupert Street

A short belch down the road brings us to our third instalment. This iteration (established 1739) underwent a total transformation in early 2018 and couldn't be more different from its Berwick Street namesake. Gone is the crowded, almost charming hangout of former times, replaced with something altogether sleeker and more modern. This pint-sized boozer has the feel more of a cocktail bar than a pub, and it's a pleasant surprise to spot several cask ales from independent brewers behind the bar. Further up-market drinking and dining spaces can be found in the basement and first floor. This is by far the swankiest of the BPs, and it's also the bluest, with a striking paint job on the outside.

W1D 6DJ

Blue Posts, 6 Bennet Street

And so we reach the last Posts. Another variation on the hanging sign awaits us. This is the best yet for bollard fans, with the blue markers placed centre of the scene. This pub has the distinction of being both the newest and oldest Blue Posts. A pub of that name has stood here since 1667, and the previous version once housed a sedan chair in its entrance. The current building is, however, only a few years old. The rebuild has added some character to what was once a bland, forgettable place. A faux-Georgian ceiling (almost blue in hue) and smart decor provide a bright, airy feel.

By this point in the pub crawl, five drinks in, you might want to order your own sedan chair, or at least an Uber, to convey yourself home.

SW1A 1RP

FICTIONAL PUBS:
AN IMAGINARY CRAWL

Some of London's finest – and indeed most notorious – pubs never actually existed.
From speakeasies frequented by wizards to bars that get blown to Kingdom Come; read your way through
these, and expect one hell of a fictional hangover tomorrow.

The Black Cross, *London Fields*
What with its fruit machine-fiddling clientele and iffy pork pie bar snacks, we've all unwittingly stepped into a Black Cross pub once or twice in our time. The setting for Martin Amis' black comedy has especially bleak consequences for Nicola Six, who finds the person who she knows is going to murder her boozing here. Does this Portobello Road pub take its inspiration from a place that once stood here, called The Golden Cross? Quite possibly.

The Duke of Burgundy,
Passport to Pimlico
A piano-jangling knees-up in this 1949 Ealing Comedy sees punters gleefully tear up their identity cards and toss them in the air like confetti. The reason? Pimlico is legally declared part of Burgundy, and the residents shun post-war rationing quicker than you can say 'Stanley Holloway'. Reminds us of when we were students, and the 24-hour drinking laws came into effect.

Korova Milk Bar,
A Clockwork Orange
It's hard to forget the icy glare of Alex at the start of Stanley Kubrick's adaptation of *A Clockwork Orange*. Alex and his droogs slurp drug-laced milk at the mannequin-festooned Korova Milk Bar, while pondering their next bout of ultraviolence on the streets of London. There's a Korova restaurant in Tufnell Park these days, although you'll have to settle for a negroni, over moloko plus.

The Leaky Cauldron,
Harry Potter
With The Leaky Cauldron, J K Rowling essentially invented the contemporary speakeasy. Think about it: stepping through an unmarked door in the City, into a candlelit den full of men in beards, knocking back curious concoctions? Sounds like a speakeasy to us.
You can get a 'real' Butterbeer these days, although you'll have to travel to the Potter studios in Watford to sink one. Plenty of other copyright-dodging,

pseudo-Potter cocktails can be found elsewhere in London.

The Lion and Unicorn,
The Long Good Friday
This fictional pub from the Bob Hoskins/ Helen Mirren gangster flick, based in London's Docklands, makes The Black Cross look like a safe bet. Spoiler: it gets blown to smithereens.

The Moon Under Water, a 1946 essay by George Orwell
Orwell's *Nineteen Eighty-Four* has 'the proles' pub, likely based on the Newman Arms in Fitzrovia (this also appeared in the film *Peeping Tom*). But his real masterstroke was The Moon Under Water, a dream bar that he concocted for an essay. Beer is served in "pleasant strawberry-pink china". There's no music. The barmaids are all middle-aged and two of them "have their hair dyed in quite surprising shades". The pub sells tobacco, aspirins, stamps and liver-sausage sandwiches. Wetherspoon founder

Tim Martin based his first pubs on Orwell's boozetopia, naming some of them The Moon Under Water – including the one you'll find in Leicester Square. Don't bother asking them to serve your bitter in strawberry-pink china, though.

The Nag's Head,
Only Fools and Horses
Nope, this is not the setting of Del Boy's epic falling through the bar (that's at some yuppy bar, remember?). The Nag's Head does, however, feature some of *Only Fool's* funniest scenes. Such as the time that Trigger talks to landlord Mike about the sex of Rodney's baby: "If it's a girl they're calling her Sigourney after an actress, and if it's a boy they're naming him Rodney… after Dave." There's an actual Nag's Head in Peckham, although as far as we know, David Jason never set foot in it.

The Queen Vic, *EastEnders*
"GET OUTTA MY PUB!" Nothing like a good East End welcome is there? Albert Square's regally named local has been the setting for rows, fires, murders, divorces, cancelled Christmasses and innumerable tomato juices for Dot Cotton. Landlords/ ladies have come and gone but Peggy Mitchell will always be the Queen, thanks to the chirpy way in which she liked to turf people out on their ear. *EastEnders* has had a number of fictional bars over the decades. Anyone remember The Dagmar? To be fair, it was only open from 1987–1988.

Samoan Joe's, *Lock, Stock and Two Smoking Barrels*
"You could fall in love with an orangutan in that". Chances are some of you have quoted Jason Statham's character in *Lock Stock*, having been presented with a particularly foliage-heavy cocktail. Decades on from this gangster classic, London still suffers from a tragic dearth of Samoan pubs.

Six Jolly Fellowship Porters,
Our Mutual Friend
"A tavern of a dropsical appearance" is how Charles Dickens rather glumly describes the Six Jolly Fellowship Porters – the pub in which shady folk assemble to fish corpses out of the Thames. It's based on a bricks-and-mortar pub – the narrow The Grapes (see page 50) in Limehouse, now part-owned by a man who appeared as David Copperfield back in 1962 – Sir Ian McKellen.

The Swan and Paedo, *Peep Show*
There's a litany of fictional sitcom pubs to drink in: The Kebab and Calculator from *The Young Ones*. The Hand and Racquet from *Hancock's Half Hour*. The Vigilante from *Citizen Smith*. The Skinner's Arms from *Steptoe and Son*. The Frog and Nightgown from *Ray's a Laugh* (us neither). But surely the greatest sitcom pub that ever was (while it existed for a small portion of series three, episode two of *Peep Show*), was The Swan and Paedo. When the ownership of a boozer falls into the unlikely hands of ne'er-do-wells

Jez and Super Hans, the former wants to call it The Swan and Tomato, while Hans is set on Free the Paedos. The resulting portmanteau tells you exactly why you should never settle on a compromise.

The Tabard, *The Canterbury Tales*
"Bifel that in that season on a day, In Southwerk at the Tabard as I lay, Redy to wenden on my pilgrymage". Although Chaucer's *Canterbury Tales* is a seminal work of fiction – in which characters try to out-story one another in the hope of scoring a free meal – The Tabard was very much a real place. Founded around 1300, it was rebuilt after the Great Fire of Southwark in 1669, and finally demolished in 1873 – presumably because its rickety old galleried ways were too comely for this world. Its neighbour, the George, remains open to thirsty pilgrims.

The Winchester Tavern,
Shaun of the Dead
Somewhere that's familiar, you know where the exits are and you're allowed to smoke (pre-smoking ban), The Winchester Tavern is supposed to be the perfect place for Simon Pegg, Nick Frost and co to have a pint and wait for the zombie apocalypse to blow over. Of course, things don't go quite according to plan: bring on the finest ever use of pool cues, Queen's 'Don't Stop Me Now' and a cast of living dead.

THE BARTENDER AND THE STAR

Ada "Coley" Coleman was the Savoy's first female head bartender – and in her time mixed drinks for Mark Twain, Marlene Dietrich, Charlie Chaplin and the Prince of Wales. Her most famous creation is the Hanky Panky, a bittersweet elixir created especially for stage actor/director/producer/manager Sir Charles Hawtrey (no relation to *Carry On* star Charles Hawtrey, who nicked his name). After he demanded something "with a bit of punch in it", Coley came up with this. Hawtrey drained the glass, exclaiming "By Jove! This is the real hanky-panky!"

Make a Hanky Panky

40ml gin
40ml sweet vermouth
2 dashes Fernet Branca
Stir with ice and strain into a coupe glass.
Add a twist of orange peel

40ml GIN

SAVOY

40ml SWEET VERMOUTH

SAVOY

TWIST OF ORANGE PEEL

SAVOY

COUPE GLASS

SAVOY

2 DASHES FERNET BRANCA

SAVOY

HEAD

LONDON'S MOST EXTRAVAGANT DRINKING EXPERIENCES

Prepare to behold some of the fanciest thirst-quenchers that have ever graced the capital – some of which you can sample today. If your wallet's up to the task.

One afternoon in 2001, six bankers made a £44k dent in the wine cellar at Gordon Ramsay's Michelin-starred Pétrus restaurant. That included a 1982 Montrachet for £1,400, and three bottles of Pétrus Pomerol ranging from £9,400 to £12,300 each. It wasn't deemed a great PR stunt, and five of the wayward bankers were subsequently given the boot. Perhaps the sixth was on the tap water.

You needn't raid a posh wine cellar to spend a pretty penny, though...

Beer fit for a Pharaoh at Harrods

With all the plotting, intrigue and fratricide that comes with being an ancient Egyptian royal, is it any wonder that a pharaoh would want a to crack open a cold one after a hard day of presiding over his empire? While Harrods' Tutankhamun Ale wasn't actually plucked from the tomb of the famous king, it was recreated "from sediment residues in old jars found in a brewery inside the Sun Temple of Nefertiti, queen of the Pharaoh Akenaten, believed to be King Tut's father". It also followed an Ancient Egyptian recipe. This pseudo-exotic concoction, brewed in Edinburgh, was dreamt up by then-Harrods owners, the Al Fayed brothers in 1996. The first bottle sold for an eye-watering £5k.

A real diamond of a cocktail at Park Tower Knightsbridge

Punters who plumped for The Park Tower Knightsbridge's Diamond Cocktail had to sip carefully, lest they ended up swallowing an actual jewel alongside their champagne and cognac elixir. If you didn't choke to death on a precious stone, the £4k bill might have done the trick. The bar is now defunct.

A very posh pot of tea at Royal China Club

Fancy a cuppa? In 2014, reports emerged that London's Royal China Club was pouring out Da Hong Pao tea for £180 a pot. Grown in the Wuyi mountains of southern China, this dark oolong tea is the most expensive in the world. Its history is steeped in legend, with one story alleging that Da Hong Pao cured the ailing mother of a Ming Dynasty emperor, who was so grateful, he ordered that the tea bushes be draped in imperial scarlet robes as a token of respect. The tea's name loosely translates as 'Big Red Robe'.

A cocktail more than two centuries in the making

The ingredients in Salvatore Calabrese's record-breaking cocktail span three whole centuries. A splash of 1770 Kummel Liqueur, some 1860 orange curaçao, and two dashes of early 1900s Angostura bitters were mixed with 1778 Clos de Griffier Vieux Cognac to create the £5,500 concoction at the Playboy Club (a cheaper version can be whipped up using modern spirits). In 2012, it smashed the Guinness World Record for the most expensive cocktail. The following year it was usurped by the Winston, which was created in Melbourne using the most expensive cognac ever sold at auction. The nerve.

The £5k sazerac at The Savoy

Get a taste of pre-Civil War New Orleans with a cocktail claimed by its creator to be as close as you can get to the original sazerac (in 21st-century London, anyway). £5,000 might sound like an awful lot for a drink comprised of just three ingredients, but the hefty price tag testifies to the quality and vintage of spirits used. The Savoy's American bar uses 1858 Sazerac de Forge, 1950s Pernod Absinthe and Peychaud's Bitters from the early 1900s. We'd rather spend the dosh on a jaunt to NOLA.

A gold latte fit for a unicorn at Saint Aymes

On the more affordable end of the spectrum, allow us to present the 24 Carat Gold Unicorn Latte. This Instagrammer's fever dream is comprised of flavoured coffee, whipped cream and a 24-carat gold topping, and is available in pink, blue or lilac. It's the brainchild of central London cafe Saint Aymes, and it can be yours for a mere £8.45. About the going rate for a coffee in London these days, no?

Liquid gold at The Bletchley

We've already seen gold and diamonds in cocktails. Well, the gin used in World War II-themed cocktail bar The Bletchley's George VI cocktail is infused with both. With a £100 price tag, it's certainly not infused with the spirit of wartime austerity, but it does come with something called a 'sparkling wine bomb', along with a golden garnish and your own personal mixologist – to borrow, rather than keep. You'll have to preorder this particular drink. With at least three day's notice.

'Press for champagne' button at Bob Bob Ricard

If ordering at the bar is beneath you, you'll love Bob Bob Ricard's 'press for champagne' button. These little beauties are installed at every table at the glam Soho restaurant, which – perhaps unsurprisingly – pours more of the sparkly stuff than any other UK dining establishment.

A wine bath in Chelsea

A spa treatment that makes Cleopatra's legendary milk baths look positively provincial: at Chelsea's Ella Di Rocco you can literally bathe in a tub of red wine. The pampering begins with a full-body Merlot scrub, before you sink into a tub of Sangiovese, Merlot and Ciliegiolo. The wines are swirled in with warm water and virgin grape juice concentrate, and we don't recommend taking a cheeky slurp during your dip. Luckily the treatment also comes with a glass. It's all about the antioxidants, apparently.

The priciest pint at Craft Beer Co.

Unfortunately it's no longer that uncommon to have to break a twenty when purchasing a couple of beers in a London pub. But you'd best hope it's not your round if your drinking buddies request a pint of Alesmith's Speedway Stout: it'll set you back £22.50, making it the UK's most expensive pint on draught. Before you cry 'daylight robbery', know that this US-imported stout ABV is 12% – about the same strength as a bottle of wine. Try it for yourself at one of The Craft Beer Co.'s bars.

£4k gin at Harvey Nichols

Got a spare £4k lying around? Blow it all on a white porcelain jar of gin, exclusively available at Harvey Nichols. At 60% ABV, Morus LXIV is sure to put hairs on your chest, and it's far too swanky to be sullied with tonic water. Instead, drinkers are instructed to enjoy it like a cask-strength Scotch: neat, or with a few drops of water to taste. The gin is made from the leaves of an ancient mulberry tree, which are hand harvested and dried prior to distillation. Each jar comes with its own stirrup cup – enjoy it on a ride with your trusty steed (you've got a steed, yes?).

Extra sparkly champagne

Well, it wouldn't be a list of extravagant drinks without a top-notch bottle of champers, would it? Around the neck of every magnum of Rare Le Secret High Jewellery Edition Ruby Champagne 1997 is a real 1.22-carat ruby in a setting inspired by the queen of excess, Marie Antoinette. Once you've emptied the bottle, you can take your adornment to the House of Mellerio's Parisian workshop and have it transformed into a piece of bling. All of this can be yours for the modest sum of £115,000 at Harrods. Keeping it real (expensive).

THE BEST PUBS NEAR LONDON'S TRAIN STATIONS

What's the best pub to go to when meeting someone near one of the big stations in London? We've chosen our favourites for all 14 of London's main termini. Each is within a five-minute walk of the mainline platforms, at least for those able to walk at 'busy Londoner pace'.

Blackfriars: The Blackfriar

Blackfriars has London's best unofficial waiting room in the jolly old shape of The Blackfriar. This gorgeous wedge of a building stands directly opposite the station. The Blackfriar rejoices in one of the capital's most unusual interiors (see page 30). It's dripping with mock-monastic embellishment, from stained glass windows to rock-hewn friars. Be sure to check out the ceiling in the dining area, whose gaudy opulence would make a Franciscan cry out in horror. The beer choice is equally splendid, with seven or eight cask pumps that'll put the pist back into trappist.

Bar to platform: 2 minutes, if the pedestrian crossing works in your favour.

174 Queen Victoria Street, EC4V 4EG

Illustration by LIS WATKINS ILLUSTRATION

MARYLEBONE

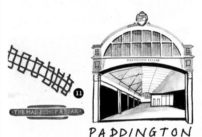

PADDINGTON

the BEST PUBS near TRAIN STATIONS

1. The Blackfriar
2. The Harp
3. The Olde Wine Shades
4. Euston Tap
5. The Draft House Seething
6. The Parcel Yard
7. Hamilton Hall
8. The George Inn
9. The Globe
10. Singer Tavern
11. The Mad Bishop and Bear
12. The Betjeman Arms
13. Market Hall Victoria
14. The Kings Arms

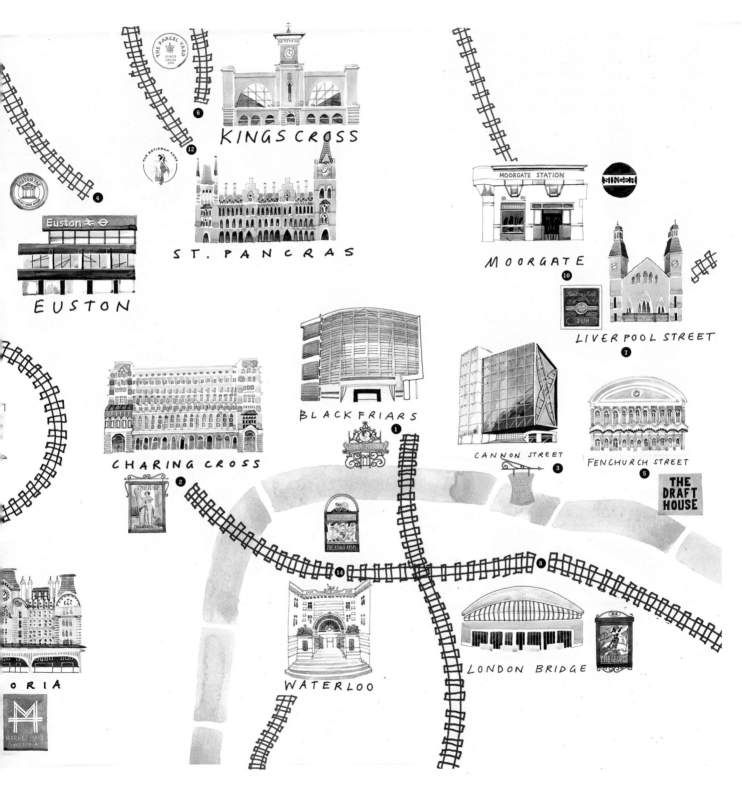

Further afield? Why bother. This pub is arguably the best in the Square Mile. But if you want something more down-to-Earth, try the **Cockpit** on St Andrew's Hill (5 mins).

Charing Cross: The Harp

Nothing in or adjacent to the station is worthy of praise, so head one block north of Strand to The Harp. Famed for its range of cask ales, and a regular winner of CAMRA awards, this is probably the best traditional pub in the West End for those who like hand-pulled tipples (see page 167). The selection has diminished a little since Fuller's asserted ownership, but this is still a notch up from its nearby rivals. If the narrow downstairs bar is packed (which it will be), try the delightful sitting room upstairs.

Bar to platform: 5 minutes.
47 Chandos Place, WC2N 4HS

Further afield: The nearby **Chandos** on St Martin's Lane has a gorgeous interior, though lacks exciting drinks (it's a Sam Smith's). Again, try the upstairs room for the best seats.

Cannon Street: The Olde Wine Shades

Cannon Street station now has its own pub, courtesy of relative newcomer the Sir John Hawkshaw (named for the chap who designed the station). While it has a good beer selection, the Hawkshaw lacks charm (and space), so doesn't make our cut. A series of short shifts through City snickleways brings the discerning drinker to The Olde Wine Shades – often touted as one of the oldest pubs in London. It's styled more as a wine bar these days, an outpost of the El Vino group, but it retains a pubby character and serves real ale in an environment that shouts out 'worship me, for I am old'.

Bar to platform: 5 minutes.
6 Martin Lane, EC4R 0DP

Further afield: We're already at our notional limits, but if you want to explore a little further, or start a pub crawl of contrasts, the **Hydrant** on Monument Street is the exact opposite of The Olde Wine Shades – brash, modern and shouty (but fun).

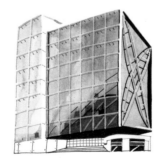

Euston: Euston Tap

Lucky old Euston boasts three above-average pubs within its purlieus. 2018 newcomer The Signal Box presides over the concourse, while old favourite the Doric Arch continues to trade beside the bus station. Easily the best option, though, can be found in the twin lodges that front Euston Road. Here, spread between two buildings, can be found the Euston Tap. With more than 40 lines of craft ale (see page 166), this place is among the best-stocked bars in London – remarkable considering how small these spaces are. Head up the precarious wrought-iron spiral staircase to find more seating and the capital's most bijou loos.

Bar to platform: 4 minutes.
173 Euston Road, NW1 2AX

Further afield: Sadly, the much-loved Bree Louise on Cobourg Street has fallen to the spade of High Speed 2. The **Exmouth Arms** on Starcross Street is bags of fun, and seems to have picked up some of the Bree's trade. It doesn't possess the same beer range, but nor does it have the smelly carpet and toilets.

Fenchurch Street: The Draft House Seething

The Square Mile's eastern terminus is overburdened with unmemorable pubs, typified by The Fen and The Windsor at its periphery. Our tip here is to head south a couple of blocks to Seething Lane, thence to find The Draft House Seething. Like other branches of The Draft House, the vibe is somewhere between that of a pub and a bar, with a dozen or so interesting kegs served from a shiny metallic counter. It gets a bit suity in the evenings, but the crowds have thinned out a little since a behemoth of a BrewDog opened nearby.

Bar to platform: 5 minutes.
14 Seething Lane, EC3R 5BA

Further afield: It's only another minute's walk away, but the aforementioned **BrewDog** offers a similarly keg-focussed plenitude, with bonus shuffleboard and seating for about 97,000 people.

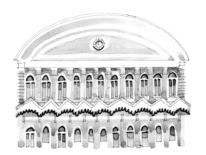

King's Cross: The Parcel Yard

Six stations in, and we finally feel confident enough to recommend a pub that's actually within the station. The Parcel Yard, at the northern end of the concourse, is always bustling but comes with a number of advantages. 1) It's so large, you can almost always find a table. 2) A big range of Fuller's ales. 3) It has a small beer terrace, from which you can laugh at the poor souls queueing up at Platform 9¾ for photographs. It's a good all-rounder, and infinitely better than the old Duke of York – a fading memory of a pub that once graced Platform 8.

Bar to platform: 1–2 minutes.
King's Cross Station concourse, N1C 4AH

Further afield: Relatively, it's a bit of a trek, but the **King Charles I** ain't that far, and offers unparalleled quantities of backstreet-boozer charm.

Liverpool Street: Hamilton Hall

Once again we're happy to recommend the station's in-built pub, Hamilton Hall. It's a fine example of an A-list Wetherspoon – a former banking hall converted for boozing. Yes, the place has the perma-reek of battered cod and vinegar, but just look at that ceiling. Like the mega-chain's other outlets, you can expect an excellent range of ales, competitively priced. The best time to catch it is 7.30am (yes, AM), when it's full of City boys necking pints to help them through the day. And we wonder why the economy tanked.

Bar to platform: 2 minutes.
Liverpool Street Station concourse, EC2M 7PY

Further afield: Head north along Bishopsgate to reach the **Crown and Shuttle** – a fine old Victorian pub, recently brought back from dereliction (some corners retain that 'lived-in' look).

London Bridge: The George Inn

'Shakespeare's Local' is a bit of a trek from the mainline platforms, but its proximity to the tube entrance on Borough High Street allows us to include it. Most readers will be aware of the George. As London's last-remaining galleried coaching inn (a seemingly obligatory phrase that all guide books include), its fame is widespread both with Londoners and tourists. Inside, a series of crooked rooms and open fires put us firmly in the 'Dickensian' category. The best seats on a warm day are in the courtyard, from where you can admire the traditional architecture while chewing over how the coaching trade was put out of business by the nearby train station*.
Bar to platform: 4 minutes to the tube (6 or 7 for mainline station).
77 **Borough High Street, SE1 1NH**

Further afield: The Horniman at Hays is often dismissed as an unmemorable Nicholson's pub for tourists, and there's some truth in that. However, the riverside views of the City skyscrapers, London and Tower Bridges, and HMS *Belfast* are simply stunning. Worth reconsidering.

Marylebone: The Globe (not that one)

You could do worse than the Victoria and Albert pub within the station. If you're after a quick half before your train departs then it's up to the job. To up the ambience, head around the corner to The Globe on Lisson Grove. This once-traditional boozer recently got a makeover to something not unlike a Draft House (see Fenchurch Street), but it still feels welcoming and characterful. The tidy range of keg beers and friendly bar staff make this one a keeper.
Bar to platform: 5 minutes.
47 **Lisson Grove, NW1 6UB**

Further afield: Head the other way to Baker Street, where the Wetherspoonian **Metropolitan Bar** is a gorgeous temple to the Met line.

Moorgate: Singer Tavern

Yes, Moorgate does count as a terminus. The oft-forgotten Northern City line concludes its rickety journey in from Hertfordshire at this station. Almost directly above, a grand old corner house called the Globe (yes, another one) is a tempting nomination, particularly given its associations with Keats, who was born here. For something more modern, and interesting, head north to the Singer Tavern, whose glazed-tiled walls recall the tube stations of Leslie Green. This is another place big on its craft ales; head downstairs to a rather nice cocktail bar if you've had enough of the beer.

Bar to platform: 5 minutes.
1 **City Road, EC1Y 1AG**

Further afield: About the same distance south lies the **Old Doctor Butler's Head**. This curiously named pub has traded from the site for centuries, and retains an 'old boozer' feel unique in this part of the City. It could hardly be more different from the Singer.

Paddington: The Mad Bishop & Bear

To be honest, we're blinded by the name. Any pub combining a deranged clergyman and a marmalade-loving ursine has to be some kind of winner (see page 10). And, it turns out, the MB&B is a thoroughly pleasant pub – perhaps because it's raised several levels above Paddington concourse so doesn't suffer from an off-putting deluge of customers like some other station pubs. A recent refit has stripped out some of the naff furnishings and breathed some new life into a place that was beginning to look a bit tired. It's a Fuller's house, so you can expect the usual run of beers and better-than-average food.
Bar to platform: 2 minutes (if you walk down the escalators).
Upper floor, Paddington Station, W2 1HB

Further afield: A plus-size branch of **The Draft House** brightens up the Paddington Basin development a short walk up Praed Street.

St Pancras: The Betjeman Arms

Until the late Noughties, 'station pub' was a dirty phrase in London. Not one of the station concourses, with the possible exception of Liverpool Street, could claim a drinking establishment of any quality. Then came the Betjeman Arms at St Pancras. This handsome pub from the Geronimo franchise combines traditional architecture with modern fittings – a good match for the wider station. The main bar area is smart enough, but head to one of the three back rooms for the most comfortable seating, and excellent food. Otherwise, sit 'outside' to admire the station's famous roof and watch the Eurostar trains come and go. The recently opened Barrel Vault (a Wetherspoon pub) at t'other end of the station has more tables but lacks the style.
Bar to platform: 5 minutes (3 for the tube)
St Pancras Station upper level, N1C 4QL

Further afield: The **Somers Town Coffee House** is equidistant between St Pancras and Euston. It is not a coffee house, but a reliable and popular booze house.

Victoria: Market Hall Victoria

Sorry Victoria commuters – although we do like the Wetherspoons (see page 66), we can't find a pub of true *excellence* within five minutes of the station. The Beer House has a little character, but would hardly find its way onto anyone's 'must visit' list. CASK is brilliant, but too far away. Instead, we're going for a bar with pub-like characteristics. Carefully make your way across the bus stands to the Market Halls – an indoor collection of eateries a bit like you find in shopping centres, but with more swagger. The two bars here serve a decent selection of craft beers in a convivial atmosphere. You'll pay a whack more than at Wetherspoons, but it's worth it. And the toilets have to be seen to be believed.
Bar to platform: 4 minutes.
191 Victoria Street, SW1E 5NE

Further afield: An even better (and much cheaper) option is to walk a bit further and enjoy the gloriously old-fashioned interior of the **Windsor Castle**… so long as you're happy with Sam Smith's beer.

Waterloo: The Kings Arms

One of our favourite pubs in inner south London, the King's Arms is two venues in one. Out front is a fine, traditional boozer, which stands amid the filmset-ready terrace housing of Roupell Street (which always seems to have a retro Citroen DS parked on it). Head through a narrow portal to the back of the pub, and you find yourself in a grand conservatory that's served bloody good Thai meals for as long as we can remember.
Bar to platform: 5 minutes.
25 Roupell Street, SE1 8TB

Further afield: The Understudy, beneath the National Theatre, is a surprisingly good bar given the tourist hotspot location. Exemplary beers served alongside chilled indie music ensure this place draws its fair share of beards and MacBooks.

*Note for pedants: We know you like to insist that people write 'railway station' rather than 'train station', but we simply won't have it. We regard this as a pointless anachronism long superseded by common usage. So there! [Pulls raspberry face.]

INSIDE THE BEEFEATERS' PRIVATE PUB IN THE TOWER OF LONDON

Despite the Tower of London attracting 2.8 million tourists each year, most of them won't have had a pint here.

The famous fortress has a pub, alright. It's just that The Keys is open exclusively to the resident 37 Beefeaters, and their special guests.

Us being *Londonist* and all, we've been invited inside. Smug so-and-sos.

'The Keys' is a reference to the Ceremony of the Keys – the ritual locking-up of the Tower, which has taken place at 9.52pm every night for around 700 years. It even went on during the Blitz, although a nearby bomb blast once delayed it by seven whole minutes.

A back and forth between two Yeoman Warders goes:

"Halt! Who goes there?"

"The Keys!"

"Whose Keys?"

"Queen Elizabeth's Keys!"

"Pass then, all's well!".

A scrupulous security system, you'll agree. You can see the pub sign swinging outside the pub, which is inside the south wall of the Tower, next to the old menagerie (look for the elephant made from wire mesh).

The keys are referenced throughout the pub – on a welcome mat, on the carpets, on the cherry red leather banquettes and on the benches outside (well, at least you can say you've visited the pub's beer garden).

Ancient ceremony, yes, but it's a recent name change: the bar – used by Beefeaters after a hard day's Beefeating for around 150 years – was previously called the Yeoman Warders Club. A sign on the door retains that name.

Inside awaits a snug warren of Beefeater related gimcrack: Beefeater figurines, Beefeater uniforms, Beefeater paintings. An axe is poised menacingly on the wall, next to a sign: 'Site of Scaffold'. Talking of menacing, the bar also sports a framed signature of Adolf Hitler's deputy, Rudolph Hess. He was imprisoned in the Tower during World War II.

What does a Beefeater drink in a Beefeater pub? Beefeater gin, of course. The bar is heavily stocked with the stuff, which is distilled a couple of miles away in Kennington. Beefeaters are given bottles of gin on their birthdays – as part of an old copyright agreement in exchange for using their image.

There are also two special brews on tap: Beefeater Bitter and Yeoman 1485 Craft Lager. You won't find these in any other bar in the world.

Your Beefeater gin or Beefeater beer will be served to you by… a Beefeater. They take it in turns to volunteer behind the bar. Although, as they're not strictly at work, they don't wear their famous uniforms.

If you ever do get the chance to have a pint in The Keys, pounce on it. But remember to dress smartly. Beefeaters might seem fluffy enough, but they're hardened military types, who love to make tourists jump out of their skins. We were this close to being turned away for being scruffy media types. You should have seen the grief that the guy without a tie got.

15 OF THE BEST
CRAFT BEER PUBS IN LONDON

Whatever your preference – well-conditioned cask ales, powerfully hopped juicy IPAs, hybrid lager styles, or the epitome of continental beer-making – you'll find something to quench your thirst in this selection of fine watering holes.

It won't have escaped the attention of many London pub-goers that the city has experienced something of a beer renaissance over the last decade. Some observers adopt even stronger hyperbole, referring to it as a revolution. Either way, we've seen a healthy surge in the popularity of non-mass-market beers in London.

We've developed a hankering for mouth-puckering sours and goses, unctuous chocolate stouts and porters, earthy saisons and wheat beers – and frankly weird concoctions that we buy in thirds, to show off to our mates.

But among the ever-increasing number of pubs serving craft beer, which, if any, are the best?

To an extent, that's an impossible question to answer. With so much choice, and new or newly revitalised pubs opening every week, how can we decide which is the 'best' for craft beer? And what do we even mean by 'craft beer' anyway?

Actually, it doesn't matter. We could spend ages getting bogged down in technical definitions about exactly what does and does not constitute a good craft beer pub, but doesn't that go against the whole ethos of enjoying great beer in a nice pub? A pub that strives to serve a regularly changing selection of high-quality beer, from a variety of independent brewers, in an enjoyable drinking environment, is a place we go to escape the tedious business of having to pigeonhole everything according to precise criteria.

Here, then, we present some of our favourite places for drinking beer.

The Arbitrager, The City

If you ever need visual proof of how space is at an absolute premium in the City, look no further than The Arbitrager. Essentially laid out as a short corridor with a bar at the end, the pub only makes a cursory nod towards the concept of seating, with most of its customers invariably concluding that this is a place where you drink standing up.

For a beery pit-stop in the middle of the Square Mile, this is a refreshing option. Friendly staff (and sometimes clientele) will talk you through the selection of 12 keg taps, dispensing beer (and occasionally a cider) from London-based craft brewers, served in ⅓ or ⅔ measures. For the beer-averse, a large array of London-made gins line the shelves. Snazzy tiling, exposed light bulbs, and a large mirror give the space an upbeat vibe, and a large historical map of London is printed on one of the walls, adorned with stickers denoting notable beery locations. A great place to kill a little – or a lot of – time.

27a Throgmorton Street, EC2N 2AN
See also: **Williams Ale & Cider House**, also near Liverpool Street.

CASK Pub and Kitchen, Pimlico

Before Craft, there was CASK. No, that's not a reference to traditional versus modern beer styles; we're talking about pub names – specifically the older cousin of the Craft Beer Co. chain: CASK Pub and Kitchen in Pimlico. In 2009 CASK set the course that Craft Beer Co. would follow a couple of years later.

Built into the structure of a blocky 1970s council estate in Pimlico, CASK is easily overlooked. But its inconspicuous entrance conceals a surprisingly bright, airy and spacious interior. And it gets better, with a bar housing 10 cask-conditioned ales from the likes of Magic Rock, Vocation, and Blackjack, and 15 keg taps dispensing a similar, but occasionally more adventurous, range. Behind the bar, several full-height fridges of beer from the UK, Europe, and the US provide a vast further variety of fermented goodness. These fridges are essentially glass-doored portals into Booze Narnia.

Soak up your beer with a posh burger or a roast on Sunday. There are few better places to spend a winter afternoon, as the setting sun casts its light through the pub's tall, narrow windows – and a jazz quartet strikes up.

6 Charlwood Street, W1V 2EE

See also: **Craft Beer Co.** pubs in Covent Garden, Clerkenwell, Islington, Old Street, Limehouse, Brixton, and the City.

Illustration by DAVID BROADBENT

The Dovetail, Clerkenwell

Jerusalem Passage – a short and easily overlooked alleyway connecting the edge of the not-very-green Clerkenwell Green and the north side of St John's Square – houses a few restaurants, a co-working office, and a Belgian bar called The Dovetail.

And oh my, The Dovetail. You could certainly just pop in for its Belgian comfort food (think moules frites and Flemish beef stew), but the stand-out offering here is the exceptional beer list. Several taps dispense a good range of popular Belgian beers into a satisfyingly comprehensive inventory of appropriately branded/shaped glasses, but the real action comes from the fridges. More than 100 bottles, covering a variety of Belgian beer styles, come listed in leather-clad menus – psalters for beer drinkers, in which every line is another tasty tribute to the god of Belgian brews. The selection rivals (and generally exceeds) pretty much any other London establishment for such a pronounced collection of trappist, lambic, flanders, blonde, amber, dubbel, tripel, quadrupel, red, saison and fruit beers.

The pub's interior is on-brand, with tiled walls giving way to wooden monastical motifs, and a tight layout of tables and chairs making the most of the economically proportioned space. Framed *Tintin* posters round off the theme nicely.

9–10 Jerusalem Passage, EC1V 4JP

See also: sister pub **The Dove** on Broadway Market, or the **Beer Merchants Tap** in Hackney Wick.

The Draft House, Old Street

Situated down an alleyway a stone's throw away from Old Street tube station, this branch of the Draft House chain is our favourite (it is, after all, where we sometimes go for post-work drinkies). Unconventionally housed in what seems to be a large concrete box at the base of a newly constructed high-rise office, the space is kitted out with a combination of The Draft House's trademark neon tubes, exposed ducts, wood, and wire caging, while the inclusion of moquette-clad furnishings underlines that stone's throw to the tube station we mentioned.

The beer selection is well curated, with the best part of 20 beers available on draught (mostly keg, with a handful of casks) representing a decent variety of styles, as well as a very handsome selection of beers from Belgium and elsewhere in the large fridges behind the bar. The food menu complements the beer selection, with chicken wings and burgers providing ample munching options. Some of it comes served on a bin lid, because east London.

Mews Unit, The Bower, 211 Old Street, EC1V 9NR

See also: a dozen other **Draft House** locations dotted around London.

The Earl of Essex, Islington

Given its slightly off-the-beaten-track location in the residential back-streets between Angel and Canonbury, it's surprising how lively The Earl of Essex can get. At popular times beer geeks flock from far and wide to hang out here. Why? Well for a start the beer selection is not just excellent, it's also rather interesting, often comprising beer from a number of brewers who tend not to feature that heavily in London's other craft beer pubs, as well as its own in-house brew and some more familiar names (Camden Town, Magic Rock, Thornbridge, etc.). Half the fun here is standing, hands on hips, and admiring the beer menu that covers one entire wall.

The food is entirely agreeable, focused more towards the gastropub audience than those looking for simple pub grub, and the woody, bright decor is immediately comfortable. Combine all this with a nice little beer garden at the back of the premises and you can begin to understand this pub's appeal.

25 Danbury Street, N1 8LE

See also: **The Island Queen**, just around the corner – a boozer dripping in big mirrors and old colonial grandeur.

Euston Tap, Euston

Housed in what must be one of the most unusual pub premises in London, the Euston Tap works hard to make the most of a rather challenging space. The Grade II-listed nature of the old Portland stone cubes in front of Euston Station, combined with the pub's popularity since it opened in 2010, means it's sometimes hard to find much space within. That said, while the main premises reside in the western stone cube, the mirror-image 'east lodge' on the other side of the station's access road also tends to open its doors at the busier times of the week, essentially doubling both the space and the beer available. When both bars are open, the Euston Tap dispenses as many as 47 different beers from keg (often pricey) and cask (more modestly priced), alongside a formidable selection of bottles and cans from the fridges that flank the bar.

The unique buildings housing the Euston Tap lend a certain cramped charm to drinking therein, although this is tempered by the almost perpetual drama that seems to befall the over-subscribed toilet facilities. On more than one occasion we've found it quicker, and less stressful, to nip over to the public loos in Euston station. Still, if you pick a quiet time, or don't mind sitting at the tables outside (looking out over a glorious vista of the traffic jams on Euston Road), you can often avoid the crush and enjoy an immense selection of craft beers in some rather unconventional surroundings. Almost enough to make you forget your impending trip to Coventry.

190 Euston Road, NW1 2EF

See also: **The Rake** in Borough Market, another minuscule pub, with barely enough room to swing a bottle of lambic.

The Harp, Covent Garden

Situated slap bang in the middle of the West End, this pub was never going to be quiet. And once you factor in the high quality of its beer – predominantly of the cask-conditioned variety – and the efficient and friendly welcome from its staff, you can see why it's popular for more than just its location. Adding to its general acclaim is an impressive list of beer-related awards, the pinnacle of which is undoubtedly CAMRA's National Pub of the Year in 2010; the massive real-ale-loving organisation essentially considered it to be the best pub in the country at the time.

This all contributes to The Harp's relentless busyness, so this might not be a sensible destination for the weary-of-foot, who would rarely be guaranteed a seat. Some respite from the (generally affable) crowd can sometimes be found in the surprisingly elegant upstairs room, but in general it's best to only visit this pub if you're happy to drink your excellent ale vertically.

47 Chandos Place, WC2N 4HS

See also: **The Hope** in Carshalton – a village-style boozer, stocked with exciting casks – and surprisingly hip kegged and canned numbers.

Italian Job, Chiswick

We once asked Michael Caine if he knew about this place. Alas, he did not. Despite the oft-noted excellence of the Italian craft brewing scene, good Italian beer often seems rather under-represented in London's craft beer pubs. Thankfully the Italian Job, a bright and cheerful cafe-like space just off Chiswick High Road, goes some way towards redressing this imbalance. The pub's 12 taps showcase a versatile variety of beer styles from Italian brewers, with a pronounced emphasis on beers from Birrificio del Ducato – a Parma-based brewery co-founded by one of the founders of the Italian Job itself.

Alongside the Italian brews are a handful of well-chosen beers from mostly London-based brewers, while a cider from Scotland's Thistly Cross also makes a regular appearance. As befits an Italian pub, decent-quality food is also on the menu, with cheeses, cured meats and olives among the snacking options, alongside a variety of accomplished burgers for those with a greater hunger. There's a TV too, should you wish to watch the rugby without being barged around by sports fans.

13 Devonshire Road, W4 2EU

See also: a larger sister pub in Notting Hill, and a bar at **Mercato Metropolitano**, near Elephant and Castle.

London Beer House, St James's

Another supremely compact drinking-hole, the diminutive London Beer House is incongruously nestled at the north end of Royal Opera Arcade – one of those rarified Georgian shopping arcades dotted around this part of London, where you could imagine Beau Brummell shopping for tights. The ground-floor premises might only accommodate a couple of dozen drinkers, but the space has been used judiciously, with nine keg taps and a couple of fridges behind the bar, and storage shelving for bottles doubling up as seating for those in need of it.

This all contributes to a pleasantly makeshift 'micropub' appearance – repurposed wood and boxes house the beer taps and provide some rudimentary shelving along a couple of the walls, while a perilously narrow staircase winds its way up to a further small seating area and a characteristically modest single-occupancy toilet. Don't visit for glamour or comfort, but do pop in for a charming oasis in what is otherwise a rather barren neighbourhood for decent brews.

17 Royal Opera Arcade, SW1Y 4UY

See also: one of London's many other fine micropubs. Page 34 has plenty of options.

Mother Kelly's, Vauxhall

Inspired by the tap rooms of New York, Mother Kelly's is one of London's most mouth-watering craft beer experiences. 20+ taps cover everything from London stalwarts (Brew By Numbers, Orbit) to guest takeovers from breweries like Põhjala in Tallinn. Have your mind broadened with bourbon oaked tripels and strawberry berliner weisses. (There are some interesting ciders too.) You can also peruse the numerous fridges that make up an entire room; this even features a decent range of non-alcoholic brews. Beers shift so quickly at Mother Kelly's, it's not unusual to have your menu swapped for a new one while you drink. That's what we call on the pulse.

Lambeth, SE1 7TW

See also: the sister pub – also beneath train arches (page 14) – in Bethnal Green.

The Queen's Head, King's Cross

The Queen's Head is one of those pubs whose minor ergonomic challenges tend to work slightly in its favour. Sure, finding an entirely comfortable drinking (or ordering) space can be a bit awkward at busy times, but here it seems to add to the place's pleasantly bustling atmosphere. This is another pub to have gained CAMRA's public approval, though curiously not for beer – the bearded ones have actually declared the Queen's Head to be a great place to drink cider.

(Side note: we were unwittingly in attendance when the Queen's Head was presented with its first London Cider Pub of the Year award by a large delegation of CAMRA dignitaries. The occasion was somewhat surreal, as apparently nobody had thought to notify the rather bemused bar staff that the presentation would be occurring. They took it in their stride.)

Don't worry if cider is not your beverage of choice – despite its apple-oriented accolades, the pub's main booze offering is beer, served from a dozen keg taps and a handful of cask pumps, alongside some great options in the fridge. It also stocks a fine selection of whiskies. Food is of the things-to-nibble-while-drinking variety – bread, cheese, cured meats, pies and suchlike. If you've a while to wait for your King's Cross train, while it away here.

66 Acton Street, WC1X 9NB

See also: sister pub **Simon the Tanner** in Bermondsey.

Southampton Arms, Kentish Town

On our first visit to the Southampton Arms, several years ago, we ordered an ale that was deliberately and vividly green in colour, served in a dimpled pint mug. We're still not sure what that was all about. It actually tasted quite good, despite its visual resemblance to washing-up liquid.

A refurbished and revitalised incarnation of an old-fashioned boozer, the Southampton Arms has managed to retain a relaxed, local feel, even at busy times. A dozen hand pumps on the bar are mostly used to dispense cask ales from independent UK brewers, and six further pumps behind the bar offer ciders. There are also a couple of keg taps, serving non-cask-conditioned beers. Food offerings seem to mostly revolve around pork – ranging from packets of scratchings (of course) to meat from a roast joint. The pub's location, between Kentish Town and Gospel Oak stations, might be mildly inconvenient for some, but once you're there you'll be happy to hang around for a while. Especially if you like pub cats.

139 Highgate Road, NW5 1LE

See also: **Tapping the Admiral**, the other side of Kentish Town. Locally brewed ale, and a juicy pork roast.

Stormbird, Camberwell

There is a phenomenon in Stormbird that we refer to as The Magic Table. However busy this contemporary Camberwell boozer gets (and it does), a lone table miraculously appears. Perhaps the real magic, though, is the beer selection: an array of pumps – most with cute, hand-drawn beer clips – runs with a constant supply of juicy IPAs, knock-out strength porters and usually a sour or two. Kernel, Mikkeller and Moor are among the usual suppliers, but you never quite know what you're going to find in this wonderland of brews.

Cask-heads are well catered for, with a choice of three or four well-priced numbers, while fridges brim with myriad exotic concoctions. Gaze out the huge windows with your brew of choice in one hand and a falafel from next door in the other, while watching buses and ambulances whiz and up down Camberwell Church Street. Magic.

25 Camberwell Church Street, SE5 8TR

See also: its family friendly sister pub in Bromley, the **Star & Garter**.

The Wenlock Arms, Hoxton

We'll always remember our first visit to the Wenlock Arms. A 15-minute stumble through cold January drizzle north of Old Street tube station eventually brought us to the door of this venerable old boozer, just as we had started to seriously mistrust our directions. As we walked in, we were greeted by a cheerful old chap wandering around with a metal bucket, urging the handful of mostly local clientele to 'bring out their dead'. Nobody batted an eyelid, of course. Eccentricities aside, it rapidly became clear that this was an unfussy, traditional, and only slightly grubby old pub, with a strong focus on serving a regularly changing selection of real ales, all in excellent condition.

Fast-forward a decade, and the pub's interior is rather less grubby. However its comfortable, relaxed atmosphere remains, as does its dedication to serving quality beers (now 10 casks and 20 kegs). It's also started brewing its own beer in the cellar, under the Block Brewery name. The pub's beery excellence has not gone unnoticed, winning CAMRA's North London Pub of the Year award five times between 1995 and 2017.

26 Wenlock Road, N1 7TA

See also: **The Old Fountain**, much closer to Old Street tube station.

The White Horse, Parson's Green

This rambling pub on Parson's Green is somewhat notorious for the perceived nature of its clientele, earning it the nickname 'The Sloany Pony'. While there's some truth in this perception, not all of the pub's customers are 'gap yah' types, and the selection of beer on offer is certainly beyond reproach.

With a wide range of cask and keg ales from a variety of UK and European brewers, as well as some big (and sometimes expensive) American craft beers, there's enough variety here to keep an eager beer drinker entertained for some time. The pub further cements its beery focus with regular festivals (including a rather excellent annual American beer festival around Independence Day) and a conspicuous tank of wonderful, golden, unpasteurised Pilsner Urquell.

1–3 Parsons Green, SW6 4UL

See also: the **Bricklayer's Arms**, a much more humble and cosy proposition, just across the river in Putney.

IT HAPPENED DOWN THE PUB...

A miscellany of alarming incidents from London's pub history.

Death by billiard ball

The Carlisle Arms on Bateman Street was the scene of London's only known death through near-inhalation of a billiard ball. In November 1893, a 24-year-old envelope cutter named Walter Cowle reckoned he could place a whole billiard ball in his mouth and still close his teeth. This he achieved, but only by accidentally blocking his windpipe and choking to death. The coroner later declared that it was a 'silly and dangerous feat to attempt', and few would argue.

When Christmas went very, very wrong

Pub landlord James John Gardiner wasn't the sort of man who welcomed live music to his pub. Just after midnight on Christmas morning 1886, a group of drinkers returned to the Rising Sun in Stockwell to sing carols. The musicians played a range of instruments including a fife, a drum and a galvanised tin bath. The noise proved unpleasant. After 15 minutes, the impromptu performance was interrupted by the report of a revolver. An angry Gardiner had fired from an upstairs window, fatally wounding the flute player Robert John Janaway, aged 23. The building on Larkhall Lane still stands, although it is no longer a pub.

Bear wrestling in Hackney

The Sebright Arms in Hackney is now a popular live music venue, but in the 19th century it served the adjacent Sebright Music Hall. It was here in December 1890 that attendant John Pinton was coaxed on stage with a performing bear. The stage manager offered 10 shillings to anyone who could throw the bear in a wrestling match. Pinton accepted the challenge and began grappling with the bruin. Unfortunately, the creature knocked him off balance and he fell awkwardly, breaking a leg and later dying of his injuries. The subsequent inquest recommended that the general public should no longer be invited to wrestle with stage bears.

House of corpses

'Pie Corner', on the corner of Cock Lane and Giltspur Street, marks the point where the Great Fire of London was held back. It is also the site of a long lost public house called the Fortune of War. While many visited the pub for refreshment, others brought a more macabre custom: this was the pub of the body snatchers. So-called resurrectionists would dig up freshly buried corpses to sell to surgeons, who needed cadavers for medical teaching. The Fortune of War served as an illicit showroom for the abominable goods.

Pub collapse kills two

October 1928, and the Nelson Arms on Lever Street, EC1, was undergoing demolition. Most of the upper floors had already gone, but a group of loyal customers were still enjoying the bar at ground floor level. Without warning, some of the remaining masonry gave way, crashing through the ceiling and burying the drinkers below. Two women were killed and six people badly injured. The rebuilt pub eventually closed in 2002, but still displays its hanging sign.

Gang of yobs inspire cult book and film

The Duke of York in Fitzrovia is normally a quiet, backstreet boozer. In 1943, however, it witnessed a frenzied attack by a 'razor gang'. A group of men stormed the pub, breaking furniture and bleeding off the beer taps. One of the customers, Lynne Burgess, confronted the gang and scolded them for wasting booze. In response, they forced her to drink pint after pint. The unfazed lady accomplished this with aplomb, earning the respect of the gang. She later related the story to her husband Anthony Burgess. It has been suggested that the incident was a key inspiration for his novel *A Clockwork Orange*; the story has never been substantiated.

THE LEGENDARY LONDONIST 12 DAYS OF CHRISTMAS PUB CRAWL

Do you have what it takes to complete the ultimate festive pub crawl? A boozy journey through the 12 days of Christmas is not for the faint hearted, but it can be done. London contains at least one pub for every true-love's gift in the song.

On the first day of Christmas my true love gave to me... a partridge in a pear tree

A gift of two parts, with a pub to match each. Londoners of a deep-south persuasion can try **The Partridge** (194 High Street, BR1 1HE) in Bromley – a handsome red-brick Fuller's pub noted for its grand interior decor. For a more central affair, head to **The Pear Tree** (14 Margravine Road, W6 8HJ) in Hammersmith. Phone ahead if you need a large space at this popular gastropub.

On the second day of Christmas my true love gave to me... two turtle doves

We have no hesitation here in recommending **The Dove** in Hammersmith (19 Upper Mall, W6 9TA), which is undeniably one of the best pubs on the River Thames (see page 49). The cosy interior and roaring fire are perfect for a sharp winter's evening, but be sure to check out the riverside terrace, too. To make it a pair of birds, head along to **The Dove** in Hackney (24–28 Broadway Market, E8 4QJ). The wood-panelled boozer has a sequence of small rooms and spaces to explore, and a fine selection of European beers.

On the third day of Christmas my true love gave to me... three French hens

There are plenty of Cocks around town, but not so many pubbish hens, and certainly no French ones. However, you can get into Gallic spirit by visiting **The French House** in Soho (49 Dean Street, W1D 5BG; see page 64), where the limited selection of beers is served in half-pint measures, just to be awkward. Stick to the wine. And don't use your phone. They're strict on house rules. Then it's on to the **Hen and Chickens Theatre Bar** in Highbury (109 St Paul's Road, N1 2NA), a cosy option with its own fringe theatre.

On the fourth day of Christmas my true love gave to me... four colly birds

A 'colly bird' is an arcane way of saying 'blackbird'. It just so happens that there's a very prominent **The Blackbird** pub in Earls Court (209 Earls Court Road, SW5 9AN), run by Fuller's. Nothing remarkable about it, but certainly a sound enough pub to sink a pint, and perhaps send out a tweet.

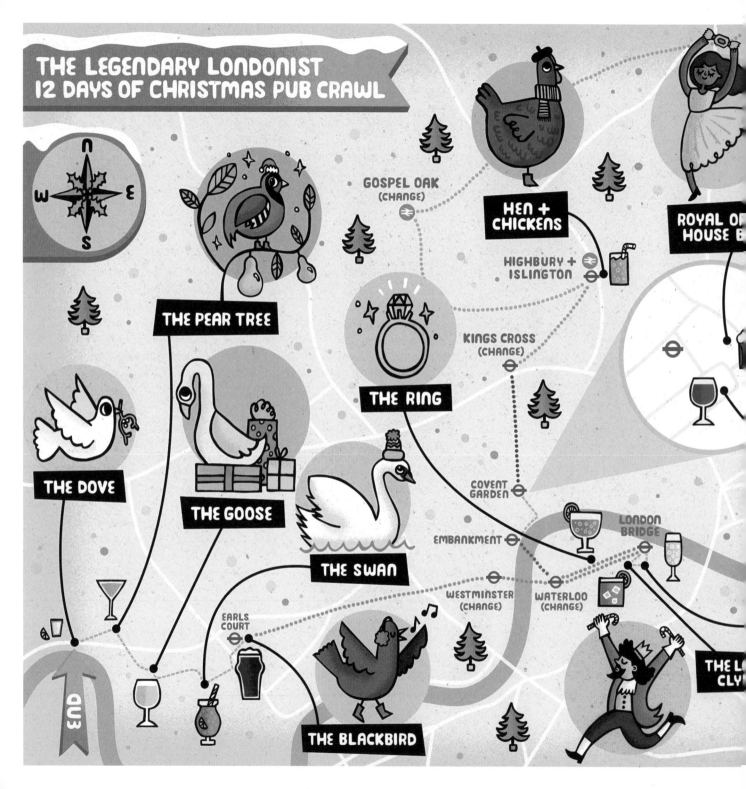

THE LEGENDARY LONDONIST
12 DAYS OF CHRISTMAS PUB CRAWL

GOSPEL OAK (CHANGE)

HEN + CHICKENS

ROYAL OP HOUSE B

HIGHBURY + ISLINGTON

THE PEAR TREE

KINGS CROSS (CHANGE)

THE RING

THE DOVE

THE GOOSE

COVENT GARDEN

THE SWAN

EMBANKMENT

LONDON BRIDGE

WESTMINSTER (CHANGE)

WATERLOO (CHANGE)

EARLS COURT

END

THE BLACKBIRD

THE L CLY

On the fifth day of Christmas my true love gave to me...
FIVE GOLD RINGS

Let's suppose for a moment that your true love gave you five tickets to visit a boxing ring, rather than a quintet of finger jewellery. In that case, **The Ring** (72 Blackfriars Road, SE1 8HA) makes perfect sense. It gets its name from a famous sporting arena also known as The Ring, which stood across the road in the first half of the 20th century. The pub is often packed with staff from Transport for London, who today occupy the vast Palestra Building on the site of the boxing ring.

On the sixth day of Christmas my true love gave to me... six geese a-laying

Have a gander at **Old Tom's Bar** (10–12 Leadenhall Market, EC3V 1PJ). This foody basement joint is named after the market's famous Victorian goose, who somehow managed to evade slaughter and lived on in the market for 37 years. The bar is decorated with genuine 19th-century tiles, which Old Tom might have seen with his own anserine eyes. Old Tom's is closed at weekends, so keep a less striking alternative, **The Goose** in Fulham (248 North End Road, SW6 1NL), in mind if you're planning to tackle the crawl.

On the seventh day of Christmas my true love gave to me... seven swans a-swimming

London presents a number of Swans to select from, if not quite seven. Perhaps the most prominent is the first-floor **Swan** (21 New Globe Walk, SE1 9DT) beside Shakespeare's Globe, which serves lovely food and also doubles as the unofficial toilets for the nearby Rose Theatre. There's also a brash **Swan** in Hammersmith (46 Hammersmith Broadway, W6 0DZ), a landlocked **Swan** in Bayswater (66 Bayswater Road, W2 3PH), and a further **Swan** in Holborn (7 Cosmo Place, WC1N 3AP).

On the eighth day of Christmas my true love gave to me... eight maids a-milking

There's a **Milkbar** in Soho, but it's all about the coffee there, and we want booze. Instead, try Southwark's **The Blue Eyed Maid** (173 Borough High Street, SE1 1HR), an area with an embarrassment of riches when it comes to pubs. We don't know if she's tried a-milking, but The Blue Eyed Maid certainly supplies a decent pint of beer.

Illustration by Freya Harrison

On the ninth day of Christmas my true love gave to me...
nine ladies dancing

Lots of pubs are named after Lords, not so many for Ladies. You could chase the dancing by going for a tipple in the **Royal Opera House** bars (Covent Garden Piazza, WC2E 9DD). This could prove an expensive option, though, we fear. Alternatively, try the **Lady Ottoline** in Clerkenwell, named after an aristocrat who enjoyed an open marriage, (11a Northington Street, WC1N 2JF), or the **Lady Mildmay** (92 Mildmay Park, N1 4PR) near Newington Green.

On the 10th day of Christmas my true love gave to me...
10 Lords a-leaping

And here they are: **Lord Abercornway** in Liverpool Street (72 Old Broad Street, EC2M 1QT), **Lord Clyde** (340–342 Essex Road, N1 3PB), another **The Lord Clyde** in Borough (27 Clennam Street, SE1 1ER), **Lord Nelson** on the Isle of Dogs (1 Manchester Road, E14 3BD), another **Lord Nelson** in Southwark (243 Union Street, SE1 0LR), **Lord Moon of the Mall** (16–18 Whitehall, SW1A 2DY), **Lord Northbrook** in Lewisham (116 Burnt Ash Road, SE12 8PU), **Lord Palmerston** (33 Dartmouth Park Hill, NW5 1HU), **Lord Raglan** in St Paul's (61 St Martins le Grand, EC1A 4ER), and

Lord Stanley (51 Camden Park Road, NW1 9BH). Other Lords are available.

On the 11th day of Christmas my true love gave to me...
11 pipers playing

If, for ladies dancing, you opted for the Royal Opera House, it is but a mere jeté to reach **The Crusting Pipe** (30 Tavistock Court, WC2E 8RF). This subterranean bar is in the basement of the Covent Garden market complex, from where you'll probably hear brass bands and carol singers while you sup. They also did a tasty afternoon tea last time we were there.

On the 12th day of Christmas my true love gave to me...
12 drummers drumming

We can only point you towards **The Drum** in Leyton (557–559 Lea Bridge Road, E10 7EQ), which was among the first pubs in the Wetherspoon chain to open. The name comes from its predecessor, a bar that had 'an eye-catching display of drums hanging from the ceiling'. Beat that.

And now for the pub crawl

We've name-checked way more than a dozen pubs above, and it would be foolhardy to attempt them in the correct order. So here's a plan to get you round one example from each of the 12 days, in a sensible route.

1. Start at The Drum.
It's a Wetherspoon, so opens at 8am, allowing you to set off early. Catch the Overground from Leyton Midland Road to Gospel Oak and change for the Highbury train.

2. Hen and Chickens
Victoria line to King's Cross, Piccadilly line to Covent Garden.

3. Crusting Pipe
Walk to next venue (2 mins).

4. Royal Opera House bar
Bakerloo + Jubilee line from Embankment to London Bridge.

5. The Blue Eyed Maid
Walk to next venue (5 mins).

6. The Lord Clyde
Walk to next venue (5 mins).

7. The Ring
Jubilee line to Westminster, change for District line to Earls Court.

8. The Blackbird
Walk, or bus along Old Brompton Road.

9. The Goose
Walk to next venue (10 mins).

10. The Pear Tree
Walk to next venue (10 mins).

11. The Swan
Walk to next venue (10 mins).

12. The Dove
And relax.

WHAT HAVE TOM AND JERRY GOT TO DO WITH EGGNOG?

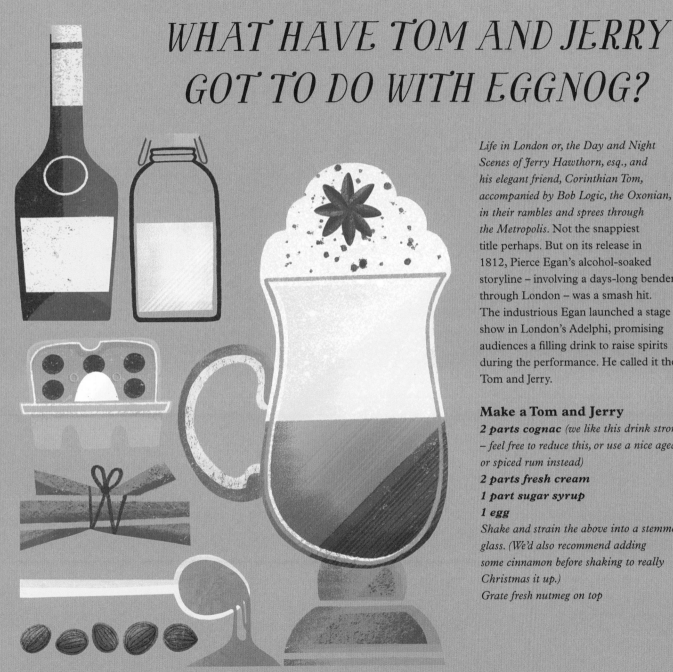

Life in London or, the Day and Night Scenes of Jerry Hawthorn, esq., and his elegant friend, Corinthian Tom, accompanied by Bob Logic, the Oxonian, in their rambles and sprees through the Metropolis. Not the snappiest title perhaps. But on its release in 1812, Pierce Egan's alcohol-soaked storyline – involving a days-long bender through London – was a smash hit. The industrious Egan launched a stage show in London's Adelphi, promising audiences a filling drink to raise spirits during the performance. He called it the Tom and Jerry.

Make a Tom and Jerry

2 parts cognac *(we like this drink strong – feel free to reduce this, or use a nice aged or spiced rum instead)*
2 parts fresh cream
1 part sugar syrup
1 egg
Shake and strain the above into a stemmed glass. (We'd also recommend adding some cinnamon before shaking to really Christmas it up.)
Grate fresh nutmeg on top

WHERE TO GET A DRINK WHEN THE CITY'S SLEEPING

The clock has struck midnight, but you're not ready to turn back into a pumpkin quite yet. Where's a reveller to go in the small hours?

London's status as a 24-hour city is… questionable. It struggles to match many of its European brethren, and though steps are being taken to remedy this – woop, night tube! – for the most part London snores the night away. That leaves just a handful of magical spots where the real night owls congregate for a final nightcap or a warming cuppa to start the day bright and early.

We've excluded clubs from this list; we're focusing on places you can drink while not having to yell at the top of your lungs to conduct any sort of conversation.

Balans Soho Society, Soho

Balans Soho Society wears a canopy that claims it's open all day and all night. That isn't quite true – opening times vary by day – but even in the wee hours of Saturday and Sunday morning, it closes for an hour and a half between 6am and 7.30am. It barely seems worth closing for such a short period, and must be especially grating for those looking for a 6.30am absinthe – oh yes, the green fairy resides here.

60–62 Old Compton Street, W1D 4UG
Times vary, but it's open until at least 5am (excluding Sundays)

Bar Italia, Soho

Wander through Soho at most hours of the day or night, and Bar Italia waits for you with its glowing neon clock. London's longest-running coffee shop opened at a time when Soho had a huge Italian community. Those regulars might've dispersed, but Bar Italia's popularity endured as the word spread about its dedication to quality coffee. It serves booze too: our perfect night/morning at Bar Italia consists of Aperol spritz at 2am, negronis at 4am, and a cappuccino at 7am for breakfast.

The upstairs room, meanwhile, hosted John Logie Baird's first public demonstration of television.
22 Frith Street, W1D 4RF
Open 7am–5am (excluding Sundays)

Blackheath Tea Hut, Blackheath

On Blackheath Common, perched on the side of the A2, you'll find a tea hut that's open 24/7. It's frequented by the emergency services, bikers and other motorists looking for a 4am cuppa to keep them going. Your tea here is going to be more builder's than matcha. There's also a selection of classic 'hut foodstuffs' – think burgers and baps, excellent for a post-midnight snack.
Goffers Road, SE3 0UA
Open 24/7

Canavan's Peckham Pool Club, Peckham

Canavan's in Peckham is a heady mash-up of pool club and nightclub. And while we said we weren't including clubs, this one's worth the exception. Firstly, it's cheap, something by no means guaranteed in Peckham since the millennials started flocking here. Secondly – as the name suggests – this is a pool club, somewhere you can do your best Ronnie O'Sullivan★, revealing your mate's shortcomings with

a cue. Thirdly, it's soundproofed with bulletproof glass. OK, that's less of a reason to go, more of a fun factoid.
For pedants: we know he plays snooker not pool, but the analogy still stands.
188 Rye Lane, SE15 4NF
Open 6pm–4am daily

Duck & Waffle, City of London

The high end option. Quite literally, as Duck & Waffle is up on the 40th floor of Heron Tower, providing glorious views of London 24/7 (see page 75). Late at night the main punters are the post-clubbing crowd from nearby Shoreditch and Farringdon, after something a little more refined than a doner kebab. An extensive drinks list includes pine needle lemonade, and a fig and chestnut Manhattan. Christmassy.
110 Bishopsgate, EC2N 4AY
Open 24/7

Hippodrome Casino, Leicester Square

Maybe not the first place that springs to mind when searching for a late-night drinking hole, but the Hippodrome Casino is open 24/7, as is its bar. Don't worry about feeling out-of-place if you're here for a drink rather than a gamble – the casino's patrons are often split evenly between gamblers and those hunting down a Winner Twist cocktail.
Cranbourn Street, WC2H 7JH
Open 24/7

Polo Bar, Liverpool Street

A hop, skip and jump down Bishopsgate from Duck & Waffle sits a very different kind of 24/7 venue. Polo Bar dates back to 1953, when Bruna Inzani opened a cafe serving proper British cafe food. More than 65 years later not much has changed, apart from the addition of a 24-hour alcohol license. In the wee hours of the morning, a cavalcade of characters come through the… well not the door; it doesn't have one. Proving just how perennially open Polo Bar is.
176 Bishopsgate, EC2M 4NQ
Open 24/7

VQ

It's all in the name. VQ's is a subtle hint to its opening hours – vingt-quatre in French, i.e. open 24 hours. Well, that's at least true for three of the mini-chain's venues. For the Euston, Clapham and Notting Hill branches, the name VQ is little more than a bare-faced lie. Anyway, in Bloomsbury, Chelsea and Aldgate you can quench your thirst with everything from champagne to chai latte, at whichever hour you wish.
Locations in Bloomsbury, Chelsea and Aldgate *are open 24/7*

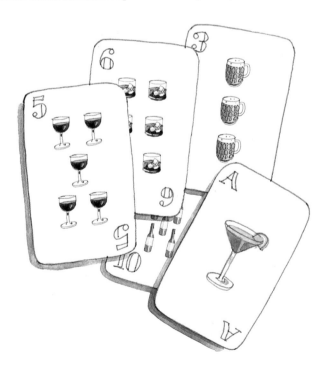

RECORD-BREAKING PUBS:
HIGHEST, SMALLEST, PRICIEST...

It's fitting that Guinness World Records come from the same family behind the uber-famous stout (which has its origins in east London). Some of these record breaking pubs serve the black stuff, too.

Oldest pub building

There is no definitive 'London's oldest pub', as we argue on page 130. It depends how you measure. In terms of bricks and mortar, though, the **Seven Stars** on Carey Street (see page 31) has one of the best shouts. Large chunks of the building are 17th-century, and a date mark declares 1602.

If we look to the suburbs, still older inns might be found. **The King and Tinker** in Enfield (see page 78) claims to be partly from the 16th century, while the **Queen's Head** in Pinner (see page 80) has a verified 16th-century staircase and panelling.

Oldest licence

Drury Lane's **White Hart** doesn't look particularly old (it isn't), but it does claim to have London's oldest licence to sell alcohol. We think this is something of a cheat though – see, again, page 131.

Smallest bar

The Dove in Hammersmith (see page 49) holds the Guinness World Record for the smallest bar. The accolade is proudly displayed in situ, just on the right as you enter. This fun-sized snug holds just three bar stools and can be inspected on Google Street View – you've very little chance of actually getting it to yourself in real life.

Smallest pub

While the Dove claims the smallest bar, it is just one space within a larger building. If we instead consider the smallest pub, then **The Rake** in Borough Market springs to mind. Unbeatable for craft beer, very much beatable for space to sit down.

Longest bar

Spurs' new **Goal Line Bar** (see page 29), running the entire length of – predictably – the goal line, clocks in at a whopping 65m – making it not just London's longest bar but, they claim, the longest in all of Europe. At least Spurs got to win *something* in 2019. (Too soon?)

Longest name

The Only Running Footman in Mayfair was often said to have the longest pub name. It's now truncated to simply The Footman, and another one of London's quirky joys has gone. In any case, Kensal Green's **Paradise by Way of Kensal Green**, with 31 characters, easily outpaces the footman. Still longer, potentially, is **Zeitgeist at the Jolly Gardeners** in Lambeth, though this is often shortened with a @, or simply called Zeitgeist.

Still longer, if a little generic, is the **Great Northern Railway Tavern** in Hornsey. The longest we've found so far is the **Jack Beard's at The Hope and Anchor** in Poplar. Including punctuation and spaces, that adds up to 35 characters.

Smallest frontage

Ye Olde Cock Tavern on Fleet Street proudly displays a sign boasting of 'the narrowest frontage of any London pub'. It should get out more. **The King's Head** on Borough High Street looks decidedly narrower to us. But the winner of this little-fought-after accolade must surely go to **The Old Ship** in Mare Street, Hackney, whose frontage is little wider than an ironing board and perhaps half the size of Ye Olde Cock. And, yes, we are aware this is turning into a comparison of cock sizes.

Most altitudinous

We can't find any hostelry that claims to be London's most elevated, so we've had to do the legwork ourselves using a topographic map. The loftiest pubs you're likely to have heard of are **The Spaniards Inn** in Hampstead (see page 123) and **The Flask** in Highgate (see page 121), both at 430 feet (the nearby **Gatehouse** is still higher, but less well-known). Both are trounced by a number of pubs on London's southern fringes. The most impressive we can find is the **Aperfield Inn**, south of Biggin Hill, which stands at 728 feet.

Most northerly, southerly, etc.

London's most epic pub crawl would take in the pubs at the four cardinal points. The most northerly is **The Plough** in Enfield. The south has **The Fox** in Coulsdon. West is the **King's Arms** in Longford, while the east has the **Old White Horse** in Upminster. And before you think it's mission impossible to visit them all in one day… some of us have done it.

Priciest

The demand for exotic craft beer has prompted many pubs to import rare, high-alcohol tipples – at a price. **The Rake** in Borough Market, if we may return to one of our favourites, has more than a few premium ales among its vast selection. In 2017, a pint of Cloudwater's North West Double IPA would set you back an eye-watering £13.40.

The record, however, currently lies with the **Craft Beer Co.**'s branch on Old Street (which happens to be the *Londonist* local). In the summer of 2018, this preposterously well-stocked venue was offering AleSmith Speedway Stout at £22.50 for a pint. The price reflects its rarity on these shores, its high alcohol content (12% ABV), and the intention that you should really buy it as a third-of-a-pint. Anyway, it's your round.

LIQUID HISTORY:
A CHRONOLOGY OF KEY EVENTS IN LONDON DRINKING

AD 43: The Romans invent London, and bring with them all manner of continental drinking habits. One of the treasures of the Roman city is a temple dedicated to Bacchus, god of wine, rediscovered in 1954.

1216: The White Hart in Covent Garden is granted a licence to sell alcohol. It's said to be the oldest-known licence in London for a pub still trading (albeit on a different site).

1364: The Worshipful Company of Vintners – the guys you had to chum up with if you wanted to flog wine in the medieval city – receive their Royal Charter. They're still going.

1415: The Old Red Lion on St John Street claims to date from this year.

1420: The Cittie of Yorke on High Holborn and The Guinea in Mayfair can be traced to this decade, although both have since been rebuilt.

1538: First mention of a pub on the site of Ye Olde Cheshire Cheese, Fleet Street.

1585: The Spaniards Inn in Hampstead is built.

1593: The Hoop & Grapes in Aldgate is constructed, one of the few City pubs to survive the Great Fire of London.

1623: London's heftiest drinker is an elephant at the Tower of London. The beast, a gift to James I from the King of Spain, reputedly died after drinking more than a gallon of wine a day.

1652: Pasqua Rosée opens London's first coffee shop, at what is now the Jamaica Wine House, Cornhill. It is, to say the least, a winning idea.

1657: London's first chocolate house is opened in Queen's Head Alley near Bishopsgate, by a Frenchman promising an "excellent West India drink". London's love for hot choccy begins.

1662: Catherine of Braganza, new wife of Charles II, moves to London. She brings with her a tradition of supping tea.

1666: The Great Fire of London destroys most of the City's ale houses. Samuel Pepys watches the fire from The Anchor on Bankside, after carefully rescuing his own stash of wine.

1706: Twinings tea shop opens on Strand. It's still there today. The brand's logo, created in 1787, is the world's oldest in continuous use.

1721: "The principal cause of all the vice & debauchery committed among the inferior sort of people" – a Middlesex magistrate commenting on the London gin craze, which gripped London for an unwholesome chunk of the 18th century.

1721: The first mention of London Porter, a dark beer that became synonymous with the capital.

1740: James Thomson supposedly composes the lyrics to 'Rule, Britannia!' at The Dove, Hammersmith.

1748: The George and Vulture, which later found wider fame in *The Pickwick Papers*, is built off Lombard Street.

1751: William Hogarth's prints *Gin Lane* and *Beer Street* are published, showing the social ills caused by the spirit, and the virtues of beer.

1769: Gordon's London Dry Gin is first distilled in Southwark.

1784: London-based James Man secures a contract to supply the Royal Navy with rum for sailors' daily 'rum tot'. The tradition continues until 1970, when it's thought that operating heavy machinery with high-strength spirit inside you might not be altogether wise.

1809: "A man may surely be allowed to take a glass of wine by his own fireside." – Richard Brinsley Sheridan, found drinking outside his Theatre Royal, which was on fire.

1814: The Great Beer Flood kills at least eight people when a giant vat of beer gives way.

1823: Henry Pimm introduces his 'No.1 Cup' at an oyster bar near the Bank of England. Thanks to clever marketing, it would become the quintessential drink of the English summer.

1835: Hoppy beer for export was developed in London in the early 19th century. By this year, the drink is being sold as India Pale Ale, or IPA.

c.1850: Karl Marx embarks on his notorious pub crawl along Tottenham Court Road, during which he drunkenly smashes the street's gas lamps.

1854: A serious cholera epidemic is traced by Dr John Snow back to a polluted Soho pump. The local pub on Broadwick Street is now named after the good doctor.

1855: It becomes illegal to extract drinking water from the tidal Thames.

1859: The first public drinking fountain is erected by the Metropolitan Drinking Fountain and Cattle Trough Association. Installed on Giltspur Street, opposite a pub, it's designed to encourage temperance. It's still there now, with two cups fixed with chains, but you can't quench your thirst at it these days.

1863: Beefeater Gin distillery is set up. The gin still has widespread availability, including within the Beefeater's own pub in the Tower of London.

1890: Gordon's Wine Bar opens on Villiers Street. It goes on to become the preferred haunt of writers, first-daters, and people having affairs.

1903: Ada Colman, the Savoy's first female bartender, invents the Hanky-Panky cocktail. Its name comes from an actor called Charles Hawtrey. But not THAT actor called Charles Hawtrey.

1909: The first Lyons' Corner House opens on Coventry Street. Curiously, the Wimpy and Burger King chains both started out in London from the same premises.

1921: Buck's Fizz is invented at Buck's Club, Clifford Street. The name would go on to inspire a Eurovision-winning quartet and a mildly humorous spoonerism.

1926: Death of Polly the parrot, world-famous mascot of Ye Olde Cheshire Cheese in Fleet Street. The stuffed bird is still to be seen in the ground-floor bar.

1951: Hollywood star Tallulah Bankhead slurps champagne from a slipper at a press conference at the Ritz.

1955: Ruth Ellis shoots dead David Blakely outside the Magdala pub in Hampstead. She becomes the last woman to be hanged in Britain.

1959: London Pride, one of London's most famous beers, is introduced by Fuller, Smith & Turner.

1961: Coca-Cola opens a factory in Sidcup. The highly moreish syrup juice is still made there.

1966: Ronnie Kray shoots dead George Cornell at the Blind Beggar pub, Whitechapel.

1979: Costa opens its first coffee shop on Vauxhall Bridge Road.

1979: The first outpost of the all-conquering Wetherspoon chain opens in Muswell Hill. It's called Martin's after the owner, but after the window-sign is accidentally smashed, Tim Martin decides to rename it after an old teacher.

1983: Dick Bradsell invents the Espresso Martini at the Soho Brasserie on Greek Street.

1985: The Queen Vic, London's most famous, albeit fictional, pub first appears in *EastEnders*. Endless characters will go on to be ordered to get out of it.

1987: "I demand to have some booze!" – Richard E Grant in *Withnail and I*, a filmic love-letter to London drinking.

1989: Del Boy falls through the bar.

1997: Caffè Nero coffee shops debut with a first venue in Frith Street, Soho.

1997: Harry Potter first sets foot into the Leaky Cauldron. The world is also introduced to Butterbeer.

1998: The first of countless branches of Starbucks opens on King's Road, Chelsea.

2001: Six bankers make a £44k dent in the wine cellar at Gordon Ramsay's Michelin-starred Pétrus restaurant. Five of them are fired.

2002: A bottle of gin is among the tributes left outside Clarence House, for the late Queen Mother. An avid lover of gin and Dubonnet, she lived to 101.

2006: "I'm the Bishop of Southwark, it's what I do." – a drunken Bishop of Southwark, caught clambering into a stranger's open-top car. He reportedly threw the contents of the car onto the pavement. All this happened on Crucifix Lane. The single greatest story in the history of London drink?

2006: Aleksandr Litvinenko's cup of tea is radioactively poisoned in the Pine Bar of the Millennium Hotel in Grosvenor Square. He dies and is later buried in a deep grave in Highgate Cemetery.

2008: Drinking on the London Underground is outlawed. Londoners mark the occasion with an almighty piss up on the Circle line.

2009: Sipsmith gin distillery is established. It is the first copper-pot gin distillery in London for almost 200 years.

2009: The Kernel brewery opens in Bermondsey. Other small breweries would follow, leading to what we now call the Bermondsey Beer Mile.

2011: The first bubble tea shop, Bubbleology, opens in Soho. Of course.

2012: Wild Card Brewery opens on a Walthamstow industrial estate, led by head brewer, Jaeger Wise. The 'brewsters' are back in town.

2013: London's first winery in centuries, London Cru in Brompton, is opened.

2015: Bompas and Parr – the Willy Wonkas of food and drink – create a walk-in, breathable cocktail room in Borough Market, on the site of an ancient monastery.

2018: *Londonist* brews its own session IPA, with a lot of help from Fourpure. Drinking in London reaches its zenith.

ABOUT THE ARTISTS

Lisa Berkshire
**theillustratedworldof
lisaberkshire.co.uk**

🐦 @lisaberkshire

📷 @lisaberkshire_illustratedworld

Lisa is an illustrator of over 25 years experience who works on commissions for publishing and design and creates work for her own ranges of prints, greetings cards, illustrated assemblage art pieces and growing range of homewares.

Amy Blackwell
amyblackwell.co.uk

🐦 @amyjpeg

📷 @amyjpeg

Amy is an artist and illustrator who lives, works and plays in the Midlands. Her lucky number is three and favourite colour this week is peach.

Josy Bloggs
josybloggs.com

🐦 @BloggsJosy

📷 @josybloggsdesign

Josy Bloggs is a designer and illustrator who lives in west Yorkshire. She began her career as an interior designer after graduating with a Masters degree in Spatial Design. She now works as a full time professional illustrator.

David Broadbent
davidbroadbent.co.uk

David Broadbent has been an illustrator for more than 15 years. He has created work that has been used for many different purposes. You will find him on the south coast of England cycling on the downs or looking out to sea.

Andy Council
andycouncil.co.uk

🐦 @AndyCouncil

📷 @andycouncil

Andy Council is a Bristol-based artist who creates composite beasts made up of architectural landmarks and other recognisable elements. He specializes in detailed illustrations and huge spray-painted murals.

Bek Cruddace

bekcruddace.co.uk

🐦 @bekcruddace

📷 BekCruddace

*Bek Cruddace is an illustrator
based in north Hampshire who
specialises in designing illustrated
maps. Since 2011 Bek has built
up a solid client base with many
return and long-term clients
combined with private commissions
and her own retail designs.*

Dave Draws Ltd

davedraws.co.uk

🐦 @DaveDraws_

📷 @dave__draws

*Dave Draws is a Manchester-based
illustrator specialising in black
and white doodle maps of cities,
highlighting well known landmarks
as well as quirky places,*

Amelia Flower

ameliaflower.co.uk

📷 @ameliaflower

*Amelia Flower is an illustrator,
living and working in London.
Amelia works digitally, using
her iPad to create her bright and
contemporary illustrations.*

Livi Gosling Illustration

livigosling.co.uk

🐦 @LiviGosling

📷 @Livi_Gosling_Illustration

*Livi Gosling is an illustrator who
lives in Hertfordshire. When's she's
not drawing at her desk, you'll find
her baking, cooking or walking
in the countryside. She draws
inspiration from both the culinary
and natural world.*

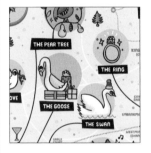

Freya Harrison

freyaharrison.com

🐦 @freyargh

📷 @freyargh

*Freya Harrison is a London-based
illustrator and designer with a love
of drawing, maps and an Aperol
spritz on a sunny evening.*

Stephanie Hofmann Illustration

stephaniehofmann.co.uk

📷 @steffi.hofmann

*Stephanie Hofmann is a German
illustrator who currently resides
in London. She has a love of the
surreal and gothic and is inspired
by most things. Her work is a
mixture of digital drawing and
hand-painted textures.*

Linzie Hunter

linziehunter.co.uk

🐦 @linziehunter

📷 @linziehunter

Linzie is a children's book author, illustrator and hand-lettering artist. Originally from Glasgow, she is now based in Peckham, south London where she creates artwork for international clients including Apple, Adobe, Nike, Marks and Spencer and HarperCollins.

Nanna Koekoek

nannakoekoek.com

🐦 @cuckoojar

📷 @cuckoojar

Nanna Koekoek is a Dutch American illustrator based in London. Besides drawing she loves pub carpets, girl groups, east coast rap, cycling, masks, food-shaped crockery, her slightly overweight cat Doris and all things yellow.

Mercedes Leon illustration

merchesico.com

🐦 @mergepsycho

📷 @merchesico

Mercedes Leon is an illustrator from Spain who loves drawing and walking around. She's living the dream in Bradford, after getting tired of living the dream in London. Now she regrets a bit, but it's alright.

Louise Lockhart

louiselockhart.co.uk

🐦 @printedpeanut

📷 @theprintedpeanut

Louise Lockhart is a freelance illustrator based in Yorkshire. She has worked on many children's books and also specialises in printed paper products and packaging. Her unique work is bright and fun, inspired by old print ephemera and vintage toys.

Lauren Rebbeck Illustration

laurenrebbeck.com

🐦 @LaurenRebbeck

📷 @laurenrebbeck

Lauren Rebbeck is a freelance illustrator who lives in the west Midlands. Lauren's background in illustration, textiles and graphic design, mixed with her love of travel, has culminated in her mixed-media, tactile and detailed illustration style, published across the world.

Kate Rochester Illustration
katerochester.com

📷 @kateroch

Kate Rochester is a designer and illustrator living in Nottingham, whose career has taken in fashion textiles, stationery, and publishing illustration. She specialises in colourful handwriting with excellent hand-drawn, collage, paint and ink skills worked into digital prints.

Janina Schröter
janina-schroeter.com

📷 @janina_schroeter

Janina Schröter is a designer and illustrator from Germany who currently works in London. She is specialised in creating hand-drawn maps.

Jane Smith
janeillustration.co.uk/blog

🐦 @DalstonScribble

📷 @janeillustration

Jane is a London-based artist/ illustrator specialising in maps, buildings, cityscapes and other subjects. She has been in London for over 35 years and finds inspiration from her surroundings. Beside illustration, Jane loves sketching and printmaking (linocut and engraving).

Mel Smith Designs
melsmithdesigns.com

🐦 @MelSmithDesigns

📷 @MelSmithDesigns

Mel Smith is a travel illustrator and map-maker, on a mission to draw her way around the globe. Incorporating striking palettes, retro styles and surface pattern she produces bold and whimsical illustrations inspired by cultural experiences and traditions.

Haydn Symons
haydnsymons.com

🐦 @haydnsym

📷 @haydnsymons

Haydn Symons is an illustrator and designer from Hampshire. Specialising in editorial, publishing to advertising illustration. With a distinctive style and commercial experience, Haydn has worked with top brands and companies including Scouts UK, Liverpool Museum and Mary Christie.

Tribambuka
tribambuka.co.uk

@tribambuka

Tribambuka, aka Anastasia Beltyukova, is an illustrator from St Petersburg, Russia, who fell in love with London after being stuck there because of the volcano Eyjafjallajökull's eruption, and has happily lived and worked there ever since.

Lis Watkins Illustration
liswatkins.com

@lineandwash

@lineandwash

Lis Watkins is a London-based illustrator specializing in watercolour, reportage drawing and hand-drawn maps.

Olivia Whitworth Illustration
liviwhit.com

@livi_whitworth

@liviwhit

Olivia is a London-based freelance illustrator with a penchant for ink and linework. She enjoys creating dense whimsical works that require closer inspection. Olivia works from her shared studio in East London, and has worked with the likes of Adidas, The Telegraph *and* Pandora.

Rebecca Lea Williams
rebsville.com

@rebsville

Rebecca is an artist and illustrator working in London. She uses watercolours and ink and her commercial commissions are varied; from editorial maps to packaging design. She opened her own online print and illustrated homewares shop last year at www.rebsville. com.

Tom Woolley Illustration
tomwoolley.com

@tcwoolley

@tomwoolley

Tom Woolley is a freelance illustrator who lives in Birmingham. His combination of vivid colours and stylised illustration create unique and distinctive artwork that has been published worldwide.

INDEX

40 Maltby Street 12
69 Colebrooke Row 118
214 Bermondsey 124

ABQ London 119
Ace Cafe 138
Aeronaut, The 72
Albany, The 113
Albertine 56
Alcotraz 52
Alexandra, The 104, 147
Alfred Le Roy 135
Allis, The 112
Altitude Sky Bar 74
American Bar at the Savoy 26
American Bar at the Stafford
  Hotel 84
Anchor & Hope 43
Angel, The 46
Antelope, The 115
Anthracite 43
Aperfield Inn 179
Aqua Shard 75
Arbitrager, The 163
Artesian 119
Artful Dodger, The 8, 108
Athenaeum, The 99
Attendant, The 41

Balans Soho Society 176
Bar & Co 135
Bar Italia 127, 176
Bar Kick 28
Bar Polski 64
Bar Story 12
Bar Three 139
Barge East 135
Basement Sate 124
Beast of Brixton, The 54
Beefsteak Club 99
Beehive, The 65
Beer Merchants Tap 165
Beer Rebellion 37

Beer Shop, The 34
Below and Hidden 55
Bermondsey Arts Club 41
Bermondsey Beer Mile 13
Berry, Bros. & Rudd 56
Bethnal Green Working Men's
  Club 142
Betjeman Arms, The 161
Betsey Trotwood 8, 108
Bird & Barrel 37
Black Cross, The 151
Black Rock 86
Blackbird, The 171, 174
Blackbook Winery 16
Blackfriar, The 30, 114, 156
Blackheath Tea Hut 176
Bletchley, The 155
Blue Anchor 96
Blue Eyed Maid, The 173, 174
Blue Posts (SW1A) 150
Blue Posts, The (W1B) 150
Blue Posts, The (W1D) 150
Blue Posts, The (W1F) 148
Blue Posts (W1T) 148
Bob Bob Ricard 155
Bodega Wine House 25
Bōkan 74
Bonnington Cafe 138
Book Club, The 139
Boot, The 107
Bounce 124
Bow Bells, The 121
Brave Sir Robin 10
BrewDog 110, 159
Bricklayer's Arms 169
Brig, The 55
Britannia 115
Broken Drum, The 37
Brooks's Club 109
Buckingham Arms 114–5
Burlock 119
Buster Mantis 13
Button's Coffee House 127

B.Y.O.C. City 124

Café Godiva 90
Café Royal 25–6
Cahoots 124
Call Me Mr Lucky 55
Callooh Callay 55
Camden Town Brewery 13
Camel & Artichoke, The 72
Canavan's Peckham Pool Club
  176–7
Candlelight Club, The 54
Candy Floss Crêperie 120
Cannick Tapps, The 114
Canvas Cafe 120
Capitol, The 65
Captain Kidd 50
Caravan 141
Carlisle Arms 170
Case is Altered, The 72
CASK Pub and Kitchen 165
Castle, The 113
Catford Constitutional 144
CellarDoor 41, 54
Cereal Killer Café 120
Champion, The 30
Chandos 158
Chapel, The 112
Chiringuito 41
Churchill Arms, The 30, 115
Claridge's 25
Cobbetts Beer Shop and
  Micropub 37
Cockpit 158
Cocktail Lounge 139
Cocktail Trading Co 119
Connaught, The 139
Coq d'Argent 103
Coral Room at The Bloomsbury
  Hotel 84
Cotton Mill, The 37
Court, The 24
Covent Garden Tea Bar 141

Craft Beer Co. 70, 155, 179
Crooked Billet 102
Crosse Keys, The 65, 114
Crown and Shuttle 159
Crusting Pipe, The 174
Cubana 62
Culpeper, The 103
Cutty Sark 51

Dar 43
Darcie & May Green 135
Defector's Weld, The 72, 112
Devil's Darling 86
Dickens Inn 108
Dirty Dicks 30
Discount Suit Company 55, 125
Distillery, The 52
Dodo, The 34–5
Dog & Fox 100
Dolphin, The 26
Doodle Bar 14
Door Hinge, The 37
Douglas Fir, The 37
Dove, The (E8) 165, 171
Dove, The (W6) 49, 171, 174, 178
Dovetail, The 165
Draft House, The 166
Draft House Seething, The 159
Draughts (E8) 13
Draughts (SE1) 13
Drum, The 174
Duck & Waffle 75, 177
Duke of Burgundy, The 151
Duke of York 170
DUKES Bar 27, 43–4, 85

Eagle, The 38
Earl of Essex, The 166
East Finchley Constitutional Club
  144
Edgar Wallace, The 114
Edgware Road 64
Effra Social 144

EL&N Café 120, 141
Elephant & Castle, The 46
Elgin, The 112
Ella Di Rocco 155
Elm Park Tavern 61
Etcetera Theatre 116
Euston Tap 113, 158, 166
Evans & Peel Detective Agency 52
Every Cloud 44
Exmouth Arms 158

Faltering Fullback, The 28
Feng Shang Princess 135–6
Finborough Theatre 116
Fire Stables 102
First Aid Box 54
Fitzrovia Belle, The 24
Flask, The 121, 179
Fortnum & Mason 21, 90
Forty Hall Vineyard 16, 58
Fountains Abbey 112
Fox, The 179
Frank's Café 104
French House, The 64, 171
Freud 125
Frolics 26

Galvin at Windows 74
Garden Bar, The 112
Garrick Club 97
Gate, The 116
Gatehouse, The 116, 179
George, The 121
George and Dragon, The 31
George Inn 107, 132, 146, 160
George Tavern, The 70
George and Vulture 107, 108
George's Bar 85
Gibson, The 44
Gidea Park Micropub 35
Gin Bar at Holborn Dining Room
    85
Globe, The (EC2) 113
Globe, The (NW1) 160
GNH Bar 119
Goal Line Bar 29, 178
Golazio 28
Gōng at The Shard 75

Good & Proper 141
Goose, The 173, 174
Gordon's Wine Bar 58
Govinda's 138
Grapes, The 51, 107
Green Man 96
Greenwood 28–9
Grenadier, The 31, 121, 123, 147
Gun, The 51

Hamilton Hall 113, 159
Hamlet Bar 29
Hampton Court Palace 58, 90
Hand in Hand 102
Hangar Micropub, The 35
Happiness Forgets 55
Harbour Arms 37
Harp, The 158, 167
Harrods 58, 154, 155
Harvey Nichols 155
Hawkes 15
Heights Bar, The 75
Hen and Chickens 171, 174
Hereford Arms, The 115
Hero of Maida 48
Hide Below 44
High Cross, The 42
Hippodrome Casino 177
Hoop & Grapes 113, 132
Hop Poles, The 110
Hop and Vine, The 35
Hope, The 167
Horniman, The 160
Hotel Chocolat 90
Hotel Indigo 96
Hummingbird Bakery 141
Hung, Drawn and Quartered,
    The 114
Hydrant 158

Ice Wharf, The 65
Iris at The Gherkin 76
Island Queen 166
Italian Job 167

Jack Horner, The 23
Jamaica Wine House 126
Jarr Kombucha 120, 141

Job Centre, The 73
John the Unicorn 73

Kanpai 16
Katzpace 116, 118
Kentish Belle, The 35
Keys, The 162
King Charles I 79, 159
King Edward VII 82
King George V 82
King Harold, The 77
King and Tinker 78–9, 178
Kings Arms, The 161
Kings Head 77
Knights Templar, The 65–6
Korova Milk Bar 151

Ladies and Gentlemen 42
Lady Mildmay 174
Lady Ottoline 174
Lamb, The 108
Lamb and Flag 108, 131
Laughing Gravy, The 10
Leaky Cauldron, The 151
Ledger Building, The 66, 70
Lemon Tree, The 93
L'Eto 141
Lexington, The 61
Library Bar, The 44
Lion and the Unicorn, The 151
Little Duck Pickery 141
Little Green Dragon 36
Little Nan's 14
Lloyd's Coffee House 127
Loft, The 104
London Apprentice, The 49
London Beer House 167
London Cocktail Club 119
London Cru 58
London Silver Vaults 58
Long Pond, The 37
Look Mum, No Hands! 29
Lord Clyde, The 174
Luggage Room, The 54
Lyon's Corner Houses 26

Mad Bishop & Bear, The 10,
    73, 160

Madison 104
Manor House 48
Maple Leaf 62
Mariage Frères 141
Market Hall Victoria 161
Mark's Bar Soho 55
Martini Bar, The 44
Maxwells 120, 140
Mayflower, The 50
Mayor of Scaredy Cat Town,
    The 55
Mercato Metropolitano 167
Merchant, The 70
Merchant House 125
Metropolitan Bar, The 112, 160
Mildmay Club 144
Milk Float, The 136
Minories, The 70
Miranda 85–6
Moby Dick, The 10
Mooboo 140–41
Moon Under Water, The 151–2
Moonshine Saloon 52
Mossy Well, The 66
MOTH Club 144
Mother Kelly's (E2) 14, 168
Mother Kelly's (SE1) 168
Mr Fogg's Gin Parlour 44
Mr Fogg's Residence 64
Mulberry Bush 96

Nag's Head, The 152
Netil360 104
Nicholas Nickleby 108
Night Tales 14
Nightjar 54
Nirvana Brewery 140
Noble Rot 58
Norfolk House Constitutional
    Club 144
Northumberland Arms, The 24

Oblix East 75
Old Bull & Bush, The 48, 123
Old Doctor Butler's Head 160
Old Fountain, The 169
Old Orchard, The 76
Old Queen's Head, The 60

Old Red Cow 93
Old Red Lion Theatre Pub 118, 132
Old Ship, The (E8) 179
Old Ship (W6) 49
Old Tom's Bar 173
Olde Wine Shades, The 158
Oliver's Jazz Bar 125
One Inn the Wood 36
O'Neill's 60
Opium 55
Orange Tree, The 93
Original Sin 125
Oriole 54
Our/London 16
Owl & Hitchhiker, The 10
Owl & Pussycat, The (E2) 11
Owl & The Pussycat, The (W13) 11, 37
Oxo Tower 104–5

Parcel Yard, The 113, 159
Park Tower Knightsbridge 154
Partridge, The 171
Pear Tree, The 171, 174
Peckham Liberal Club 145
Penny Farthing, The 37
Pepper St Ontiod 73
Permit Room 139–40
Persepolis 138–9
Pineapple, The 147
Pinoli's 26
Plough, The 179
Plumstead Radical Club 145
Polo Bar 177
Porchester, The 48, 112
Porterhouse, The 29
Postcard Teas 21
Pratts & Payne 73
Prince Alfred 115
Prince Frederick 81
Prince of Wales 60
Princess of Wales, The 114
Punch Room 86
Pyrotechnists Arms, The 73

Queen Elizabeth, The (E4) 78
Queen Elizabeth, The (SE17) 78

Queen of Hoxton 105
Queen Vic, The 152
Queen's Head (E14) 82
Queen's Head (HA5) 80–81, 178
Queen's Head (WC1) 168
Queen's Larder, The 82

Radicals & Victuallers 29
Radio Rooftop 105
Radius Arms, The 36
Rake, The 166, 178, 179
Real Ale Way 37
Red Lion, The 114
Redemption Bar 138
Reform Club 99
Renegade London Wine 14, 16, 58–9
Restaurant Story 42
Resting Hare, The 11
Reverend JW Simpson 125
Rex Whistler Restaurant 59
Richard I 77
Ring, The 173, 174
Rising Sun (EC1A) 123
Rising Sun, The (W1T) 23
Ritzy, The 60
River Ale House, The 36
Robin Hood (SM1) 11
Robin Hood, The (EN2) 11
Robin Hood & Little John 11
Rochester Castle, The 66
Rocket, The 66
Rose & Crown 100
Royal China Club 154
Royal Oak 80
Royal Opera House 174
Royal Vauxhall Tavern 118
R.S. *Hispaniola* 136
Rusty Bucket, The 37

SACK 86
Saint Aymes 155
St Pancras Champagne Bar 59
Samoan Joe's 152
Savoy, The 26, 155
Seven Stars, The 31, 178
Shakespeare, The 113
Shayona 64

Sherlock Holmes, The 31
Ship, The 49–50
Ship & Shovell, The 73
Simon the Tanner 168
Singer Tavern 160
Six Jolly Fellowship Porters 152
Sky Pod Bar 76
Small Beer Brew Co. 140
Somers Town Coffee House 161
Southampton Arms 168
Southwark 31
Spaniards Inn, The 107, 123, 132, 179
Star & Garter 169
Stormbird 169
Sushi Samba 75–6
Swan and Paedo, The 152
Swan, The (SE1) 173, 174
Swan, The (SW19) 102
Sydney Arms, The 29
Sylvan Post, The 73
Sympathetic Ear, The 37

Tabard, The 152
Tabard Theatre 118
Tamesis Dock 136
Tankard, The 105
Tapping the Admiral 168
Tate Modern 59, 76
Tattershall Castle 136
Tayyabs 139
TCR Lounge Bar 24
Tea House Theatre 21
Teddington Constitutional Club 145
Terroirs Wine Bar 59
Theatre503 118
Tierra Peru 62
Tom King's Coffee House 127
Tosier's Chocolate House 90
Trafalgar St James 105
Trailer Happiness 52
Troubadour 52
Tufnell Park Tavern 61
Twinings 21

Understudy, The 161
Union Tavern 112
Upminster Taproom 37

Vagabond Wines 16
Vauxhall's Tea House Theatre 141
Vertigo 42 76
Viaduct Tavern, The 123
Victorian Bath House, The 52
Vintners' Hall 59
Volunteer, The 123
VQ 177

Walrus & The Carpenter, The 11
Walthamstow Trades Hall 145
Wanstead Tap, The 14
Warrington, The 86
WC 42
Wenlock Arms, The 169
Wetherspoons, Victoria 66
White Hart (N16) 77
White Hart (WC2) 131–2, 178
White Horse, The 81, 169
White Swan, The 49
White's 97
Widow's Son, The 146
Wigmore Hall 59
Willesden Working Men's Club 145
William the Conqueror 77
William IV, The 82
Winchester Tavern, The 152
Windsor Castle 115, 161
Wood Green Social Club 145

Ye Old Mitre 108
Ye Olde Cheshire Cheese 108, 132
Ye Olde Swiss Cottage 48
Ye Olde Watling 114
Yeotown Kitchen 140
Yumchaa 141

Zander Bar 178
Zeret Kitchen 64
Zetland Arms 115

CREDITS

Londonist and AA Media Ltd would like to thank the following artists and copyright holders for their assistance in the preparation of this book:

Feature illustrations: 8–9, 10, 11, 107, 108 *Pubs Named After Fictional Characters* © Mel Smith Designs; **19**, 20, 21 *Tea Town* © Tribambuka; **22**, 24 *Karl Marx's Rowdy Tottenham Court Road Pub Crawl* © Nanna Koekoek; **32–3** *Red Lion* © Andy Council; **39** *Pop Goes The Weasel* © Livi Gosling Illustration; **40**, 41, 42 *London toilets you can drink in* © Janina Schröter; **47**, 48 *Tube stations* © Tom Woolley Illustration; **50–51** *A Riverside Crawl of the Thames* © Louise Lockhart; **53**, 54, 55 *London Speakeasy Illustrated Map* © Josy Bloggs; **56–7**, 59 *Illustrated Map* © Amelia Flower; **62–3**, 64 *Drink your way around the world* © Linzie Hunter; **71** *The Docklands Light Ale-way* © Mercedes Leon Illustration; **78–9**, 80–81 *Kings and Queens* © Amy Blackwell; **89** *London Chocolate Houses* © Lauren Rebbeck Illustration; **94–5**, 96 *Drink your way through the Rainbow* © Bek Cruddace; **98** *Illustrated map of London's Gentlemen's Clubs* © Haydn Symons; **101** *Oliver Reed's Wimbledon Run* © Kate Rochester Illustration; **110–11**, 112, 113, 115, **endpapers** *The Circle Line Pub Crawl* © Olivia Whitworth Illustration; **117** *Theatre Pubs of London* © Lisa Berkshire; **122** *Haunted London Pubs* © Stephanie Hofmann Illustration; **130–31**, 132 *The Oldest Pubs in London* © Rebecca Lea Williams; **142–3** *London Pubs Doodle Map* © Dave Draws Ltd; **148**, **149**, 150 *Blue Posts Pubs Map - London's West End* © Jane Smith; **156–7**, 158, 159, 160, 161 *Best Pubs Near London's Train Stations* © Lis Watkins Illustration; **164–5**, 166, 168, 169 *London pubs* © David Broadbent; 171, **172–3**, 174 *12 Days of Christmas Pub Crawl* © Freya Harrison

Cocktail illustrations: 17, 27, 45, 69, 87, 109, 129, 137, 153, 175 © Lauren Rebbeck Illustration

Additional illustrations: 2, 5, 7, 28, 29, 34, 35, 36, 37, 43, 44, 65, 84, 85, 86, 103, 104, 105, 106, 144, 145, 180, 181, 182, 183 © Mercedes Leon Illustration; 6, 15, 16, 67, 74, 75, 76, 119, 120, 127, 139, 140, 154 © Lauren Rebbeck Illustration; 12–13, 30, 31, 60, 61, 124, 125, 136, 177, 178–9 © Lis Watkins Illustration; 25, 72, 73, 83, 91, 92, 134, 147, 162 © Freya Harrison

A note on the venues

We've tried to find a definitive 'correct' answer to how we present the names of pubs, but many can't consistently decide if 'The' is part of their name or not even on their own signs, frontages and websites. It's an editor's nightmare. If you find any inconsistencies, please pretend it's a deliberate nod.

The majority of the the pubs, bars and other drinking establishments featured here were open at the time of writing but, the food and drink business being what it is, we can't guarantee that they'll remain that way. We'd suggest checking online prior to planning any visits. Think of this book as a memorial to any subsequent closures, and raise a glass to the dearly departed.

A note on the text

All information and esoterica contained within is believed to be correct at the time of printing – or, in the case of more contentious facts, to be supported by at least one additional source. We apologise for any errors you may find and will do our best to correct them in any subsequent editions.

Writing for this title was contributed by

Matt Brown, Maire Connor, Sam Cullen, Deserter, Dave Haste, Lydia Manch, Steve Manktelow, Lettie McKie, Will Noble, Ben O'Norum, Laura Reynolds, Harry Rosehill and Peter Watts.